GLOBAL ECONOMIC STUDIES

MILLENNIUM CHALLENGE CORPORATION

ECONOMIC ASSISTANCE FOR DEVELOPING NATIONS

GLOBAL ECONOMIC STUDIES

Additional books in this series can be found on Nova's website
under the Series tab.

Additional E-books in this series can be found on Nova's website
under the E-books tab.

ECONOMIC ISSUES, PROBLEMS AND PERSPECTIVES

Additional books in this series can be found on Nova's website
under the Series tab.

Additional E-books in this series can be found on Nova's website
under the E-books tab.

MILLENNIUM CHALLENGE CORPORATION

ECONOMIC ASSISTANCE FOR DEVELOPING NATIONS

LAUTARO B. ROJAS

EDITOR

Nova Science Publishers, Inc.

New York

NOTICE TO THE READER

The Publisher has taken reasonable care in the preparation of this book, but makes no expressed or implied warranty of any kind and assumes no responsibility for any errors or omissions. No liability is assumed for incidental or consequential damages in connection with or arising out of information contained in this book. The Publisher shall not be liable for any special, consequential, or exemplary damages resulting, in whole or in part, from the readers' use of, or reliance upon, this material. Any parts of this book based on government reports are so indicated and copyright is claimed for those parts to the extent applicable to compilations of such works.

Independent verification should be sought for any data, advice or recommendations contained in this book. In addition, no responsibility is assumed by the publisher for any injury and/or damage to persons or property arising from any methods, products, instructions, ideas or otherwise contained in this publication.

This publication is designed to provide accurate and authoritative information with regard to the subject matter covered herein. It is sold with the clear understanding that the Publisher is not engaged in rendering legal or any other professional services. If legal or any other expert assistance is required, the services of a competent person should be sought. FROM A DECLARATION OF PARTICIPANTS JOINTLY ADOPTED BY A COMMITTEE OF THE AMERICAN BAR ASSOCIATION AND A COMMITTEE OF PUBLISHERS.

Additional color graphics may be available in the e-book version of this book.

Library of Congress Cataloging-in-Publication Data

Millenium Challenge Corporation : economic assistance for developing nations / editor, Lautaro B. Rojas.
   p. cm.
 Includes index.
 ISBN 978-1-62100-584-1 (hardcover)
 1. Humanitarian assistance, American--Developing countries. 2. Millennium Challenge Corporation (U.S.)
I. Rojas, Lautaro B.
 HV555.D44M55 2011
 338.91'7301724--dc23
                                2011035680

Published by Nova Science Publishers, Inc. † New York

CONTENTS

PREFACE

This book explores the Millenium Challenge Corporation which provides economic assistance to developing nations. The Millenium Challenge Corporation (MCC), now in its seventh year of operations provides aid to developing countries that have demonstrated a commitment to ruling justly, encouraging economic freedom and investing in people. MCC provides assistance to eligible countries through multiyear compact agreements to fund specific programs targeted at reducing poverty and stimulating economic growth. MCC has received appropriations for fiscal years 2004 through 2010 totaling about $9.5 billion and has set aside about $8.1 billion of this amount for compact assistance.

Chapter 1- The Millennium Challenge Corporation (MCC) provides economic assistance through a competitive selection process to developing nations that are pursuing political and economic reforms in three areas: ruling justly, investing in people, and fostering economic freedom.

Chapter 2- MCC and the partner country determine the compact structure before the compact is signed. However, the structure of some compacts has been altered during implementation.

At signature, Cape Verde's compact focused on water and infrastructure projects on four islands. Compact funds support the upgrade and expansion of the Port of Praia, which is Cape Verde's busiest port and handles half of the country's cargo. At signature, 10 percent of Cape Verde's land was arable, and agricultural productivity was low; approximately 85 percent of food was imported (70 percent in the form of food aid). In May 2008, MCC restructured the Cape Verde compact in response to project rescoping, increased input costs, and currency fluctuations.

Chapter 3- The Millennium Challenge Corporation (MCC) was established in 2004 to help developing countries reduce poverty and stimulate economic growth through multiyear compact agreements. As of June 2011, MCC had signed compacts with 23 countries totaling approximately $8.2 billion in assistance. MCC asks countries to develop compacts with a focus on results and effective monitoring and evaluation. MCC sets targets, which may be revised, to measure the compact results. In late 2010, the Cape Verde and Honduras compacts reached the end of the 5-year implementation period. This report, prepared in response to a congressional mandate to review compact results, examines the extent to which MCC has (1) achieved performance targets and sustainability for projects in Cape Verde and Honduras and (2) assessed progress toward the goal of income growth and poverty reduction. GAO analyzed MCC documents and interviewed MCC officials and stakeholders in Washington, D.C., Cape Verde, and Honduras.

In: Millenium Challenge Corporation
Editor: Lautaro B. Rojas

ISBN: 978-1-62100-584-1
© 2012 Nova Science Publishers, Inc.

Chapter 1

MILLENNIUM CHALLENGE CORPORATION[*]

Curt Tarnoff

SUMMARY

The Millennium Challenge Corporation (MCC) provides economic assistance through a competitive selection process to developing nations that are pursuing political and economic reforms in three areas: ruling justly, investing in people, and fostering economic freedom.

Established in 2004, the MCC differs in several respects from past and current U.S. aid practices:

- the competitive process that rewards countries for past actions measured by 17 objective performance indicators;
- the pledge to segregate the funds from U.S. strategic foreign policy objectives that often strongly influence where U.S. aid is spent;
- its mandate to seek poverty reduction through economic growth, not encumbered with multiple sector objectives;
- the requirement to solicit program proposals developed solely by qualifying countries with broad-based civil society involvement;
- the responsibility of recipient countries to implement their own MCC-funded programs, known as compacts;
- a compact duration limited to five years, with funding committed up front;
- the expectation that compact projects will have measurable impact;
- an emphasis on public transparency in every aspect of agency operations.

In February 2011, the Obama Administration issued its FY2012 budget, requesting $1.125 billion for the MCC, a 2% increase from the enacted FY2010 appropriation and a 25% increase over the final FY2011 appropriation. Following a series of continuing appropriations, in April 2011, Congress approved H.R. 1473 (P.L. 112-10), providing $900 million for the MCC in FY2011. After applying a .2% across-the-board non-defense

---

[*] This is an edited, reformatted and augmented version of a Congressional Research Service publication, CRS Report for Congress RL32427, from www.crs.gov, dated May 3, 2011.

rescission, the MCC receives $898 million in FY2011, a 19% decrease from the FY2010-enacted level.

Congress authorized the MCC in P.L. 108-199 (January 23, 2004). Since that time, the MCC's Board of Directors has approved 23 grant agreements, known as compacts: with Madagascar (2005), Honduras (2005), Cape Verde (2005), Nicaragua (2005), Georgia (2005), Benin (2006), Vanuatu (2006), Armenia (2006), Ghana (2006), Mali (2006), El Salvador (2006), Mozambique (2007), Lesotho (2007), Morocco (2007), Mongolia (2007), Tanzania (2007), Burkina Faso (2008), Namibia (2008), Senegal (2009), Moldova (2009), Philippines (2010), Jordan (2010), and Malawi (2011).

MCC issues include the level of funding to support MCC programs, the impact of budget reductions on MCC programs, the rate of program implementation, the results of MCC compacts, and procurement and corruption concerns.

MOST RECENT DEVELOPMENTS

On April 15, 2011, the Full-Year Continuing Appropriations Act of 2011 (P.L. 112-10, H.R. 1473) was signed, providing $900 million for the MCC in FY2011. After applying a .2% across-the-board non-defense rescission, the MCC receives $898 million in FY2011, a 19% decrease from the FY2010-enacted level.

In February 2011, the Obama Administration issued its FY2012 budget, requesting $1.125 billion for the MCC, a 2% increase from the enacted FY2010 appropriation and a 25% increase over the final FY2011 appropriation.

On January 5, 2011, the MCC Board approved a $350.7 million compact for Malawi (signed on April 7, 2011) focusing on electric power development. The Board also selected Ghana and Georgia as eligible to develop new, second compacts.

INTRODUCTION

In a speech on March 14, 2002, President Bush outlined a proposal for a new program that would represent a fundamental change in the way the United States invests and delivers economic assistance. The resulting Millennium Challenge Corporation (MCC) is based on the premise that economic development succeeds best where it is linked to free market economic and democratic principles and policies, and where governments are committed to implementing reform measures in order to achieve such goals. The MCC concept differs in several fundamental respects from past and current U.S. aid practices:

- the competitive process that rewards countries for past actions measured by 17 objective performance indicators;
- the pledge to segregate the funds from U.S. strategic foreign policy objectives that often strongly influence where U.S. aid is spent;
- its mandate to seek poverty reduction through economic growth, not encumbered with multiple sector objectives;
- the requirement to solicit program proposals developed solely by qualifying countries with broad-based civil society involvement;

- the responsibility of recipient countries to implement their own MCC-funded programs, known as compacts;
- a compact duration limited to five years, with funding committed up front;
- the expectation that compact projects will have measurable impact;
- an emphasis on public transparency in every aspect of agency operations.

The original proposal also differed from previous aid efforts in the size of its commitment to reach an annual level of $5 billion within a few years, an aim never even approximately met.

Congress approved the new initiative in January 2004 in the Millennium Challenge Act of 2003 (Division D of P.L. 108-199).[1] To manage the initiative, Congress authorized the creation of a Millennium Challenge Corporation (MCC), an independent government entity separate from the Departments of State and the Treasury and from the U.S. Agency for International Development (USAID).[2] The MCC headquarters staff level is currently about 258, with a handful of additional employees in each compact country.[3] On December 8, 2009, Daniel Yohannes was sworn in as the new Chief Executive Officer (CEO) of the MCC. A Board of Directors oversees the MCC and makes the country selections. It is chaired by the Secretary of State and composed of the Secretary of the Treasury, the USAID Administrator, the U.S. Trade Representative, the Corporation's CEO, and four individuals from the private sector appointed by the President drawn from lists submitted by Congressional leaders.[4]

Since its inception, Congress has closely followed MCC implementation. The 112th Congress will likely consider MCC funding issues and conduct oversight hearings on operations of the Corporation.

MCC POLICY AND PROGRAMS

From the time the MCC Board of Directors held its initial meeting to establish the program and agree to Corporation by-laws on February 2, 2004, procedures and policies have continued to evolve. Program implementation moves chronologically through a number of steps: candidate countries are identified, eligibility criteria are formulated, compact and threshold-eligible countries are selected, compact programs are developed and proposed, and those approved are funded and carried out. Elements in this process are discussed below.

Selection of Candidate Countries

The selection of initial candidate countries is fairly straightforward and based on the authorizing statute. Countries must fall into specific economic categories determined by their per capita income status (as defined and ranked by the World Bank). MCC participation is limited to all low- and lower-middle-income countries (the former with per capita incomes below $1,905 and the latter between that figure and $3,945 in FY2011), a total of 84 in FY2011. Countries in the low-income group compete with other countries in the low-income group; countries in the lowermiddle-income group compete with each other.

As the relative income status of countries changes from year to year, their MCC eligibility is affected, often negatively. For FY2011, two countries—Azerbaijan and Albania, the latter with a threshold program—have moved from lower-middle-income to upper-middle income status and are, therefore, now ineligible for further MCC assistance. Namibia signed a compact in 2008 and, therefore, continues its program regardless of the upper-middle income status gained in FY2010.

Countries that move from low-income to lower-middle-income status may be affected negatively by having to compete against countries at a higher level of development. In addition, under the MCC legislative authority, only a quarter of total MCC assistance in any year is available for lower-middle-income country compacts, severely limiting the possibility that such countries will be selected or funded. For FY2010, this would have affected the chances of countries like Indonesia and the Philippines, which would have been in a better position to obtain a compact had they remained in the low-income group. In September 2009, the MCC Board announced that, for countries that move from low to lower-middle-income status, it will consider their performance relative to both their old income group and the newer one for a period of three years. Further, the FY2010 Consolidated appropriations (P.L. 111-117, H.R. 3288, Division F) allows transitioning countries already selected in FY2009 to maintain their candidacy for eligibility and, if reselected, draw on the same source of funds as when they were first selected. A possible compact for Indonesia, reselected in FY2010, will therefore be funded as though in the low-income group.[5]

In addition to the income ceiling, countries may be candidates only if they are not statutorily prohibited from receiving U.S. economic assistance. For FY2011, 11 countries were excluded for this reason. Most had been barred in prior years as well.[6] One, Madagascar, excluded in FY2010 because of an undemocratic change in government, was one of the first compact countries and, in losing its eligibility, had its program terminated early.

In August 2010, the MCC transmitted to Congress its annual notification of candidate countries, listing 55 low-income countries and 29 lower-middle-income countries (see *Table 4* and *Table 5*).

Eligible Country Selection Criteria and Methodology

As noted earlier, the MCC provides assistance to developing nations through a competitive selection process, judged by country performance in three areas:

- Ruling justly—promoting good governance, fighting corruption, respecting human rights, and adhering to the rule of law.
- Investing in people—providing adequate health care, education, and other opportunities promoting an educated and healthy population.
- Economic freedom—fostering enterprise and entrepreneurship and promoting open markets and sustainable budgets.

Country selection is based largely, but not exclusively, on a nation's record measured by 17 performance indicators related to these three categories, or "baskets." Countries that score above the median on half of the indicators in each of the three baskets qualify. Emphasizing the importance of fighting corruption, the indicator for corruption is a "pass/fail" test: should a country fall below the median on the corruption indicator, it will be disqualified from consideration unless other, more recent trends suggest otherwise. (See *Table 6* below for a complete list of the 17 performance indicators.)

The choice of criteria on which to base the eligibility of countries for MCC programs is one of the most important elements in MCC operations. They are a key statement of MCC development priorities as they ultimately determine which countries will receive U.S. assistance. Perhaps of equal significance, the current indicators themselves have become prominent objectives of some developing countries in what former CEO Danilovich called the "MCC effect."[7] Countries seeking eligibility are said to be moving on their own to enact reforms and take measures that would enable them to meet MCC criteria.

Pursuant to reporting requirements set in the MCC legislation, each year the Corporation sends to Congress an overview of the criteria and methodology that would be used to determine the eligibility of the candidate countries in that fiscal year. The criteria have been altered and refined, sometimes dramatically, over time.

As noted above, the main criteria is that a country has demonstrated a commitment to good governance, economic freedom, and investments in its people (especially in health and education). In addition to criteria originally proposed by the Bush Administration, lawmakers included four other matters on which to evaluate a country's performance. These relate to the degree to which a country recognizes the rights of people with disabilities; respects worker rights; supports a sustainable management of natural resources; and makes social investments, especially in women and girls. For each of these, the MCC has sought to use supplemental data and qualitative information to inform its decisions on compact eligibility. The latter two factors have led to the development of new indicators.

With regard to the requirement added by Congress regarding social investments in women and girls, at first the MCC reported it would draw on girls' primary enrollment rates to supplement the four social investment performance indicators. But in FY2005, an indicator measuring girls' primary education completion rates replaced a broader measure used in FY2004 that did not disaggregate primary education graduation by gender.

Beginning with the FY2005 selection process, the MCC lowered the inflation rate threshold from 20% to 15%, making it somewhat more difficult to pass this test (only 6 of the 63 candidate countries failed this test for FY2004). For FY2006, the Corporation added a new indicator—the Cost of Starting a Business—that replaced a Country Credit Rating. The Corporation believed that not only did the new indicator have a strong correlation with economic growth, but that it was a measurement that might encourage governments to take action in order to improve their scores. Since the initial use of the indicator Days to Start a Business, MCC candidate countries had introduced many business start-up reforms, the results of which were reflected in a lowered median for this category. MCC officials hoped that adding an indicator for the Cost of Starting a Business would stimulate additional policy improvements. They believed that the Country Credit Rating indicator was not as well linked to policy reforms and that it had a greater income bias than other MCC indicators.

Efforts to develop a measurement to assess a country's commitment to policies that promote sustainable management of natural resources as required by Congress led to the adoption of two new indicators, first used as supplemental information in determining FY2007 MCC eligibility and then integrated with all the other indicators beginning with the FY2008 eligibility process. The Natural Resources Management index is a composite of indicators: whether the country is protecting at least 10% of its biomes, the percentage of population with access to sanitation and clean water, and child mortality levels. It has been placed in the Investing in People basket, raising the number of those indicators to five. The Land Rights and Access index looks at whether land tenure is secure and access to land is equitable, and the number of days and cost of registering property. It has been placed in the Economic Freedom basket. That basket remains at six indicators, because, beginning in FY2008, the MCC collapsed the Days to Start a Business and Cost of Starting a Business indicators into one Business Start-Up indicator.

In the explanatory statement accompanying the FY2009 Omnibus appropriations (P.L. 111-8), Congress urged the Board of Directors to consider establishment of an indicator that would take into consideration the votes and positions of countries in international institutions with regard to human rights issues. The MCC explored this option and noted in its September 2009 criteria report that as indicators measuring commitment to human rights within a country already exist and a country's voting record could be influenced by political goals, the suggested indicator was not appropriate.

Selection of Eligible Countries

Shortly after release of the performance criteria, the MCC publishes a scorecard, showing where each candidate country's performance falls in relation to the other candidate countries in its peer group (i.e., low-income countries "compete" with other low-income countries and lower-middleincome countries with other lower-middle-income countries). Some time later, the MCC Board meets to select countries eligible to apply for compact assistance.

A review of the history of MCC selections suggests that the Board is guided by, but not entirely bound to, the outcome of the performance indicator review process; board members can apply discretion in their selection. Performance trends, missing or old data, and recent policy actions might come into play during selection deliberations.

Just because a country passes the requisite number of qualifying indicators does not mean that it will be selected for compact eligibility. This can be due to a variety of reasons, not least of which is the limited funding available to support compacts. The Board is not required to give a reason for its selections and only occasionally offers one. Most often it appears that a country passes half or more of the qualifying indicators in each basket, but is not selected because it scores very poorly—perhaps in the lowest 25th percentile—in one or more of the remaining indicators. For example, in FY2005, the Philippines passed 13 of the then-16 indicators, but was not made eligible, because it scored "substantially below" the median on tests for health expenditures and fiscal policy, and that more recent trends indicated the fiscal policy situation was deteriorating further.[8] In FY2006, Bhutan, China, and Vietnam passed enough hurdles but were not chosen based on very low scores on political rights and civil liberties; Uganda passed 12 of the 16 indicators and did not fall significantly below the median on the other four, but was not selected for unexplained reasons.

At times, countries have been deemed compact eligible without meeting a sufficient number of qualifying factors or with weak scores in some qualifying areas. In most such cases, the Board takes into consideration recent policy changes or positive trend lines. For example, in FY2004, the program's first year, several countries were selected despite having failed the so-called "pass-fail" corruption indicator. Mozambique, which failed on corruption and each of the four "investing in people" indicators, was chosen based on supplemental data that was more current than information available from the primary data sources. This evidence, the Board felt, demonstrated Mozambique's commitment to fighting corruption and improving its performance on health and education. In FY2004, Cape Verde scored poorly on the Trade Policy indicator, but the Board took into account the country's progress towards joining the World Trade Organization and implementing a value added tax to reduce reliance on import tariffs. Lesotho did not score well on the measurement for Days to Start a Business. The MCC Board, however, took note of Lesotho's creation of a central office to facilitate new business formation and saw positive performance on other factors related to business start-ups. In FY2011, Georgia was invited to submit a proposal for a second compact despite failure in the investing in people basket; supplemental information attributing an insufficient score in immunization rates to a temporary shortage of one vaccine helped the Board toward a positive decision.

Even prior to its selection in FY2007, the possible choice of Jordan had come in for severe criticism from some quarters. Freedom House, the organization whose annual Index of Freedom is drawn upon for two of the "Ruling Justly" indicators, had urged the MCC Board to bypass countries that had low scores on political rights and civil liberties. It argued that countries like Jordan that fall below 4 out of a possible 7 on its index should be automatically disqualified. Jordan, however, did well on three of the other indicators in this category. Several development analysts further argued that Jordan should not be selected, because it is one of the largest recipients of U.S. aid, has access to private sector capital, and is not a democracy.[9] In selecting Jordan, the MCC Board appears not to have been swayed by these arguments.

The Board has, at times, selected a country and then, in future years, and prior to approval of a compact, de-selected it if its qualifying scores worsened or other factors interceded. Although the Gambia was selected in FY2006, its eligibility for MCC assistance was suspended by the MCC Board in June 2006 because of "a disturbing pattern of deteriorating conditions" in half of the 16 qualifying factors. Among the problems cited in this case were human rights abuses, restrictions on civil liberties and press freedom, and worsened anti-corruption efforts.[10] For the 2008 selection process, the MCC Board eliminated Sri Lanka because of the resurgent civil strife that would make a compact problematic. In the FY2009 selection round, the Board decided not to reselect several countries that had been eligible in previous years—Bolivia, Timor-Leste, and Ukraine. In FY2008 and FY2009, both Ukraine and Timor-Leste failed the corruption indicator. Timor-Leste, in addition, failed the "investing in people" basket in those years. Bolivia, however, had passed its indicator test in every year. A hold put on MCC consideration of its compact proposal in FY2008 and its exclusion from eligibility in FY2009 appeared likely due to the political tensions existing between it and the United States rather than its performance in development-related matters.

A number of countries have remained eligible despite failing performances in years following their selection. For example, Indonesia, selected in FY2009, and now in the process of preparing a compact proposal, fails the corruption indicator and investing in people basket in FY2011. Cape Verde, selected in FY2010 for a second compact, also fails the investing in people basket in FY2011. Both countries remain compact-eligible. Indonesia, because Congress has allowed it to be judged and funded as a lower income country, in which case it passes the selection requirements. Cape Verde remains eligible, because revised data for FY2011 on expenditures for primary education was received from UNESCO after the score was tabulated indicating it would have passed that indicator and the investing in people basket.

Countries that are already implementing compacts generally appear unaffected by a decline in performance indicators. Nine of the 19 countries implementing compacts as of January 2011 would not qualify in FY2011.[11] Georgia and Vanuatu have failed three years in a row; Armenia, El Salvador, Mail, and Mozambique have failed four years in a row. Morocco has failed for five years straight.[12]

In not strictly following the rule of the performance indicators, the MCC argues that the indicators themselves are imperfect measures of a country's policies and performance. The indicators often suffer from lag time, reflecting when the raw data was derived as much as a year or more previously. A country's position *vis-a-vis* its peers may also fluctuate considerably from year to year without reflecting any significant change in the country's policies. Countries following reasonable policies may fall behind the performance criteria when other countries are improving faster—thereby raising the bar. A shift in position from the low income to lower-middle income group can similarly alter a country's scores as it competes with countries more likely to achieve better indicators than ones in the lower income group. They may also fail when new criteria are introduced which countries have not had an opportunity to address and when institutions measuring performance refine or revise their indicators.

Country Selection—FY2011

In its FY2011 selection round, the MCC Board reselected countries currently in the process of preparing their compact proposals—Indonesia, Zambia, and Cape Verde—and selected Ghana and Georgia as eligible to develop second compacts.

Table 1. Compact-Eligible Countries: FY2011

Low-Income Countries	Lower-Middle-Income Countries
Ghana	Cape Verde
Zambia	Georgia
Indonesia ((a lower-middle income country, but for eligibility and funding, treated as a low-income country until FY2012)	

MCC Compacts

MCC compacts are grant agreements, none more than five-years in length (as required by the MCC authorization), proposed and implemented by countries selected by the MCC Board. Details of each compact and significant developments in their implementation are provided below (under Compact Descriptions).

As of April 2011, 36% of MCC compact funding was in the transport sector, mostly roads; 20% was targeted on agriculture; 9% on health, education, and community services; 9% on water supply and sanitation; 8% on energy; 4% on governance, and 2% on financial services. Counting all 23 compact countries to date, 58% of compact funding has gone to sub-

Saharan African countries, 12% to North Africa and the Middle East, 10% to the former Soviet Union, 10% to Latin America, and 10% to Asia and the Pacific.

Since its inception, the MCC has designed guidelines and procedures for project development and implementation that are followed by all MCC compact countries. These are described below.

Compact Development

Once declared as eligible, countries may prepare and negotiate program proposals with the MCC. Only those compact proposals that demonstrate a strong relationship between the proposal and economic growth and poverty reduction will receive funding.

While acknowledging that compact proposal contents likely will vary, the MCC expects each to discuss certain matters, including a country's strategy for economic growth and poverty reduction, impediments to the strategy, how MCC aid will overcome the impediments, and the goals expected to be achieved during implementation of the compact; why the proposed program is a high priority for economic development and poverty reduction and why it will succeed; the process through which a public/private dialogue took place in developing the proposal; how the program will be managed and monitored during implementation and sustained after the compact expires; the relationship of other donor activities in the priority area; examples of projects, where appropriate; a multi-year financial plan; and a country's commitment to future progress on MCC performance indicators.

Countries designate an entity, usually composed of government and non-government personnel, to coordinate the formulation of the proposal and act as a point of contact with the MCC. In many cases, a high level of political commitment to the program—country leadership identifying themselves closely with the success of the compact—helps propel compact development forward and continues into implementation.

The MCC did not set hard deadlines for compact submissions in order to allow countries adequate time to conduct a national dialogue over the contents of the program proposal. Underscoring the MCC concept of "country-ownership" and the requirement of broad public participation in the development of MCC programs embodied in MCC authorization language, the compact development entity typically launches nationwide discussions regarding the scope and purpose of the MCC grant, with meetings held at the regional and national level that include representation of civil society and the business community. In Namibia, the National Planning Commission charged with developing the compact, identified 500 issues as a result of public discussions held throughout the country on the question "What will unlock economic development in your region?", narrowing them down to 77, and then just to several.[13] Burkina Faso's consultations reportedly included 3,100 people in all 13 regions.[14]

Public consultation combined with analysis of constraints to growth help focus a country on the range of sectors and possible activities that might go into a compact proposal. Concept papers are developed around many of these ideas. During each step in the development process, the MCC provides feedback to keep the country within MCC parameters.

The eventual result of these public deliberations and concept papers are compact proposals. These proposal often exceed MCC's budget capacity, forcing a process of further prioritization and elimination. Tanzania reportedly suggested a package worth $2 billion; with the elimination of irrigation and education options, they were able to bring it down to $700 million. Namibia's first proposal, at $415 million, was whittled down to $305 million by eliminating irrigated agriculture and roads projects.

Proposals are developed by a country with the guidance of and in consultation with the MCC. To assist in compact development, the MCC may, under section 609(g) of its authorizing statute, provide so-called pre-compact development grants to assist the country's preparatory activities. Among other things, these grants may be used for design studies, baseline surveys, technical and feasibility studies, environmental and social assessments, ongoing consultations, fees for fiscal and/or procurement agents, and the like. For example, in June 2009, the MCC provided Jordan with a pre-compact development grant of $13.34 million, not counted as part of the final compact. It was used for feasibility studies and other assessments for water and wastewater projects.

One feature of compact proposals is the requirement that sustainability issues be addressed. In the case of road construction, this might mean provisions committing the government to seek to establish transport road funds, a fuel levy or some other tax to pay for road maintenance in future. For example, as a condition of its compact, Honduras increased its annual road maintenance budget from $37 million to $64 million.[15]

Once a proposal is submitted, the MCC conducts an initial assessment, then, on the basis of that assessment, launches a due diligence review that closely examines all aspects of the proposal, including costs and impacts to see if they are worthy of MCC support. Included in the review is an economic analysis assessing anticipated economic rates of return for the proposed projects and estimating the impact on poverty reduction. At the same time, MCC staff work with the country to refine program elements. Finally, the MCC negotiates a final compact agreement prior to its approval by the MCC Board. The compact is signed but does not enter into force until supplemental agreements on disbursements and procurement are reached.[16]

When the compact enters into force the clock begins to tick on compact implementation and the total amount of funds proposed for the compact are formally obligated (held by the U.S. Treasury until disbursed). Because of the difficulties encountered in trying to undertake a complex set of projects within a set five-year time span, MCC has increasingly sought to front load many planning activities prior to compact signing or entry-into-force, including feasibility studies and project design, which in the case of infrastructure can be a lengthy process. Usually, the first year of operations is consumed by contract design and solicitation for services. In the case of Burkina Faso, however, one analyst noted that the passage of a full year between signing and entry-intoforce combined with early action on staff and planning, allowed an estimated 60% of procurement to be initiated before entry-into-force.[17]

Compact Implementation

The MCC signed its first compact, with Madagascar, on April 18, 2005, an event that was followed by four other signings in 2005—with Honduras, Cape Verde, Nicaragua, and Georgia. In 2006, six more agreements were signed: Benin, Vanuatu, Armenia, Ghana, Mali and El Salvador. In 2007, four compacts were signed—with Mozambique, Lesotho, Morocco, Mongolia. In 2008, three, with Tanzania, Burkina Faso, and Namibia were signed. In 2009, one compact, with Senegal was signed. Compacts with Moldova, the Philippines, and Jordan were signed in 2010. So far in 2011, one compact with Malawi was signed.

Typically, by the time of signing, the entity that was established as point of contact during program development segues into the compact management and oversight body, the "accountable entity" usually known as the MCA. Its board is usually composed of government and non-government officials, including representatives of civil society. The government representatives are usually ministers most closely associated with compact project sectors. The MCA itself may take a variety of forms. In Tanzania, it is a government parastatal established by presidential decree under the Ministry of Finance. In Namibia, it is a separate unit within the ministry-level government National Planning Commission.

MCA staff will include fiscal and procurement agents, in many cases duties contracted out and in some cases, where the capacity is available, undertaken in-house. In the case of Namibia, for example, procurement started as a contracted function, and, when capacity improved, the contractor was replaced by an MCA-staffed procurement office. The MCA is also responsible for ensuring that accountability requirements concerning audits, monitoring, and evaluation take place. Environmental, gender, and other social requirements embedded in the compact agreement are its responsibility as well. Held to a strict five-year timetable and limited budget, the MCA faces a daunting challenge for most developing countries. For many countries, the process of getting the MCA set up, staffed, and operating was very time consuming and difficult, in some cases causing delays in implementation.

As, perhaps, the most important aspect of compact implementation, MCC procurement processes are a good example of how the MCC is building government capacity at the same time that it provides development project assistance and maintains accountability oversight for the use of U.S. funds. MCC-supported procurements are fixed-price contracts, putting the burden on the contractor to get the work done to meet the agreed price. The MCC has a set of standards and guidelines for all its project contracting. The MCC requires that procurements are preceded by a price reasonableness analysis to ensure that bids are realistic. An independent evaluation panel is selected for each discrete procurement, with all members requiring MCC approval to ensure that appropriate technical expertise is represented. The panel's report is also vetted by the MCC.

Reportedly, several countries have adopted this methodology for their procurements. Cape Verde is applying it to all public procurements. Honduras says it will maintain the program management unit to deal with projects funded by other donors and will apply MCC guidelines for procurement.[18]

The MCC itself has only a very small staff located in-country, composed chiefly of a Resident Country Director and a deputy. To assist in oversight of infrastructure projects, which account for more than half of MCC activities, MCC will often hire an independent engineering consultant. Close cooperation and guidance is also provided by MCC Washington headquarters expert staff at all points of implementation, on procedure as well as on sector technical support. MCC has to sign off on all major steps during implementation, including each disbursement. To reduce the risk of corruption, funding is transferred periodically and directly to contractors following a determination that project performance has continued satisfactorily. An appealing feature of MCC contracts to international contractor firms is that payment is made by the United States Treasury, not the compact country.

Following completion of a compact, as is the case with Honduras and Cape Verde which closed in 2010, and will be the case with five more in 2011, the MCC conducts impact evaluations using independent evaluators. Results of the first evaluations are expected to be made public within the year.

As projects are implemented, events may require that changes be made to compact plans. In 2007 and 2008, for example, the convergence of a depreciating U.S. dollar and rising costs for the machines and material necessary for the many infrastructure projects conducted by MCC meant that MCC projects were faced with having less funding than envisioned to meet the agreed-on objectives. At the time, at least six projects were scaled-back from original plans or supplemented by financing from other sources. In 2010, increased costs due to design changes and higher construction costs led to the re-allocation of nearly $40 million for a Ghana transportation project. A re-allocation of project resources was made unnecessary when bids on Tanzania's rural roads came in higher than budgeted, because the Tanzania government committed funds to make up for the shortfall. The number of boreholes to be drilled under a rural water supply project in Mozambique was reduced from 600 to 300-400 because the amount allocated for construction were insufficient. Although the MCC is trying to address potential changes by requiring more frequent portfolio reviews and early identification of high risk projects, projects planned for a five-year life span are likely to undergo revision at some point. Changes in country policy performance, however, are less foreseeable and carry more serious consequences. These are discussed below.

Compact Suspension and Termination

Throughout the entire process from candidacy to eligibility through development and implementation of a threshold program or compact, countries are expected to maintain a level of performance on the criteria reasonably close to that which brought them to their MCC threshold or compact-eligible status. On more than one occasion and for a variety of reasons, MCC programs have been suspended or terminated.

Section 611(a) of the Millennium Challenge Act of 2003 provides that, after consultation with MCC's Board of Directors (Board), the CEO may suspend or terminate assistance in whole or in part if the CEO determines that (1) the country or other entity receiving MCC aid is engaged in activities which are contrary to the national security interests of the United States; (2) the country or entity has engaged in a pattern of actions inconsistent with the criteria used to determine the eligibility of the country or entity; or (3) the country or entity has failed to adhere to its responsibilities under its compact. This policy applies to MCC assistance provided through a compact, for compact development and implementation, and assistance through a threshold agreement.[19] All compacts contain language providing that MCC may terminate the compact if the government engages in a pattern of action inconsistent with the criteria used to determine the eligibility of the country for assistance. This is the standard compact language that has been cited in most, if not all, prior MCC compact terminations.

In addition, all countries at all points of the process are affected by certain strictly applied foreign assistance restrictions in the Foreign Assistance Act of 1961 and in annual appropriations legislation. For example, restrictions on aid to countries whose governments are deposed by a military coup prevent countries from being considered for MCC candidacy, eligibility, or continued threshold or compact implementation.[20]

Application of legislative restrictions varies according to circumstances. The MCC has four steps available to it as responses to any perceived violations of its performance rules. It may warn a country of its concerns and potential consequences. It may place a program or part of a program on hold. These actions are both preliminary steps that can be taken by management without immediate concurrence of the Board. The two further steps, suspension and termination, must be made by the Board of Directors.

In all cases when some possible violation of MCC standards has been brought to the attention of the agency, the MCC Department of Policy and Evaluation conducts a review of the evidence and presents it with a recommendation to the Board. The Board does not uniformly follow the recommendation made. If a determination is made to hold, suspend, or terminate, it may be further determined to affect a whole or only part of the compact.

The MCC has suspended or terminated programs in the following cases:

- Threshold programs have been suspended or terminated in Niger, due to undemocratic actions taken by its leadership contrary to the MCC's governance criteria; Yemen due to a pattern of deterioration in its performance criteria; and Mauritania due to aid prohibitions on governments deposed by a coup. See Threshold Program section below for details.
- Compact eligibility was suspended in the Gambia because of "a disturbing pattern of deteriorating conditions" in half of the 16 qualifying factors.
- Compacts have been suspended or terminated, in whole or part, in Nicaragua, because of the actions of the government inconsistent with the MCC eligibility criteria in the area of good governance; in Honduras, because of an undemocratic transfer of power contrary to the Ruling Justly criteria; and in Madagascar, due to a military coup. In Armenia, MCC put a hold on a portion of the compact due to poor performance in a range of governance indicators, but the Board did not formally vote to suspend. See Compact Descriptions section below for details.

In as much as there have been only 23 compacts and 23 threshold agreements to date, the number of holds, suspensions, or terminations suggests that the MCC takes seriously its legislative mandate by moving to address violations of its performance standards. These prior instances of MCC program suspension and termination indicate that the MCC is most likely to apply Sec. 611(a) in response to an undemocratic transfer/retention of power, a violation of the Ruling Justly eligibility criteria. However, observers have noted instances in the past in which MCC has not taken action to restrict eligibility to countries with questionable records on political rights and civil liberties, for instance Jordan.[21] And, as noted above, a number of compact countries have failed one or more of their qualifying indicators for one or more years in a row during the period of compact implementation.

Compact Descriptions

Descriptions and key developments in the 23 compacts are provided below in alphabetical order (also see *Table 3*). Compact funding totals include administrative and monitoring costs.

Armenia

The five-year, $236 million compact concentrates on the agricultural sector, investing in the rehabilitation of rural roads ($67 million) and improving irrigation ($146 million). The program anticipates that it will benefit about 750,000 people, 75% of Armenia's rural population, by improving 943 kilometers of rural roads and increasing the amount of land under irrigation by 40%.

Misgivings have been raised both prior to and during implementation of the Armenia compact. In September 2005, during compact development, the MCC expressed concerns with Armenian officials regarding slippage on two of the governance indicators and matters raised by international groups concerning political rights and freedoms in the country. Moreover, the MCC Board delayed final approval of the compact following the November 27, 2005, constitutional referendum, after allegations of fraud, mismanagement, limited access by the press, and abuse of individuals were raised. In signing the compact on March 27, 2006, the MCC issued a cautionary note, signaling that Armenia must maintain its commitment to the performance indicators or risk suspension or termination of the compact. On March 11, 2008, the MCC issued a warning that assistance might be suspended or terminated in response to the government's actions, including the imposition of a state of emergency and restrictions on press freedoms.[22] In the autumn of 2008, the Armenian government used $17 million of its own funds to begin a road segment when there was some question of whether the MCC would continue its support. In December 2008, then-MCC CEO Danilovich noted that Armenia had since moved forward on a number of reforms addressing MCC concerns and he expected MCC support to resume in the spring of 2009.[23] However, on March 11, 2009, the MCC Board of Directors declined to lift the funding hold for the rural roads component of the Armenia compact until an interim review session could be held prior to its normal June 2009 meeting in order to assess the status of democratic governance in Armenia. On June 10, 2009, the MCC Board allowed the hold to continue on financial support for the roads project. One board member noted that the hold on funding was, in effect, a termination, as the work, if reapproved, could not be completed within the compact lifespan.[24]

Benin

The five-year, $307 million compact focuses on four sectors—land rights, reducing the time and cost of obtaining property title; financial services, helping micro, small, and medium-sized businesses; justice reform, assisting the judicial systems capacity to resolve business and investment claims; and market access, improving the Port of Cotonou. The compact's goal is to benefit five million people, bringing 250,000 of the population out of poverty by 2015.

Burkina Faso

The five-year, $480.9 million compact has four elements. A rural land governance project ($59.9 million) will focus on improving legal and institutional approaches to rural land issues, including registration and land use management. An agriculture project ($141.9 million) will target water management and irrigation, diversified agriculture, and access to rural finance in specific regions of the country. A roads project ($194.1 million) will improve rural roads. The education effort ($28.8 million) will build on the country's MCC threshold program and construct additional classrooms and provide daily meals to children. The education project will be administered by USAID.

Cape Verde

The five-year, $110 million compact, completed in October 2010, has focused largely on improving the country's investment climate, transportation networks, and agriculture productivity. The program's goal has been to increase the annual income in Cape Verde by at least $10 million.

The compact evolved around three projects. In support of private sector development, $2.1 million and additional participation with the International Finance Corporation was used to remove constraints to private sector investment by creating a commercial credit information bureau and stimulate other reforms. The MCC invested $83.2 million primarily for port construction to help link the nine inhabited islands and roads and bridges to improve transportation links to social services, employment opportunities, and local markets. By investing $11.4 million to increase the collection and distribution of rainfall water and strengthen agribusiness services, including access to credit, the project hoped to increase agricultural production and double the household income of farmers.

Cape Verde is the first compact country to be made eligible for a second compact.

El Salvador

The five-year, $461 million compact addresses economic growth and poverty reduction concerns in El Salvador's northern region where more than half the population lives below the poverty line. Education as well as water and sanitation, and electricity supply ($95.1 million); support for poor farmers and small and medium-sized business ($87.5 million); and transportation, including roads ($233.6 million) are the chief elements of program.

Georgia

The $295 million, five-year agreement with Georgia, ended in April 2011. It focused on reducing poverty and promoting economic growth in areas outside of the capital, where over half the population lives in poverty. The compact was divided into two projects. The first and the largest component ($211.7 million) concentrated on infrastructure rehabilitation, including roads, the north-south gas pipeline, water supply networks, and solid waste facilities. The Enterprise Development Project ($47.5 million) financed an investment fund aimed at providing risk capital and technical assistance to small and medium-sized businesses, and support farmers and agribusinesses that produce commodities for the domestic market.

The program expected to reduce the incidence of poverty by 12% in the Samtskhi-Javakheti region; provide direct benefits to 500,000 people and indirectly benefit over 25% of Georgia's population; reduce the travel time by 43% to Tbilisi, the capital, from regional areas, thereby cutting transportation costs for farmers, businesses, and individuals needing health and other social services; and lower the risk of a major gas pipeline accident and improve the reliability of heat and electricity to over one million Georgians.

On September 4, 2008, the Bush Administration proposed a $1 billion aid initiative for Georgia, of which one component was adding $100 million to the existing compact. An amendment to the compact was signed on November 20, 2008. Complementing or completing projects begun in the original compact, it is directed at road projects, water and sanitation facilities, and a natural gas storage facility.

Georgia has been selected as eligible for a second compact.

Ghana

The five-year, $547 million compact focuses on agriculture and rural development. Poverty rates in the three targeted geographic areas are above 40%. The agriculture component ($241 million) will provide training for farmer-based organizations, improve irrigation, provide greater access to credit, and rehabilitate local roads. The transport component ($143 million) will seek to reduce transport costs to farmers by improving key roads, such as the one between the capital and the airport, and an important ferry service. Rural development programs ($101 million) will construct and rehabilitate education, water, and electric facilities, among other activities.

Ghana has been selected as eligible for a second compact.

Honduras

The five-year, $205 million (originally $215 million) compact with Honduras, completed on September 17, 2010, focused on two objectives—rural development and transportation. The rural development project, representing $68.3 million of the compact, assisted small and medium-size farmers to enhance their business skills and to transition from the production of basic grains to more high-value horticultural crops, such as cucumbers, peppers, and tomatoes. The project provided farmers with the appropriate infrastructure and necessary training for producing and marketing these different crops. More than 7,000 farmers were trained, of which 6,029 significantly increased production of horticulture crops. About 422 kilometers of rural roads were also upgraded, helping farmers transport their goods to markets at a lower cost. The original objective was 1,500 kilometers, but increased construction costs limited that figure.

The transportation project, totaling $119.2 million of the compact, sought to improve the CA-5 major highway linking Honduran Atlantic and Pacific ports and major production centers in Honduras, El Salvador, and Nicaragua. Almost 50 kilometers of the CA-5 were completed of 107 originally planned and 45 of 68 kilometers in secondary roads before an undemocratic change in government contrary to MCC's Ruling Justly criteria—the removal of President Zelaya from office by a coalition of civilian and military institutions—led to the September 9, 2009, MCC termination of these two planned activities in the transportation sector. The termination affected about $10 million in funding, including $4 million for the CA-5 road project. Already contractually obligated programs were continued.[25]

Honduras has not been selected as eligible for a second compact due to concerns over governance.

Jordan

The five-year, $275.1 million compact is solely aimed at the water sector. In the governorate of Zarqa, it will reduce water loss by rehabilitating the water supply and distribution network from reservoir to household ($102.5 million) and will improve the sewage system by replacing or rehabilitating sewage lines ($58.22 million). In a partnership with the private sector, the compact will also expand a wastewater treatment plant originally built by USAID ($93.03 million).

Lesotho

The five-year, $362.6 million compact has three elements. A water sector project ($164 million) will focus on both industrial, supporting garment and textile operations, and domestic needs. It will also support a national watershed management and wetlands conservation plan. A health project ($122.4 million) will seek to strengthen the health care infrastructure, including renovation of up to 150 health centers, improved management of up to 14 hospital out-patient departments, construction and equipping of a central laboratory, and improved housing for medical staff and training for nurses. A private sector development project ($36.1 million) will address a wide range of legal and administrative obstacles to increased private sector activity, including development of land policy and administration authority, implementation of a new payments and settlement system, and improvement of case management of commercial courts.

Madagascar

The Madagascar compact, MCC's first signed agreement, started out as a four-year, $110 million program, was extended to five years because of start-up delays, and then terminated prematurely because of a coup. The project had three objectives: (1) to increase land titling and land security ($36 million), (2) to expand the financial sector and increase competition ($36 million), and (3) to improve agricultural production technologies and market capacity in rural areas ($17 million). After restoring 149,000 land rights documents, digitizing another 128,000, formalizing land rights for 12,800 families, constructing two new bank branches, and providing agriculture technical assistance to 34,450 farmers and 290 small businesses and farmers associations, the compact ended in May 2009, with little more than a year remaining in the compact's five-year span and $88 million of the $110 project committed.

Malawi

The five-year, $350.7 million Malawi compact focuses on just one sector—electric power. The program aims to reduce power outages, reduce costs to business and homes, and improve the economic environment. One element will upgrade and modernize generation and distribution capacity ($283 million); another will reform electric power supply institutions in the country ($25.7 million).

Mali

The five-year, $461 million compact emphasizes an increase in agricultural production and expansion of trade. About half the funds ($234.6 million) support a major irrigation project, including modernization of infrastructure and improvements in land tenure. Improvements in the airport ($89.6 million) target both passenger and freight operations. Due to rising construction costs and changes in currency valuations, $94.6 million in funds originally intended for construction of an industrial park at the airport have been reallocated to the airport project.

Moldova

The five-year, $262 million compact addresses agriculture and roads. On the agriculture side, $101.77 million will be provided to repair large irrigation systems supporting high-value fruits and vegetables, to support the legal transfer for these systems to water user organizations, to facilitate financing facilities for farmers and entrepreneurs. USAID will provide technical assistance to improve market access for high-value agriculture. The compact will also provide $132.84 million to repair a major bridge and highway leading toward Ukraine, facilitating commercial traffic between the two countries.

Mongolia

The most significant part of the original five-year, $285 million compact was intended to stimulate economic growth by refurbishing the rail system, including infrastructure and management ($188.38 million). However, in April 2009, the government of Mongolia informed the MCC that it would not be able to implement the $188 million rail component of its compact, because Russian members of the joint Mongolian-Russian rail company would not allow an audit of the company.

The MCC has decided to use $52 million of this amount to expand the three other original projects in the compact. These include support for improvements in the property registration and titling system ($23.06 million) and the vocational education system ($25.51 million), and an attempt to reform the health system to better address non-communicable diseases and injuries, which are rapidly increasing in the country ($17.03 million). In December 2009, the MCC Board approved a further restructuring of the compact, utilizing remaining funding from the terminated rail component of the compact to target $47.2 million at energy and environmental projects and $79.7 million at rehabilitating a road and bridge.

Morocco

The five-year, $697.5 million compact has multiple components, all aimed at increasing private sector growth. These include efforts to increase fruit tree productivity ($300.9 million), modernize the small-scale fisheries industry ($116.2 million), and support artisan crafts ($111.9 million). In addition, the compact will fund financial services to micro-enterprises ($46.2 million) and will provide business training and technical assistance aimed at young, unemployed graduates ($33.9 million).

Mozambique

The five-year, $506.9 million compact, like most other compacts, targets specific districts, in this case the less prosperous North of the country. The compact has four components. Water and sanitation services will be improved ($203.6 million), a major road will be rehabilitated ($176.3 million), land tenure services will be made more efficient ($39.1 million), and steps will be taken to protect existing coconut trees, improve coconut productivity, and support diversification to other cash crops ($17.4 million). The long-term objective is to reduce the projected poverty rate by more than 7%.

Namibia

The five-year, $304.5 million compact focuses on education, tourism, and agriculture. The education project ($145 million) will improve school infrastructure and training, vocational and skills training, and textbook acquisition. The tourism project ($67 million) will target management and infrastructure in Etosha National Park, the premier wildlife park in Namibia, and build ecotourism capacity in the country. The agriculture project ($47 million) will focus on land management, livestock support, and production of indigenous natural products.

Nicaragua

The five-year, $175 million compact with Nicaragua, ending in May 2011, focused on promoting economic growth primarily in the northwestern region of the country, where potential opportunities exist due to the area's fertile land and nearby markets in Honduras and El Salvador. The compact had three components: (1) to strengthen property registration ($26.5 million), (2) to upgrade primary and secondary roads between Managua and Leon and to provide technical assistance to the Ministry of Transportation ($92.8 million), and (3) to promote higher-profit agriculture activities, especially for poor farmers, and to improve water supply in support of higher-value sustainable agriculture.

On June 10, 2009, the MCC Board voted to terminate assistance for activities not yet contracted under the Nicaragua compact. These activities had been suspended since the end of 2008 because of the actions of the Nicaraguan government inconsistent with the MCC eligibility criteria, specifically in the area of good governance. Nicaragua first received a warning, then projects were put on hold, and then activities not yet contracted were suspended in December 2008 as the credibility of Nicaragua's municipal elections was seriously questioned. In July 2009, due to government actions that "limited the activity of political opposition, civil society, media elections and observers" prior to the municipal elections,[26] and were judged by MCC to be a pattern of action "inconsistent with the criteria used by MCC to determine eligibility for assistance,"[27] compact funding was partially terminated. The termination affected activities not yet contracted, a property regularization project and a major road, together amounting to about $62 million.

Philippines

The five-year, $434 million compact has three components. Computerization of the revenue collection process is expected to raise tax revenues and reduce tax evasion, while improving the impartiality of tax administration ($54.4 million). Support for small-scale, community development projects, designed and implemented by rural communities, is intended to strengthen local governance and participation in development activities ($120 million). Rehabilitation of 222 kilometers of road linking two provinces is meant to reduce transport costs and increase incomes ($214.4 million).

Senegal

The five-year, $540 million compact targets two infrastructure needs—roads and irrigation, both largely intended to support the agricultural sector in Senegal. The road rehabilitation project ($324 million) seeks to improve two key roads, one connecting major towns and neighboring countries to the capital and the other connecting the agricultural area of the Casamance to the rest of Senegal. The irrigation project ($170 million) will develop up to 10,500 hectares of land and prevent abandonment of 26,000 hectares. It will also address land tenure issues.

Tanzania

The five-year, $698 million compact focuses on three key economic infrastructure issues. A transport sector project ($373 million) will improve major trunk roads, select rural roads, general road maintenance capabilities, and upgrade an airport. An energy sector project ($206 million) will lay an electric transmission cable from the mainland to Zanzibar and will rehabilitate the existing distribution system to unserved areas. A water sector project ($66 million) will expand a clean water treatment facility serving the capital, reduce water loss in the capital region, and improve the water supply in Morogoro, a growing city.

Vanuatu

The $65.7 million, five-year compact, completed in April 2011, targeted improvements broadly in multiple types of infrastructure, including roads, wharfs, an airstrip, and warehouses. The objective was to increase the average per capita income by 15%, by helping rural agricultural producers and providers of tourism-related goods and services. The compact further aimed to help strengthen Vanuatu's Public Works Department in order to enhance capacity to maintain the country's entire transport network.

Anticipated Compacts in FY2011 and FY2012

In addition to the compact signed with Malawi in April 2011 (discussed above), the MCC anticipates possible approval of compacts with Zambia, Cape Verde, Indonesia, Ghana, and Georgia in FY2011 and FY2012. At this stage, the government of Zambia has conducted an analysis of poverty reduction strategies and has identified issues that will help guide its future compact proposal. Cape Verde is developing a second compact. A compact with Indonesia was anticipated for FY2012, but budget cuts and other considerations may mean a smaller grant with Indonesia is approved in FY2011, leaving the other countries to compete for FY2012 funding.

Threshold Programs

In order to encourage non-qualifying countries to improve in weak areas, the MCC has helped governments that are committed to reform to strengthen their performance so that they would be more competitive for MCC funding in future years. Congress provided in authorizing legislation that not more than 10% of MCC appropriations could be used for such purposes, stating that the funding could be made available through USAID. Subsequent foreign operations appropriations have made 10% of new MCC appropriations available for this so-called threshold assistance.[28]

In the first part of 2010, the threshold program underwent a review, the conclusions of which have only recently begun to emerge and have not yet been published in formal policy guidance. Up through mid-2010, the threshold programs sought chiefly to assist countries make policy reforms and institutional changes in areas where they failed to meet the MCC performance criteria with the stated goal of helping them improve those indicators. Those countries deemed eligible for the program had to submit concept papers identifying where and why the country failed to pass specific indicators; make proposals for policy, regulatory, or institutional reforms that would improve the country's performance on these indicators;

and note types of assistance, over a two-year maximum period, required to implement these reforms. If the MCC, in consultation with USAID, determined that the concept paper showed sufficient commitment to reform and a promise of success, the country would prepare a threshold country plan that specifically established a program schedule, the means to measure progress, and financing requirements, among other considerations. USAID has been charged with overseeing the implementation of nearly all threshold country plans, including working with countries to identify appropriate implementing partners such as local, U.S., and international firms; NGOs; U.S. government agencies; and international organizations. Like regular MCC compacts, funding is not guaranteed for each country selected for the threshold program, but is based on the quality of the country plan.

Although eight threshold country programs have been followed by compact eligibility, some Members of Congress and others raised concerns regarding the efficacy of threshold programs. It has been variously argued that two years is insufficient time to alter the indicators; that some countries passed the indicators before the threshold program could begin; that, by funding reform to improve an indicator, the threshold program undermines the principle that countries should themselves be responsible for reform and MCC eligibility; and that programs should focus on better preparing countries to implement compacts rather than on enabling them to qualify for eligibility. [29] In response to an explanatory statement accompanying the FY2009 Omnibus appropriations that suggested an assessment of the programs be undertaken before more are approved, the MCC did not select any new countries for threshold eligibility for FY2010 and did not request funding for the program in its FY2011 budget.

The MCC briefed its board in June 2010 and announced in September 2010 a new approach to threshold programs. While maintaining the basic purpose of helping countries become compact-eligible as required by the authorizing language, the MCC will no longer focus on changing specific indicator scores. Rather, it will focus on constraints to economic growth, like those identified for compact countries, but maintain the former threshold program focus on reforming policies. Working on resolving constraints to growth would have the benefit of helping MCC and the board become more familiar with potential compact countries as well as of beginning to work on policy reforms for problem sectors that would likely be among the ones addressed in compact projects. Despite this statement of policy, the MCC has not selected new eligible countries for the FY2011 round and requested no threshold funding for FY2012.

To date 23 threshold programs worth a total of about $495 million have been awarded to 21 countries, two of which have received second programs. Currently 6 countries are receiving threshold assistance: Rwanda, Liberia, Albania (second program), Timor-Leste, Paraguay (second program), and Peru. Of those countries that have completed programs, Indonesia, Moldova, Burkina Faso, Jordan, Malawi, the Philippines, Tanzania, and Zambia, have either begun or are eligible for compacts.

Threshold countries are subject to the same performance rules as compact countries. Two countries—Mauritania and Yemen—have had their threshold eligibility terminated prior to program implementation, the former because of a coup and the latter due to deterioration in qualifying indicators.[30] One country—Niger—had its active threshold program suspended as its governance performance deteriorated.[31]

Funding levels for threshold programs differ, ranging from $6.7 million for Guyana to $55 million for Indonesia. Of the programs ongoing or completed, most have sought to improve country scores on the corruption indicator. Several countries have multiple objectives. Indonesia and Peru, for example, target both corruption and immunization indicators. Liberia's program focuses on girls' education and land rights. Timor-Leste targets corruption and childhood immunization.

SELECT ISSUES

Concerns regarding the MCC have been expressed at various points in time on its level of funding, the speed of program implementation, the size of compacts, the sectors supported, impact on development, the role of USAID, aspects of procurement, and the risk of corruption. These issues are discussed below.

Table 2. MCC Appropriations: FY2004-FY2012
(in $ billions)

	FY 2004	FY 2005	FY 2006	FY 2007	FY 2008	FY 2009	FY 2010	FY 2011	FY 2012
Request	1.300	2.500	3.000	3.000	3.000	2.225	1.425	1.280	1.125
Enacted Appropriation	0.994	1.488	1.752	1.752	1.544	0.875	1.105	0.900	
Post- Rescission Appropriation	0.989	1.480	1.751	1.746	1.484	0.871	1.081	0.898	

Note: P.L. 110-252 rescinded $58 million in FY2008 appropriation. P.L. 111-226 rescinded $50 million from unobligated amounts; MCC applied it to the 2004-2010 fiscal years. H.R. 1473 includes an across-the-board 0.2% rescission.

Funding

When the MCC was proposed, it was expected that, within a few years, the level of funding would ramp up to about $5 billion per year. For a variety of reasons, not least of which is the limitation on available funding for foreign aid, the MCC never achieved anywhere near that level of funding. In fact, in each year since the MCC was established, its enacted appropriation has been well below the President's request. At $1.1 billion, the FY2010 pre-rescission appropriation was $320 million or 22% below the request. The FY2011 pre-rescission appropriation of $900 million is 30% below the request and the second lowest appropriation in its eight-year history.

In determining the appropriation level, Congress has to weigh the benefits of the MCC program against all other foreign assistance programs as well as against other non-foreign policy needs. A consequence of diminished appropriations is that the agency may provide fewer compacts each year to fewer countries than originally anticipated. An additional effect may be that, if few compacts are offered annually, the incentive for countries to reform on their own in order to meet eligibility requirements—the so-called MCC effect—could be lost.

MCC Appropriations Request and Congressional Action for FY2011

On February 1, 2010, the Obama Administration issued its FY2011 budget, requesting $1.280 billion for the MCC, a 16% increase over the FY2010 pre-rescission appropriation level. On June 30, the House State, Foreign Operations Appropriations subcommittee approved a draft FY2011 bill, never reported out of committee. The bill would have provided $1.105 billion for the MCC. On July 29, the Senate Appropriations Committee reported S. 3676, the FY2011 State, Foreign Operations appropriations, also providing $1.105 billion for the MCC, $174.7 million below the request and equal to the FY2010 appropriation level. The Senate bill also contained extensive amendments to the MCC authorization (see below).

Following a series of continuing appropriations, in April 2011, Congress approved H.R. 1473 (P.L. 112-10), providing $900 million for the MCC. After applying a .2% across-the-board nondefense rescission, the MCC receives $898 million in FY2011, a 19% decrease from the FY2010 enacted level.

On August 10, 2010, Congress rescinded $50 million from unobligated balances of the MCC in FY2009 and prior fiscal years, one of dozens of rescissions included in P.L. 111-226, an act that funded a number of domestic programs.

MCC Appropriations Request and Congressional Action for FY2012

In February 2011, the Obama Administration issued its FY2012 budget, requesting $1.125 billion for the MCC, a 2% increase from the enacted FY2010 appropriation and a 25% increase over the final FY2011 appropriation.

Authorizing Legislation and MCC Reform

Although the requirement of an authorization of foreign aid programs has been routinely waived in annual Foreign Operations appropriations bills, as the FY2011 Continuing Appropriations measure did in the case of currently unauthorized foreign aid programs, including the MCC (section 1108, P.L. 112-10), it is possible that an MCC reauthorization measure will be considered in the 112th Congress.

A previous effort, in the 109th Congress (2006), was reported by the House International Relations Committee (H.R. 4014, H.Rept. 109-563), but received no further consideration. That bill would have made a number of policy modifications to the original legislation and would have authorized MCC appropriations ("such sums as may be necessary") for fiscal years 2007 through 2009. Early in 2010, the Administration proposed a number of changes to MCC legislative authorities, including provisions on eligibility of countries moving from one income status to another, compact extensions, and concurrent compacts. Provisions on these issues were included in section 609 of the Foreign Relations Authorization Act, S. 2971 (Kerry), introduced on January 29, 2010, and were largely maintained in section 405 of the amended version of S. 2971 reported by the Senate Foreign Relations Committee on April 27, 2010. A somewhat similar set of authorization provisions was included in section 7075 of the Senate version of the FY2011 State, Foreign Operations appropriations, S. 3676.

With regard to the MCC, these two pieces of legislation would have

- extended the potential eligibility of selected countries that transition from low-income status to lower-middle income status, or the reverse, as though they remained in their former income status for the year of transition and two subsequent years. S. 3676 requires retention of the former status; S. 2971 allows it. This provision addresses a matter raised first in the FY2010 Consolidated appropriations (H.R. 3288, P.L. 111-117). However, the latter also allowed countries that moved in FY2009 to the upper-middle-income class, a group technically banned from MCC assistance, to maintain their lower-middle status for several years. No such provision is included in either S. 3676 or S. 2971.
- allowed a compact to exceed five years in length, up to seven years. This provision is deemed necessary in view of the difficulties that recipient countries may have in implementing complex projects within a limited timeframe.
- allowed two concurrent compacts (more than one at the same time), in order to give the MCC flexibility to do smaller, staggered projects, instead of wrapping them all in one compact. The MCC argues that concurrent compacts could be implemented as a recipient country is prepared to do so, thereby speeding up the implementation process. For example, some infrastructure projects require more planning than do technical assistance projects. S. 3676 contains additional provisions that would allow concurrent compacts only up to two years after an initial compact and would limit compact funding to any one country to 15 years.
- redefined low- and lower-middle income status to place the lowest 75 countries in the low-income group and the remaining lower-middle income countries in the lower-middle income level. Without this change, there would be 55 countries in the low-income and 29 in the lower-middle level in FY2011. This move is a response to the continually shifting classification of candidate countries that determines who they compete against for compact eligibility and the level of funding available to support their compacts (only 25 % of appropriations are available to the lower-middle group each year).

Some form of these authorization proposals may be considered in the 112th Congress.

Compact Size

During its first five years, the MCC was criticized for supporting compacts that were either too small or too large based on the dollar size of the grants. A closely examined characteristic of the early compacts was their lower-than-anticipated funding level. While Bush Administration officials had said repeatedly that compacts would be funded at various levels depending on the nature and potential impact of the proposal, the presumption in its first years was that the MCC grant would represent a sizable increase in U.S. assistance to the eligible country. In order to realize its potential as a "transformational" aid program and to provide sufficient incentives to countries requesting "breakthrough" projects, the MCC said that the size of its grants must place MCC assistance among the top aid donors in a country.[32]

Some had estimated that once the Corporation's budget reached the $5 billion annual level originally suggested, each compact would be supported with annual resources in the $150-$200 million range.[33] These levels could vary up or down depending on many factors, such as the number of people living in poverty, the size of the economy, and the scope of the proposed projects.

Most of the first several compacts, however, did not meet the anticipated financial allocation thresholds. Madagascar's four-year, $110 million compact roughly doubled U.S. assistance to the country, but did not place MCC assistance among the top donors. France was the largest bilateral donor, disbursing on average $189 million per year, 2001-2004. The European Commission's aid program, 2001-2004, averaged $82 million per year, while the World Bank's International Development Association was Madagascar's largest source of concessional assistance of about $209 million lent in each of 2001 through 2004.[34] The $110 million compact for Madagascar was also not very large relative to the country's population. Of the 16 qualified countries for FY2004, Madagascar had the fourth largest population (16.4 million), and might have been expected to receive one of the larger MCC grants given its population size and its per capita income.

For Honduras (a $215 million MCC program over five years), Georgia ($295 million over five years), and Armenia ($236 million over five years), the United States was the top bilateral donor without the MCC program, and will likely remain in that position as MCC grants are disbursed. But the MCC Compact for Honduras called for only a slightly higher annual amount ($43 million) than U.S. economic assistance provided ($34 million) at the time, while Georgia's compact averaged only about three-fourths and the Armenia compact only about two-thirds of the annual level of their recent American aid. While these were not insignificant amounts of new resources, they were far less than Bush Administration officials had suggested previously.[35]

In contrast, the early five-year compacts with Cape Verde ($110 million), Benin ($307 million), and Vanuatu ($66 million) represented a substantial investment by the United States, relative to the size of recent American aid and the size of their economies. USAID, which last provided direct bilateral assistance to Cape Verde in the mid-1990s, does not maintain a mission presence, allocating small amounts of aid through regional programs. The compact's $22 million annual average placed the United States second to Portugal, Cape Verde's former colonial power, as the leading donor, and represented more than a quarter of total bilateral development aid grants from all sources compared with figures for 2003 and 2004. Likewise, the United States does not maintain a bilateral program with Vanuatu, limiting direct aid to the Peace Corps. The $13 million annual average of the Vanuatu program places the United States as the country's top aid donor, along with Australia. In Benin, USAID manages an annual bilateral economic aid program of about $15 million, compared with the $61 million annual size of the MCC compact. The Benin compact likely places the MCC as the top aid donor, together with France.[36]

This issue of compact size was a priority of Ambassador Danilovich following his September 2005 confirmation hearing to be the MCC's new CEO. He noted that the MCC was "meant to create transformative programs," and to do so he said that "future compacts will generally need to be larger than those signed thus far." Ambassador Danilovich cautioned, however, that with limited resources but larger compacts, fewer countries would receive funding if MCC was to achieve its transformational goal.[37] After assuming the CEO position, he moved the MCC towards larger compacts and placing the MCC as the largest donor in recipient countries. In 2005, the average amount of compacts signed in that year was $181 million, in 2006, $364 million, in 2007, $463 million, and in 2008, $495 million.

Apparently, in the view of some in Congress, the move to larger compacts went too far. In the explanatory statement accompanying the FY2009 Omnibus appropriations (P.L. 111-8), the MCC was urged to limit compact size to under $350 million in order to "ensure that the MCC does not become overextended, that existing compacts are meeting their goals, and future compacts are of a manageable size."

Speed of Implementation

A recurrent criticism of the MCC, especially in Congress, has been the seemingly slow speed of implementation, reflected, in the view of some, by the limited amount of disbursements relative to available funds. This view is, to some extent, a cause of cuts in MCC funding from the Administration request and of threatened rescissions from amounts already appropriated during the past few years. As of the end of September 2009, of the $6.4 billion obligated for MCC compacts up to that point, only $889 million, or 14%, had been disbursed.

There are some good reasons for this spending rate. The MCC was a new initiative, and it took time to develop methods of operation, including settling on the rules of eligibility and the requirements of compact proposals. Further, the countries themselves are responsible for developing proposals, and they have problems common to most developing countries in managing complex programs to meet donor requirements of accountability. The GAO found that for five signed compacts in Africa—Madagascar, Cape Verde, Benin, Ghana, and Mali— the process of going from eligibility to compact signature took between 12 and 31 months. Four of these compacts entered into force about five months after compact signature.[38]

Once launched, compacts may be slow to get underway. For example, Honduras and Cape Verde, both in their fourth year had disbursed only 29% and 40%, respectively, of their total grants by end of March 2009. Among the causes for these low rates are delays by compact countries in filling managerial positions. The nature of many of the compacts is also responsible for the delays. Typically, infrastructure projects are slow to disburse funds in the early years, the majority of activity being the design and planning of projects rather than actual construction.

Whatever the causes, the MCC responded to the criticisms by shifting its organizational focus from the early emphasis on compact development to compact implementation. In October 2007, it announced a reorganization aimed at facilitating implementation. Spending has speeded up in the past year, representing 28% of total compact obligations as of September 2010.

Compact Sectors

One feature of the first series of compacts drew particular attention. Most of the early compacts included a similar sector concentration, focusing on agriculture and transportation infrastructure projects. While these activities are well justified, the similarity across Compacts surprised some observers. Given the wide diversity of conditions in each of the countries, plus the MCC's willingness to support all types of programs—the agency's only requirement is that projects be able to project the amount of economic growth and poverty reduction that will be generated— many had expected to see a greater degree of variation among the compacts. Some believe that social sectors, including those in health and education, should be receiving greater attention in compact design. Others had expected greater variety in aid delivery mechanisms, and are concerned that the MCC is reluctant to approve sector grants and other types of budget support assistance. While there can be greater accountability risks associated with budget support aid, countries that qualify for MCC support are selected because they have already demonstrated stronger performance in managing resources and fighting corruption.[39]

As more compacts are signed, some diversity in programs is creeping in—four of the more recent ones, in Lesotho, Mozambique, Tanzania, and Jordan, feature a water and sanitation component.

The Morocco compact includes micro-credit and artisan crafts support among its projects. Burkina Faso and Namibia have education components.

Compact Outcomes and Impact

The MCC places considerable weight on demonstrating results. During project development, it predicts a set of outcomes that help determine which projects will be funded. During implementation, it gathers data to establish baselines and monitor performance. And, at project completion, it supports independent evaluations of achievements. It promises to release these findings to the public, regardless of the results, with the intention of improving the agency's performance in meeting its purpose of reducing poverty through economic growth.

In its first seven years of existence, however, some observers have complained about the lack of measurable results.[40] There are some possible reasons for this, most prominently the slow speed of compact implementation noted above. The first compact programs have only just ended in late 2010. As a result, it will likely be some time before a serious analysis of actual impacts can be undertaken. In the meantime, some reporting on outcomes has emerged. For instance, according to the MCC, the number of new registered businesses in Albania has grown by 20,000, and the time and cost of starting a business in Paraguay has fallen by nearly half. In March 2009, the MCC issued an independent impact analysis of the Burkina Faso Threshold Program, which constructed 132 primary schools and provided other assistance to increase girls' enrollment rates. It found that enrollment increased for both genders, by about 20%, and for girls over boys, by 5%.[41] With the recent completion of compacts in Honduras, Cape Verde, Vanuatu, and Georgia, close of compact independent assessments are expected to more thoroughly enumerate outcomes and impacts.

A 2007 GAO report highlighted a concern, that, in the case of Vanuatu, projected impacts had been overstated. The GAO noted that the MCC estimated a rise from 2005 per capita income in Vanuatu of about 15% ($200) by 2015 when the data suggest it would rise by 4.6%. Although the MCC states that the compact would benefit 65,000 poor, rural inhabitants, the data, according to the GAO, do not establish the extent of benefit to the rural poor. Further, the MCC projections assume continued maintenance of projects following completion, whereas the experience of previous donors is that such maintenance has been poor.[42] The MCC response was that, although there may be varying views on the degree of benefit, both agencies agree that the underlying data show that the compact will help Vanuatu address poverty reduction.[43]

In lieu of results from the compacts, MCC officials have pointed to the impact made by the MCC process itself. Under the so-called MCC effect, many countries are said to be establishing reforms in an effort to qualify under the 17 indicators. Yemen has been cited in this regard, because, following its suspension from the threshold program in 2005, it approved a number of reforms to address indicators where its performance had lapsed (and subsequently was reinstated and then later suspended for different reasons). Both the House and Senate approved resolutions in 2007 (H.Res. 294 and S.Res. 103) noting the role the MCC played in encouraging Lesotho to adopt legislation improving the rights of married women.

Role of USAID

How USAID would participate in the MCC initiative was a concern of Congress and members of the development community when the MCC was established. Section 615 of the MCC authorizing legislation requires the Corporation's CEO to coordinate and consult with USAID and directs the Agency to ensure that its programs play a primary role in helping candidate countries prepare for MCC consideration. USAID maintains missions in most of the eligible countries and might be expected to support MCC programs in some way.

USAID's role to date has varied. In cases where there is a USAID mission, the views of mission personnel on potential compact proposals have been requested, and several MCC projects appear to expand on activities from earlier USAID projects. In Namibia, for example, the MCC based its community-based natural resource management efforts on USAID's successful efforts to establish conservancies. Almost all MCC threshold programs have been implemented by USAID, and USAID is the implementor of the Burkina Faso compact education project, continuing efforts it led in that country's threshold program to increase primary school completion rates for girls.

One question of concern to the development community is how USAID would adjust its own programs in countries receiving MCC compacts. Then-USAID Administrator Natsios told the House Appropriations Committee on May 13, 2004, that the Agency would not withdraw from or cut programs in MCC countries, but would not increase spending either. Nonetheless, some critics continue to express concern that MCC funding is not always additive, as had been the pledge, but substitutes for portions of previous USAID bilateral development aid programs. In its FY2008 report on the State/Foreign Operations bill (H.Rept. 110-197), the House Appropriations Committee expressed the view that MCC aid should be "a complement," not a substitute, to the current aid program.

Procurement Policy

In the course of implementing compacts, the entity that MCC sets up with partner governments signs hundreds of contracts each year to procure equipment, construct infrastructure, or obtain technical expertise. Under MCC rules, compact procurement processes are based on World Bank procedures, not U.S. federal acquisition requirements or the compact country's own rules. To counter corruption, build capacity, and achieve the maximum value for the cost of goods and services, MCC-approved rules feature transparent, competitive bidding from all firms, regardless of national origin. According to the MCC, companies from 54 countries have won MCC procurement contracts, U.S. firms winning the most with 15% of the total.

In August 2010, Senator Jim Webb raised the concern that some of these contracts had been won by Chinese government-owned firms. In a letter to the MCC, he argued that contracts awarded to Sinohydro Corporation for construction work in Mali and Tanzania supported Chinese foreign policy efforts to expand influence in Africa and harmed U.S. business. In October 2011, the MCC amended its procurement guidelines to prohibit contracts with state-owned enterprises (SOEs), except in the case of educational, research, and statistical units of government not formed for a commercial purpose. Its chief stated reason for making the change is to ensure a level playing field for competing firms. As of June 30, 2010, $325 million or about 10% of MCC contracts had gone to SOEs.

Corruption

With developing countries themselves implementing MCC-funded programs, corruption is a major concern of the MCC, in the selection process, in threshold programs, and in compact implementation.

Aiming to safeguard U.S. aid dollars, MCC programs are designed to prevent corrupt contracting. Among other things, MCC requires a transparent and competitive process and mandates separation of technical and financial elements of a bid. The MCC reviews each decision made by the procurement entity and must register approval for many of them, and it provides funds directly to contractors rather than through the government implementing entity. MCC argues that, in following this process, recipient governments learn how to do procurement in a corrupt-free way.

The degree to which a country controls corruption is one of the performance indicators that help determine whether a country should be eligible for compact funding. In fact, it is the only "pass-fail" indicator. Passing the indicator, however, does not mean there is little or no corruption—an unrealistic expectation for most developing countries. It only demonstrates that a country's performance is above the median relative to other countries at the same economic level. Further, as suggested in the discussion of country selection, the MCC board does not depend on indicator scores alone to determine the selection process. These scores change from year to year, depending on fresh data and the relative scores of competing countries. Taking this into account, the MCC board uses discretion by looking at a number of factors, including the many underlying data sources that make up indicators, as well as recent steps taken by the government in question to address corruption (or, in some cases, recent increased allegations of corruption). Accordingly, a country can be selected that technically falls near or below the median if mitigating factors occur. Alternatively, countries that pass the corruption indicator may be the subject of intense debate over incidences of alleged corruption. Because of data lags, countries passing the indicator may fail a year or two later, once a compact is in place. This can be true of all the indicators, particularly when a country "graduates" into a higher income category, thereby changing the medians.

Table 3. MCC Compacts

Country	Compact Signed	Compact Size (millions)	Entry Into Force	Compact Focus	GNI per capita	Popula-tion Living Below $2 p/day (%)	Human Development Index Ranking[a]	Other U.S. Econ. Aid: FY2010 (millions)[b]
Armenia	Mar. 27, 2006	$236 5 years	Sept.29,2006	-Agriculture/ irrigation -Rural roads	$3,100	43.4%	76	$41.4
Benin	Feb. 22, 2006	$307 5 years	Oct. 6 2006	-Land and property -Financial services -Judicial improvement -Port reha[b]	$750	75.3%	134	$35.5
Burkina Faso	July 14, 2008	$481 5 years	July 31 2009	- Rural land governance- Agriculture - Roads- Education	$510	87.6%	161	$6.0
Cape Verde	July 4, 2005	$110 5 years	Oct. 17, 2005	-Agriculture-Transport/roads -Private sector	$3,010	40.2	118	$0.0
El Salvador	Nov. 29, 2006	$461 5 years	Sept. 20, 2007	-Education -Transport//roads -Small business/farm development	$3,370	20.5%	90	$29.4
Georgia	Sept. 12, 2005	$295 5 years	April 7, 2006	-Infrastructure/ gas -Transport/ roads -Agriculture/ business	$2,530	34.2%	74	$59.9
Ghana	August 1, 2006	$547 5 years	Feb. 16, 2007	-Agriculture -Transport -Rural Development	$700	63.3%	130	$138.2
Honduras completed	June 13, 2005	$215 5 years	Sept. 29, 2005	-Agriculture -Transport/roads	$1,820	34.8%	106	$49.5
Jordan	Oct. 25, 2010	$275.1 5 years	-	-Clean Water and Sanitation	$3,740	11.0%	82	$363.0
Lesotho	July 23, 2007	$362.6 5 years	Sept. 17, 2008	-Water sector -Health sector -Private sector	$1,030	61.1%	141	$28.1

Country	Compact Signed	Compact Size (millions)	Entry Into Force	Compact Focus	GNI per capita	Popula-tion Living Below $2 p/day (%)	Human Development Index Ranking[a]	Other U.S. Econ. Aid: FY2010 (millions)[b]
Madagas-car (termina-ted May 2009)	April 18, 2005	$110 4 years	July 27, 2005	- Land titling/ Agriculture - Financial sector	$420	88.7%	135	$69.4
Malawi	April 7, 2011	$350.75 years	—	-Electric power	$280	91.0%	153	$127.6
Mali	Nov. 13, 2006	$460.8 5 years	Sept. 17, 2007	-Irrigation-Transport/ airport -Industrial park	$680	82.0%	160	$107.3
Moldova	Jan. 22, 2010	$262 5 years	—	-Agriculture - Roads	$1,590	28.9%	99	$19.0
Mongolia	Oct. 22, 2007	$285 5 years	Sept. 17, 2008	-Transport/rail-Property Rights -Voc Ed -Health	$1,630	38.8%	100	$7.5
Morocco	August 31, 2007	$697.5 5 years	Sept. 15, 2008	-Agriculture/ Fisheries -Artisan Crafts -Financial Serv/ Enterprise Support	$2,790	24.3%	114	$21.5
Mozambique	July 13, 2007	$506.9 5 years	Sept. 22, 2008	-Water and Sanitation -Transport -Land Tenure/ Agriculture	$440	92.9%	165	$364.2
Namibia	July 28, 2008	$305 5 years	Sept. 16, 2009	- Education - Tourism - Agriculture	$4,290	62.2%	105	$102.8
Nicaragua	July 14, 2005	$175 5 years	May 26, 2006	- Land titling/ Agriculture - Transport roads	$1,000	37.5%	115	$34.1
Philippines	Sept. 23, 2010	$434 5 years	—	-Revenue Reform Community Dev -Road Rehab	$1,790	43.8%	97	$103.5

Table 3. (Continued)

Country	Compact Signed	Compact Size (millions)	Entry Into Force	Compact Focus	GNI per capita	Popula-tion Living Below $2 p/day (%)	Human Development Index Ranking[a]	Other U.S. Econ. Aid: FY2010 (millions)[b]
Senegal	Sept. 16, 2009	$540 5 years	—	-Roads Irrigation	$1,030	71.3%	144	$105.1
Tanzania	Feb. 17, 2008	$698 5 years	Sept. 15, 2008	Transport/roads airport -Energy -Water	$500	91.3%	148	$463.0
Vanuatu	March 2, 2006	$66 5 years	April 28, 2006	-Transport rehab -Public Works Dept.	$2,620	NA	Not ranked	$0.0

Sources: Population Living Below $2 Per Day—data from the World Bank, World Development Indicators, 2010; Gross National Income per capita (Atlas method)—2009 data from the World Bank, World Development Indicators. Human Development Index Rank—from UNDP, Human Development Report, 2010. MCC Information: MCC.

[a] The Human Development Index (HDI) is compiled by the U.N. Development Program and is published annually in the UNDP Human Development Report. It is a composite index that measures the average achievements in a country in three basic dimensions of human development: a long and healthy life, as measured by life expectancy at birth; knowledge, as measured by the adult literacy rate and the combined gross enrolment ratio for primary, secondary, and tertiary schools; and a decent standard of living, as measured by GDP per capita in purchasing power parity (PPP) U.S. dollars. The most recent report (2010) evaluates 169 countries, with number 1 having the best HDI and number 169 scoring the worst in the Index.

[b] Other U.S. Economic Aid is defined here as Global Health and Child Survival, Development Assistance, Economic Support Fund, and Assistance to Europe, Eurasia, and Central Asia accounts.

Table 4. MCC Low-Income Candidate Countries—FY2011

Criteria: Per capita income $1,905 and below, and not prohibited from receiving other U.S. economic assistance.

Compact Eligible Countries (FY2011) are in Bold
Compact Countries are followed with (C)
Threshold Eligible Countries (FY2011) are in Italics
Threshold Program Countries are followed with (TC)

Africa		East Asia/Pacific		
Benin (C)	Tanzania (C)	Cambodia		
Burkina Faso (C)	Togo	Kiribati		
Burundi	Uganda (TC)	Indonesia (TC) (a lower-middle income country, but for eligibility and funding, treated as a low-income country until FY2012)		
Cameroon	**Zambia**	Laos		
Central African Rep		Mongolia (C)		
Chad		Papua New Guinea		
Comoros		Philippines (C)		
Congo, Dem Rep of		Solomon Islands		
Congo, Rep of		Vietnam		
Djibouti				
Ethiopia				
Gambia				
Ghana (C)				
Guinea		**Latin America**		
Guinea-Bissau		Bolivia		
Kenya (TC)	**South Asia**	Guyana (TC)		
Lesotho (C)	Afghanistan	Haiti		
Liberia (TC)	Bangladesh	Honduras (C)		
Malawi (C)	India	Nicaragua (C)		
Mali (C)	Nepal			
Mauritania	Pakistan			
Mozambique (C)		**Mid-East**		
Niger (TC)		Yemen		
Nigeria				
Rwanda				
Sao Tome and Principe (TC)	**Eurasia**	**Europe**		
Senegal (C)	Kyrgyz Rep. (TC)	—		
Sierra Leone	Moldova (TC) (C)			
Somalia	Tajikistan			

The MCC attempts to address this concern by looking for a pattern of behavior on the part of the government in order to judge the severity of any proposed corrective action.

In 2010, there were suggestions from Congress that the MCC should take the issue of corruption more into account in judging compact country behavior. During hearings with the MCC CEO, the House State, Foreign Operations Appropriations Sub-committee Chair and Ranking Member raised concerns regarding the absence of termination guidelines based on a pattern of corruption.[44]

In 2009 and 2010, several members of Congress noted their concern regarding provision of MCC funding to corrupt countries.[45] Specifically, they each referred to the case of Senegal, whose leader installed a monument to the country's independence estimated to cost between $24 million and $70 million. The $540 million compact with Senegal was signed in September 2009. Despite corruption reports, Senegal scores in the 74th percentile of the FY2011 Control of Corruption indicator formulated by the World Bank. The MCC says it has looked at but found no pattern of corrupt behavior since signing the Senegal compact that would justify suspending or closing the compact program. It has notified the Senegalese government that any decline in policy performance, regardless of indicator scores, could jeopardize the compact.

Table 5. MCC Lower-Middle-Income Candidate Countries—FY2011

Criteria: Per capita income between $1,906 and $3,945, and not prohibited from receiving other U.S. economic assistance.
Compact Eligible Countries (FY2011) are in Bold
Compact Countries are followed with (C)
Threshold Eligible Countries (FY2011) are in Italics
Threshold Program Countries are followed with (TC)

Africa	East Asia/Pacific	Latin America
Angola	Marshall Islands	Belize
Cape Verde (C)	Micronesia	Ecuador
Swaziland	Samoa	El Salvador(C)
	Thailand	Guatemala
	Timor-Leste (TC)	Paraguay (TC)
	Tonga	
	Tuvalu	
	Vanuatu (C)	
	South Asia	**Mid-East**
	Bhutan	Egypt
	Maldives	Jordan (C)
	Sri Lanka	Morocco (C)
		Tunisia
	Eurasia	**Europe**
	Armenia (C)	Kosovo
	Georgia (C)	
	Turkmenistan	
	Ukraine (TC)	

Table 6. MCC Performance Indicators for FY2011

Ruling Justly	Investing in People	Economic Freedom
Control of Corruption Source: World Bank Institute http://www.worldbank.org/wbi/governance	Public Primary Education Spending as % of GDP Sources: UNESCO and National governments	Inflation Source: IMF World Economic Outlook
Voice and Accountability Source: World Bank Institute http://www.worldbank.org/wbi/governance	Primary Girls' Education Completion Rate Source: UNESCO	Fiscal Policy Source: National governments and IMF World Economic Outlook

Ruling Justly	Investing in People	Economic Freedom
Government Effectiveness Source: World Bank Institute http://www.worldbank.org/wbi/governance	Public Expenditure on Health as % of GDP Source: World Health Organization (WHO)	Trade Policy Source: The Heritage Foundation, Index of Economic Freedom http://www.heritage.org/research/features/index/
Rule of Law Source: World Bank Institute http://www.worldbank.org/wbi/governance	Immunization Rates: DPT and Measles Source: World Health Organization (WHO)	Regulatory Policy Source: World Bank Institute http://www.worldbank.org/wbi/governance
Civil Liberties Source: Freedom House http://www.freedomhouse.org/template.cfm?page=15&year=2006	Natural Resource Management: Eco-Region Protection, Access to Clean Water and Sanitation, Child Mortality Sources: Columbia Center for Int'l Earth Science Info Network (CIESIN) and Yale Center for Env. Law and Policy (YCLEP)	Business Start-Up: Days and Cost of Starting a Business Source: World Bank http://www.doingbusiness.org
Political Rights Source: Freedom House http://www.freedomhouse.org/template.cfm?page=15&year=2006		Land Rights and Access Source: Int'l Fund for Agricultural Development (IFAD) and Int'l Finance Corporation

End Notes

[1] When first proposed and in its early years, the initiative was known as the Millennium Challenge Account. Today, both the program and the funding account in the foreign operations budget are more commonly known by the name of the managing entity, the MCC. For a more in-depth discussion of the original MCC proposal and issues debated by Congress in 2003, see CRS Report RL31687, *The Millennium Challenge Account: Congressional Consideration of a New Foreign Aid Initiative*, by Larry Nowels.

[2] The decision to house the initiative in a new organization was one of the most debated issues during early congressional deliberations. The Bush Administration argued that because the initiative represents a new concept in aid delivery, it should have a "fresh" organizational structure, unencumbered by bureaucratic authorities and regulations that would interfere in effective management. Critics, however, contended that if the initiative was placed outside the formal U.S. government foreign aid structure, it would lead to further fragmentation of policy development and consistency. Some believed that USAID, the principal U.S. aid agency, should manage the program, while others said that it should reside in the State Department. At least, some argued, the USAID Administrator should be a member of the MCC Board, which had not been proposed in the initial Administration request. The MCC's status remained unchanged under Secretary of State Rice's realignment of foreign aid authorities, announced on January 19, 2006. While gaining policy and budget authority over nearly all USAID and State Department foreign aid programs, the new Director of Foreign Assistance in the State Department played a more limited role in other agency activities, developing an overall U.S. government development strategy and only providing "guidance" to foreign aid programs delivered through other agencies like the MCC.

[3] MCC, *Agency Financial Report, Fiscal Year 2010*, p. 15.

[4] Current private sector board members are Mark Green, former congressman and ambassador to Tanzania, serving his first term, and Alan Patricof, co-founder of a venture capital corporation, serving his second term. First terms run three years and second terms run two years. Two board seats are currently vacant.

[5] The Philippines moved to the lower-middle income level in FY2010, signed a compact as a low-income country in FY2010, and has now returned to low-income status in FY2011.

[6] Various types of aid restrictions applied to these countries. For several—Sudan, Cote d'Ivoire, and Madagascar— U.S. aid was blocked because an elected head of government had been deposed by a military coup. For Uzbekistan, legislation banned assistance to the central government. Aid restrictions imposed on nations not cooperating in counternarcotics efforts (Burma), that are on the terrorist list (Sudan, Syria, North Korea), or in

arrears on debt owed the United States (Syria, Sudan) also applied. Notwithstanding these and other restrictions, each country remained eligible for humanitarian assistance from the United States.

[7] MCC Public Outreach Meeting, February 15, 2007.

[8] Comments by Paul Applegarth, then MCC CEO, at a State Department Foreign Press Center Briefing, November 9, 2004.

[9] Freedom House, "Millennium Challenge Corporation Should Hold Countries to Higher Standards of Democratic Governance," November 2, 2006, http://www.freedomhouse.org; Sheila Herrling, Steve Radelet, and Sarah Rose, "Will Politics Encroach in the MCA FY2007 Selection Round? The Cases of Jordan and Indonesia," Center for Global Development, October 30, 2006, http://www.cgdev.org.

[10] MCC Press Release, "The Gambia Suspended From Participation in MCC Compact Program," June 15, 2006.

[11] These are Armenia, Burkina Faso, El Salvador, Georgia, Mali, Mongolia, Morocco, Mozambique, and Vanuatu.

[12] For further discussion, see Casey Dunning, Owen McCarthy, and Sarah Jane Staats, Center for Global Development, *Round Eight of the MCA*, December 3, 2010.

[13] Tanzania and Namibia examples in this section are based on author interviews.

[14] Rebecca Schutte, *Burkina Faso Field Report*, Center for Global Development, July 2009.

[15] MCC, *Policy Reforms Matter*, September 9, 2010.

[16] Details on each of the negotiated compacts can be found at the MCC website: http://www.mcc.gov.

[17] Rebecca Schutte, Center for Global Development, *Burkina Faso Field Report*, July 2009, p. 1.

[18] Marco Bogran, Acting General Director, MCA-Honduras, and Ariane Gauchat, Associate Director, MCC, *MCC Hosts Public Event: Lessons Learned from MCC's First Compacts*, February 22, 2011, pages 9 and 32.

[19] "MCC Policy on Suspension and Termination", available at http://www.mcc.gov/mcc/bm.doc/07-suspensionandterminationpolicy.pdf.

[20] Most recently, section 7008 in P.L. 111-117, Division F, the State, Foreign Operations Appropriations, FY2010.

[21] Freedom House, Press Release, "Millennium Challenge Corporation Should Hold Countries to Higher Standards of Democratic Governance, November 2, 2006, available at http://www.freedomhouse.org/template.cfm?page=70&release=435; Sheila Herrling, Steve Radelet, and Sarah Rose, "Will Politics Encroach in the MCA FY2007 Selection Round? The Cases of Jordan and Indonesia," Center for Global Development, October 30, 2006, http://www.cgdev.org.

[22] See letters of John Danilovich to Armenia President Robert Kocharyan on December 16, 2005 and March 11, 2008 on MCC website.

[23] MCC, Public Outreach Meeting Transcript, December 12, 2008, p. 12.

[24] Lorne Craner at Public Outreach Meeting, June 11, 2009.

[25] See MCC Congressional Notification, September 17, 2009, at http://www.mcc.gov/mcc/bm.doc/cn-091709-honduras.pdf.

[26] MCC Press Release, "MCC Urges Nicaraguan Government to Respect Democracy," available at http://www.mcc.gov/mcc/countries/nicaragua/ni-documents/release-112508-nicaragua.shtml .

[27] From Nicaragua country page of MCC website, available at http://www.mcc.gov/mcc/countries/ nicaragua/ index. shtml.

[28] Initially, assistance for threshold countries was authorized only for FY2004.

[29] One such critic, Sheila Herrling, has since become the MCC Vice President for Policy and Evaluation . See "Precedent-Setting Board Meeting for Team Obama," *MCA Monitor Blog*, June 9, 2009, Center for Global Development website http://blogs.cgdev.org/mca-monitor.

[30] Mauritania, made eligible in 2007, saw its eligibility terminated in 2008, prior to development of a threshold program agreement, due to aid prohibitions on governments deposed by a coup. Yemen, made threshold eligible in 2004, was suspended by the Board in November 2005, as a result of a consistent "pattern of deterioration" in its policy performance on selection criteria.30 Following a series of government reforms, Yemen's threshold status was reinstated in February 2007 and a threshold agreement valued at $20.6 million was approved in September 2007. In October 2007, however, the Chair and ranking member of the Senate Foreign Relations Committee noted their concern regarding the Yemen decision, in particular noting that, while Yemen had made reforms, its performance indicators had not yet shown improvement. The Members emphasized that, even if the MCC moved forward with the Yemen threshold program, "such compromises should never extend to the Compact program itself." In the end, implementation was postponed on October 27, 2007, pending a review, and its program has never been resumed.

[31] In September 2009, the MCC Board warned that Niger appeared to be moving away from its reform agenda, jeopardizing its $23 million threshold program. Niger's threshold program was suspended in December 2009 due to "political events that were inconsistent with the criteria used to determine eligibility for MCC

assistance," when President Tandja dissolved parliament and dismissed the constitutional court after it ruled that a referendum to extend his presidential term was illegal. See MCC Congressional Notification, December 17, 2009, available at http://www.mcc.gov/mcc/bm.doc/cn-121709-niger.pdf.

[32] See, for example, Millennium Challenge Corporation FY2005 Budget Justification, p. 7. Found at http://www.mcc.gov/about/reports/congressional/budgetjustifications/budget_justification_fy05.pdf.

[33] Prepared statement of Steve Radelet, Senior Fellow at the Center for Global Development, before a hearing of the House International Relations Committee, April 27, 2005.

[34] Organization for Economic Cooperation and Development (OECD), Geographical Distribution of Financial Flows to Aid Recipients, 2000/2004: 2006 edition.

[35] For example, USAID Administrator Natsios remarked in an October 22, 2002 speech at the American Embassy in London that "we estimate in most countries the MCA will provide funding 5 to 10 times higher than existing levels" of U.S. assistance.

[36] Geographical Distribution of Financial Flows to Aid Recipients, 2000/2004: 2006 edition.

[37] Prepared statement of John J. Danilovich, before the Senate Committee on Foreign Relations, September 27, 2005.

[38] Government Accountability Office, Millennium Challenge Corporation: Progress and Challenges with Compact in Africa, Testimony, June 28, 2007, GAO-07-1049T.

[39] James Fox and Lex Rieffel, The Millennium Challenge Account: Moving Toward Smarter Aid. The Brookings Institution, July 14, 2005, p. 24.

[40] For example, the Senate Appropriations Committee report (S.Rept. 110-425) on its version of the FY2009 State/Foreign Operations appropriations explained a proposed cut to the MCC by noting the small compact disbursement rate (4% of total compact funding at the time) and the lack of tangible results to date as factors. The committee stated its intention to support future compacts "if current country compacts are shown to be cost effective and achieving results."

[41] MCC Public Board Meeting, June 11, 2009. Mathematica Policy Research, Inc., Impact Evaluation of Burkina Faso's BRIGHT Program, March 2009.

[42] Government Accountability Office, Millennium Challenge Corporation: Vanuatu Compact Overstates Projected Program Impact, July 2007, GAO-07-909.

[43] Testimony of Rodney Bent before the House Committee on Foreign Affairs, Subcommittee on Asia, the Pacific, and the Global Environment, July 26, 2007.

[44] Hearing with Daniel Yohannes, MCC CEO, April 14, 2010.

[45] "For Senegal: U.S. Aid, 164-ft. Statue," The Washington Times, August 16, 2010.

In: Millenium Challenge Corporation
Editor: Lautaro B. Rojas

ISBN: 978-1-62100-584-1
© 2012 Nova Science Publishers, Inc.

Chapter 2

MILLENNIUM CHALLENGE CORPORATION: SUMMARY FACT SHEETS FOR 17 COMPACTS[*]

United States Government Accountability Office

July 14, 2010
Congressional Committees

The Millennium Challenge Corporation (MCC), now in its seventh year of operations, is to provide aid to developing countries that have demonstrated a commitment to ruling justly, encouraging economic freedom, and investing in people. MCC provides assistance to eligible countries through multiyear compact agreements to fund specific programs targeted at reducing poverty and stimulating economic growth. MCC has received appropriations for fiscal years 2004 through 2010 totaling about $9.5 billion and has set aside about $8.1 billion of this amount for compact assistance. As of June 2010, MCC had signed compacts with 20 countries totaling approximately $7.1 billion; of the 20 compacts, 18 compacts had entered into force, obligating a total of approximately $6.3 billion. The President has requested approximately $1.3 billion in additional funds for MCC for fiscal year 2011, of which MCC plans to use about $1.1 billion for compact assistance to countries currently eligible for compacts.

Enclosed are fact sheets for 17 of the MCC compacts that had entered into force as of December 2009.[1] The fact sheets summarize each country's

- general country characteristics and location,
- timeline of key compact events as of June 2010,
- per capita income relative to MCC income criteria,
- performance on MCC's eligibility indicators,
- compact characteristics and structure,
- compact funding and project allocations as of December 2009, and
- planned and actual compact fund disbursements through December 2009.[2]

---

[*] This is an edited, reformatted and augmented version of theUnited States Government Accountability Office publication GAO-10-797R, dated July 14, 2010.

SCOPE AND METHODOLOGY

We compiled and summarized data from a number of sources to develop these fact sheets, including our previous reporting on MCC, as follows:

- To provide a general overview of each country's characteristics, we used information from the World Bank and from the Central Intelligence Agency World Fact Books.
- To develop timelines of key compact events, we analyzed MCC data from its fiscal year 2009 financial report and our previous reporting.
- To depict countries' income categorization, we compared World Bank data on per capita gross national incomes (GNI) with MCC's income eligibility thresholds published in its annual candidate country reports.
- To summarize country performance on MCC eligibility indicators, we used data from MCC's annual candidate country scorecards and eligible country reports.
- To summarize each compact's characteristics and structure, we reviewed and analyzed MCC's compacts, compact summaries, and monitoring and evaluation plans at compact signature, and the fiscal year 2011 Congressional Budget Justification. These summaries reflect the compact structure as of December 2009 and expected beneficiaries recalculated as of fiscal year 2009. Expected results are reported as of compact signature, however MCC continues to modify expected results as projects evolve and as new data becomes available.
- To analyze compact allocations, disbursements, and commitments, we compiled public information from MCC's quarterly reports on compact obligations, disbursements, and commitments published in the *Federal Register* and from MCC's quarterly country status reports.[3] The planned disbursements we report are based on MCC's financial plan projections at compact signature and as of December 2009 and on the assumption that compact funds are disbursed evenly throughout the compact term and implementation year. One country, Mongolia, had a major reallocation of funds that MCC approved at the end of 2009; however, the reallocations were not implemented until January 2010. Although the implementation date for these reallocations was outside our scope, we have included information on the reallocations using MCC's most current financial plan.

To clarify and confirm our understanding of this information, we met with MCC officials.

We determined that World Bank gross national income per capita data were sufficiently reliable to depict countries' income categorization as compared to MCC's eligibility cutoffs.

We further determined that MCC financial data were sufficiently reliable for our purposes based on our review of U.S. Agency for International Development Inspector General Audits of MCC's internal controls and financial statements. We did not independently assess the reliability of MCC's projections of all countries' compact results in this review and have noted this accordingly on each fact sheet.[4] We conducted our work from January 2010 to July 2010 in accordance with sections of GAO's Quality Assurance Framework relevant to our objectives. This framework requires that we plan and perform the engagement to obtain sufficient and appropriate evidence to meet our stated objectives and discuss any limitation in our work. We believe that the information and data obtained, and the analysis conducted, provide a reasonable basis for any findings and conclusions.

Agency Comments and Our Evaluation

We provided a draft of the fact sheets to MCC for review. MCC provided written comments about the draft, which we have reproduced in enclosure I. Regarding the rate of funds disbursement, MCC stated that the pace is, in some cases, slower than projected when the compacts were signed. MCC notes that the disbursement lags can be attributed to a number of factors, which MCC and the partner countries are addressing. Regarding projected compact beneficiaries and results, MCC noted that, as a part of its monitoring and evaluation, MCC periodically reviews and revises compacts' results and beneficiaries in light of evolving project designs or additional data.

We also received and incorporated as appropriate a number of technical comments from MCC.

Emil Friberg, Jr. (Assistant Director), Miriam Carroll Fenton, and Suneeti Shah Vakharia made significant contributions to this report. Jena Sinkfield, Etana Finkler, Ernie Jackson, Reid Lowe, and Amanda Miller provided technical assistance.

David B. Gootnick
Director, International Affairs and Trade

Armenia Compact Fact Sheet

Coutry Characteristics

Located in the Caucasus region of Asia, Armenia has a population of about 3.1 million. It is a lowermiddle-income country. Its economy is based primarily on services and industry, which respectively constitute 48 and 34 percent of its gross domestic product (GDP). Agriculture constitutes 19 percent of GDP but employs about 46 percent of the labor force. After the breakup of the Soviet Union in 1991,

ENCLOSURE I: COMMENTS FROM THE MILLENNIUM CHALLENGE CORPORATION

MILLENNIUM
CHALLENGE CORPORATION
UNITED STATES OF AMERICA

June 28, 2010

Mr. David B. Gootnick
Director, International Affairs and Trade
U.S. Government Accountability Office
441 G Street, NW
Washington, DC 20548

Dear Mr. Gootnick:

Thank you for the opportunity to provide comments on the GAO report entitled "Millennium Challenge Corporation: **Summary Fact Sheets for 17 Compacts Entered into Force.**" MCC appreciates GAO's summaries of our compacts that reduce global poverty through the promotion of sustainable economic growth, and wishes to clarify certain points regarding the pace of our disbursements as well as the dynamic nature of our project evaluation process.

Compact Disbursement Rates

MCC acknowledges that the pace of its disbursements, in some cases, is slower than projected by the general financial plans developed when individual compacts were signed. These lags are attributed to a number of factors being addressed by MCC and our partner countries.

First, as a result of more project feasibility work being conducted during the compact development process, MCC has greater certainty on project costs and is therefore able to develop more complete financial plans at the time of compact signing. Second, implementing units, known as MCAs, are now established and mobilized earlier, allowing procurements to begin sooner after compact signature, which in turn allows for earlier disbursements. Third, during implementation, MCC requires MCAs to update their detailed financial plans on a quarterly basis. This process provides MCC with revised quarterly projections for the remainder of the compact term; these projections form the basis of our annual corporate disbursement and commitment targets. MCC makes these targets public and reviews them with various stakeholders.

These changes have significantly improved MCC's disbursement performance against the corporate targets over the past two years without compromising its oversight model. Increases in the pace of MCC's disbursements has resulted in an increase in the on-the-ground work completed which has allowed MCC to begin showing the related output and outcome results of its investments.

Dynamic Evaluation of Expected Beneficiaries & Results

As noted in the GAO report, MCC undertook a major effort in December 2009 to ensure that consistent definitions of beneficiaries are used across compacts. This has resulted in updates to a number of the project beneficiary estimates.

MCC periodically reviews compacts' benefits and beneficiaries. MCC project designs may evolve or be refined during program implementation, and additional data impacting assumptions in the economic model may become available. Consequently, projections of expected benefits and beneficiaries may also change. MCC provides updated estimates in publicly available documents such as monitoring and evaluation plans as they are available.

We have greatly appreciated working with the GAO in the development of these documents. If you have any questions, please do not hesitate to contact me.

Sincerely Yours,

Patrick C. Fine
Department of Compact Implementation

Source: Map Resources (map).

Armenia implemented some economic reforms, but geographic isolation, a narrow export base, and monopolies in important business sectors made it vulnerable to the deterioration in the global economy. After several years of high economic growth, Armenia faced an economic recession, with GDP declining by at least 15 percent in 2009. Its economy is further challenged by high transportation costs. The country is landlocked, and its borders with Azerbaijan and Turkey have been closed since the early 1990s.

Conpact Timeline

During compact development, MCC and an eligible country negotiate project proposals and the compact's terms. After the compact is signed, the country finalizes administrative requirements, such as procurement and disbursement agreements.

When the compact enters into force, MCC obligates funds and compact implementation begins. MCC's statute limits compact implementation to 5 years.

Armenia was 1 of 16 countries that MCC selected as eligible in its first eligibility round. As of June 30, 2010, 75 percent of the compact's 5- year period had elapsed.

Key Events for Armenia Compact

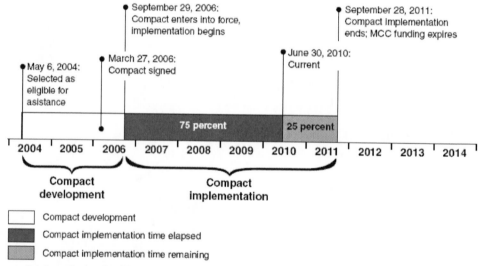

Source: GAO analysis of Millennium Challenge Corporation data.

ARMENIA

MCC Candidate Criteria

Each fiscal year, MCC uses per capita gross national income (GNI) data to identify two pools of candidate countries—low-income and lower-middle-income—based on World Bank lending thresholds. Also, a candidate country must not be statutorily barred from receiving U.S. assistance. By law, MCC can use up to 25 percent of compact assistance each year for new compacts with lower-middle-income countries.

Armenia was classified as a low-income country from 2004 through 2007. In 2008, Armenia's rising GNI per capita lifted it to lower-middle-income status.

MCC Eligibility Criteria

MCC's board uses quantitative indicators to assess a candidate's policy performance. To meet MCC's criteria, a country must pass the control of corruption indicator and at least half of the indictors in each of three categories. To pass an indicator, a country must score above the median in its income group. However, the board may select a country as eligible even if it does not meet the criteria. Once MCC has signed a compact with a country, MCC continues to work with it—even if it fails the criteria—as long as its actions are not inconsistent with the criteria. If a country's policy performance declines, the board can suspend or terminate the compact.

Armenia met MCC's eligibility criteria each year from 2004 through 2007 as a low-income country. In 2008, it rose to lower-middle-income status and each year since then has failed to meet the criteria for that group.

MCC SELECTION CRITERIA

Armenia GNI Per Capita

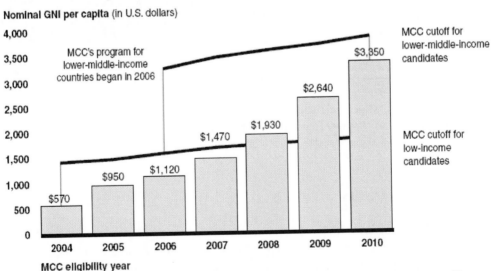

Source: GAO analysis of World Bank World Development Indicators and MCC income cutoffs.

ARMENIA'S PERFORMANCE ON MCC ELIGIBILITY INDICATORS

Indicator category	MCC eligibility year	2004	2005	2006	2007	2008	2009	2010
	MCC Income group	Low	Low	Low	Low	Lower-middle	Lower-middle	Lower-middle
Ruling Justly	Political Rights	X	✓	X	X	X	X	X
	Civil Liberties	X	✓	✓	X	X	X	X
	Voice and Accountability	✓	✓	✓	✓	X	X	X
	Government Effectiveness	✓	✓	✓	✓	✓	✓	✓
	Rule of Law	✓	✓	✓	✓	X	X	X
	Control of Corruption	✓	✓	✓	✓	X	X	X
Investing in People	Girls' Primary Education Completion[a]	✓	✓	✓	✓	X	✓	✓
	Primary Education Expenditures	X	X	X	✓	✓	✓	✓
	Health Expenditures	X	X	X	X	X	X	X
	Immunization Rates	✓	✓	✓	✓	X	X	X
	Natural Resource Management (2008-2010)					✓	✓	✓
Economic Freedom	Country Credit Rating (2004-2005)	✓	✓					
	Days to Start a Business (2004-2007)	✓	✓	✓	✓			
	Cost of Starting a Business (2006-2007)			✓	✓			
	Business Start-up (2008-2010)					✓	✓	✓
	Inflation	✓	✓	✓	✓	✓	✓	✓
	Fiscal Policy	✓	✓	✓	✓	X	X	X
	Trade Policy	✓	✓	✓	✓	✓	✓	✓
	Regulatory Quality	✓	✓	✓	✓	✓	✓	✓
	Land Rights and Access (2008-2010)					✓	✓	✓
	Indicator performance results	Passed	Passed	Passed	Passed	Failed	Failed	Failed
	MCC eligibility determination	Eligible	Eligible	Eligible	Eligible	Eligible	NA[b]	NA[b]

✓ Passed (scored above the median)　X Failed (scored at the median or below)　☐ NA for that year

Source: GAO analysis of Millenium Challenge Corporation Data.
[a]In 2004, the indicator was "Primary Education Completion."
[b]In 2009, MCC stopped making an eligibility determination for countries with existing compacts.

Compact Characteristics

MCC and the partner country determine the compact structure before the compact is signed. However, the structure of some compacts has been altered during implementation.

At signature, Armenia's compact focused on reducing rural poverty by increasing the agricultural sector's economic performance. At that time, more than 1 million Armenians (35 percent of the population) were dependent on semisubsistence agriculture. In June 2009, MCC put a hold on funding for the Rural Road Rehabilitation Project because of concerns about the status of democratic governance in Armenia. MCC will not resume funding for any future road construction under the compact. MCC also rescoped the Irrigated Agriculture Project.

Compact Summary

Structure of Armenia Compact, as of December 2009

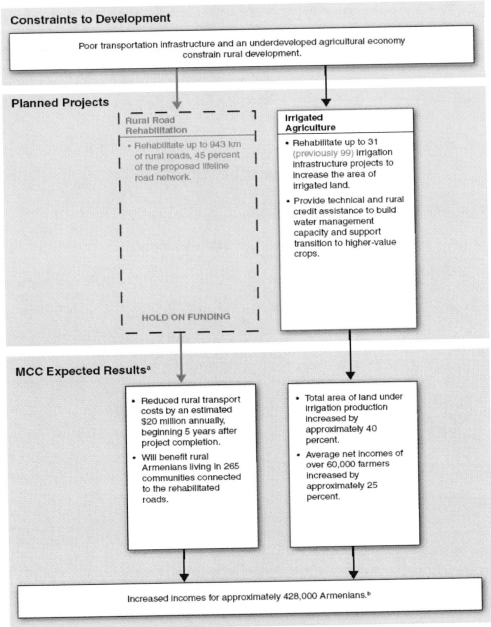

Constraints to Development

Poor transportation infrastructure and an underdeveloped agricultural economy constrain rural development.

Planned Projects

Rural Road Rehabilitation

• Rehabilitate up to 943 km of rural roads, 45 percent of the proposed lifeline road network.

HOLD ON FUNDING

Irrigated Agriculture

• Rehabilitate up to 31 (previously 99) irrigation infrastructure projects to increase the area of irrigated land.

• Provide technical and rural credit assistance to build water management capacity and support transition to higher-value crops.

MCC Expected Results[a]

• Reduced rural transport costs by an estimated $20 million annually, beginning 5 years after project completion.

• Will benefit rural Armenians living in 265 communities connected to the rehabilitated roads.

• Total area of land under irrigation production increased by approximately 40 percent.

• Average net incomes of over 60,000 farmers increased by approximately 25 percent.

Increased incomes for approximately 428,000 Armenians.[b]

Source: GAO analysis of Millennium Challenge Corporation data.

[a] MCC expected results are reported as of compact signature, except the number of beneficiaries with increased incomes. The hold on funding for the Rural Road Rehabilitation Project may affect results.

[b] In fiscal year 2009, MCC recalculated the number of expected beneficiaries using a standardized methodology. At compact signature, MCC reported the compact would benefit approximately 750,000 people.

Expected Results

This graphic presents MCC's expectations of selected compact results at compact signature and at the end of fiscal year 2009.

The Armenia compact is one of five compacts for which GAO has independently verified the reliability of MCC's result projections. In June 2008, GAO reported that MCC made analytic errors in its original projections of the Armenia compact's impact. Correcting these errors reduces MCC's expected impact on income in rural areas and on poverty (GAO-08-730).

MCC has modified the Armenia compact but only partially recalculated the expected results.

COMPACT FUNDING

Armenia Compact Project Allocations

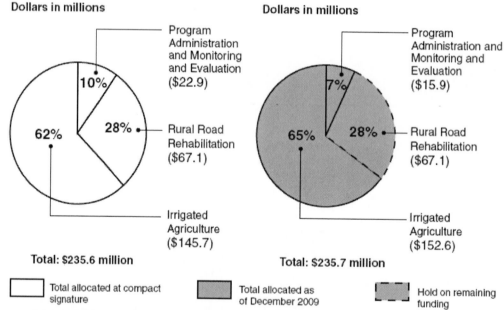

Dollars in millions

10%
62%
28% — Program Administration and Monitoring and Evaluation ($22.9)
— Rural Road Rehabilitation ($67.1)
— Irrigated Agriculture ($145.7)

Total: $235.6 million

Dollars in millions

7%
65%
28% — Program Administration and Monitoring and Evaluation ($15.9)
— Rural Road Rehabilitation ($67.1)
— Irrigated Agriculture ($152.6)

Total: $235.7 million

☐ Total allocated at compact signature   ▨ Total allocated as of December 2009   ▨ Hold on remaining funding

Source: GAO analysis of Millennium Challenge Corporation data.

Note: The difference in total compact funds allocated at compact signature and as of December 2009 is due to rounding.

Compact Project Funding

MCC and the country may reallocate funds among projects during implementation. In some cases, MCC has also changed the overall compact obligation.

At signature (March 2006), MCC obligated $235.6 million for the Armenia compact. As of December 2009, the overall obligation amount had not changed, however, nearly $7 million had been reallocated from Program Administration and Monitoring and Evaluation funds to the Irrigated Agriculture Project. In addition, because MCC put a hold on funding for the Rural Road Rehabilitation Project, approximately $59.0 million of compact funds will not be disbursed or reallocated.

Compact Disbursements

At compact signature, MCC develops a disbursement plan for the compact. MCC disburses funds as the country begins implementing projects. According to MCC, any funds not disbursed within 120 days after the compact ends would return to MCC for reprogramming.

As of December 2009, MCC had disbursed $54.0 million (approximately 23 percent) of compact funds, compared with the $153.4 million (approximately 65 percent) that it had planned to disburse as of that date.

Although it is not shown in the graphic, in addition to the above disbursements, $80.8 million has been committed under the compact for pending expenses as of December 2009.

Armenia Compact Planned and Actual Disbursements

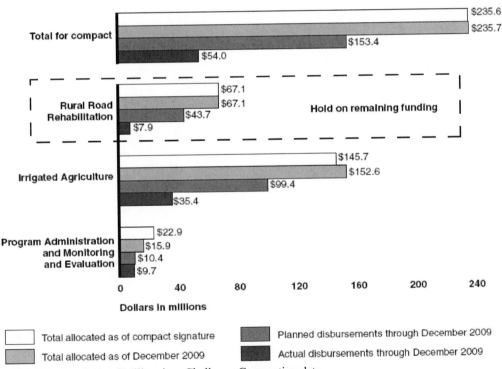

Source: GAO analysis of Millennium Challenge Corporation data.

Notes: We base planned disbursements on MCC's projections for the fiscal quarter ending December 2009. We assume that funds are disbursed evenly throughout each year. Actual disbursements by project may not add up to total disbursements because some disbursements are pending allocation to projects and are reflected in the total but not in the projects.

BENIN COMPACT FACT SHEET

Map of Benin

Source: Map Resources (map).

Country Characteristics

Located in coastal West Africa, Benin has a population of approximately 8.7 million. It is a low-income country. Its economy is based on services, which constitute 52 percent of its gross domestic product; industry and agriculture constitute another 15 and 33 percent, respectively. The economy has experienced some positive growth in the last few years, with the real economic growth rate averaging 4.2 percent from 2007 through 2009. However, the global economic slowdown has negatively affected Benin's growth. The current government, which entered office in 2006, has emphasized efforts to fight corruption and accelerate Benin's economic growth.

Compact Timeline

During compact development, MCC and an eligible country negotiate project proposals and the compact's terms. After the compact is signed, the country finalizes administrative requirements, such as procurement and disbursement agreements. When the compact enters into force, MCC obligates funds and compact implementation begins. MCC's statute limits compact implementation to 5 years.

Benin was 1 of 16 countries that MCC selected as eligible in its first eligibility round. As of June 30, 2010, 75 percent of the compact's 5-year period had elapsed.

Key Events for Benin Compact

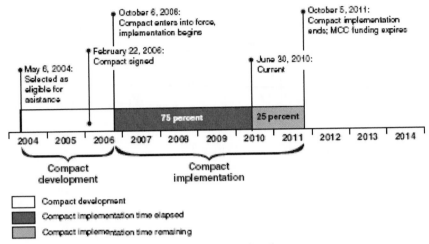

Source: GAO analysis of Millennium Challenge Corporation data.

MCC SELECTION CRITERIA

MCC Candidate Criteria

Each fiscal year, MCC uses per capita gross national income (GNI) data to identify two pools of candidate countries—low-income and lower-middle-income—based on World Bank lending thresholds. Also, a candidate country must not be statutorily barred from receiving U.S. assistance. By law, MCC can use up to 25 percent of compact assistance each year for new compacts with lower-middle-income countries.

Benin has been classified as a low-income country every year since MCC began operations in 2004.

MCC Eligibility Criteria

MCC's board uses quantitative indicators to assess a candidate's policy performance. To meet MCC's criteria, a country must pass the control of corruption indicator and at least half of the indictors in each of three categories. To pass an indicator, a country must score above the median in its income group. However, the Board may select a country as eligible even if it does not meet the criteria. Once MCC has signed a compact with a country, MCC continues to work with it—even if it fails the criteria—as long as its actions are not inconsistent with the criteria. If a country's policy performance declines, the Board can suspend or terminate the compact.

Benin met MCC's eligibility criteria in 2004 through 2006. In 2007 through 2009, it did not meet the criteria because it either failed the corruption indicator or more than three Investing in People indicators. Benin met all criteria in 2010.

Benin GNI Per Capita

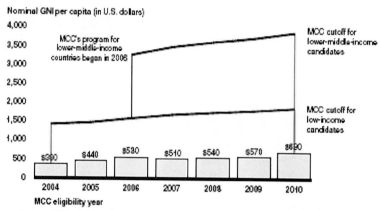

Source: GAO analysis of World Bank World Development Indicators and MCC income cutoffs.

Benin's Performance on MCC Eligibility Indicators

Indicator category	MCC eligibility year	2004	2005	2006	2007	2008	2009	2010
	MCC income group	Low	Low	Low	Low	Low	Low	Low
Ruling Justly	Political Rights	✓	✓	✓	✓	✓	✓	✓
	Civil Liberties	✓	✓	✓	✓	✓	✓	✓
	Voice and Accountability	✓	✓	✓	✓	✓	✓	✓
	Government Effectiveness	✓	✓	✓	✓	✓	✓	✓
	Rule of Law	✓	✓	✓	✓	✓	✓	✓
	Control of Corruption	✓	✓	✓	X	X	✓	✓
Investing in People	Girls' Primary Education Completion[a]	X	X	X	X	X	X	X
	Primary Education Expenditures	X	✓	✓	✓	✓	X	✓
	Health Expenditures	✓	X	X	X	✓	✓	✓
	Immunization Rates	✓	✓	✓	✓	✓	X	X
	Natural Resource Management (2009-2010)						X	X	✓
Economic Freedom	Country Credit Rating (2004-2005)	✓	✓					
	Days to Start a Business (2004-2007)	✓	✓	✓	✓			
	Cost of Starting a Business (2006-2007)			X	X			
	Business Start-up (2008-2010)					X	X	X
	Inflation	✓	✓	✓	✓	✓	✓	✓
	Fiscal Policy	✓	✓	✓	✓	✓	✓	✓
	Trade Policy	X	X	X	X	X	X	X
	Regulatory Quality	✓	✓	✓	✓	✓	✓	✓
	Land Rights and Access (2008-2010)					X	X	X
	Indicator performance results	Passed	Passed	Passed	Failed	Failed	Failed	Passed
	MCC eligibility determination	Eligible	Eligible	Eligible	Eligible	Eligible	NA[b]	NA[b]

✓ Passed (scored above the median)   X Failed (scored at the median or below)   ☐ NA for that year

Source: GAO analysis of Millennium Challenge Corporation data.

[a] In 2004, the indicator was "Primary Education Completion."

[b] In 2009, MCC stopped making an eligibility determination for countries with existing compacts.

COMPACT SUMMARY

Structure of Benin Compact, as of December 2009

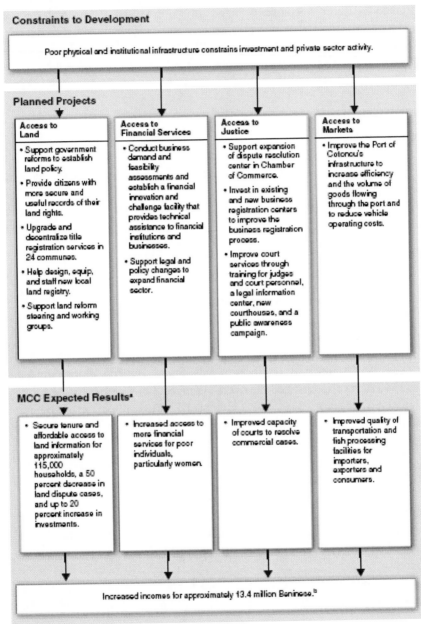

Constraints to Development

Poor physical and institutional infrastructure constrains investment and private sector activity.

Planned Projects

Access to Land	Access to Financial Services	Access to Justice	Access to Markets
• Support government reforms to establish land policy. • Provide citizens with more secure and useful records of their land rights. • Upgrade and decentralize title registration services in 24 communes. • Help design, equip, and staff new local land registry. • Support land reform steering and working groups.	• Conduct business demand and feasibility assessments and establish a financial innovation and challenge facility that provides technical assistance to financial institutions and businesses. • Support legal and policy changes to expand financial sector.	• Support expansion of dispute resolution center in Chamber of Commerce. • Invest in existing and new business registration centers to improve the business registration process. • Improve court services through training for judges and court personnel, a legal information center, new courthouses, and a public awareness campaign.	• Improve the Port of Cotonou's infrastructure to increase efficiency and the volume of goods flowing through the port and to reduce vehicle operating costs.

MCC Expected Results[a]

• Secure tenure and affordable access to land information for approximately 115,000 households, a 50 percent decrease in land dispute cases, and up to 20 percent increase in investments.	• Increased access to more financial services for poor individuals, particularly women.	• Improved capacity of courts to resolve commercial cases.	• Improved quality of transportation and fish processing facilities for importers, exporters and consumers.

Increased incomes for approximately 13.4 million Beninese.[b]

Source: GAO analysis of Millennium Challenge Corporation data.

[a] MCC expected results are reported as of compact signature, except the number of beneficiaries with increased incomes.

[b] In fiscal year 2009, MCC recalculated the number of expected beneficiaries using a standardized methodology. At compact signature, MCC reported the compact would benefit approximately 5 million people.

Compact Characteristics

MCC and the partner country determine the compact structure before the compact is signed. However, the structure of some compacts has been altered during implementation.

At signature, Benin's compact aimed to improve core physical and institutional infrastructure and increase private sector activity and investment. At that time, one-third of Benin residents lived in poverty; 1 percent of Benin households held a formal title to land, with a majority of the rural population relying on oral customary land rights; and only a small fraction of the population owned a bank account.

Expected Results

This graphic presents MCC's expectations of selected compact results at compact signature and at the end of fiscal year 2009.

GAO has not independently verified the reliability of MCC's results projections for this compact. Previous GAO work has identified several problems with the methodology used to determine compact results. (See GAO-08-730 and GAO-07-909.)

COMPACT FUNDING

Compact Project Funding

MCC and the country may reallocate funds among projects during implementation. In some cases, MCC has also changed the overall compact obligation.

At signature (February 2006), MCC obligated $307.3 million for the Benin compact. As of December 2009, the overall obligation amount and project allocations had not changed.

Compact Disbursements

At compact signature, MCC develops a disbursement plan for the compact. MCC disburses funds as the country begins implementing projects. According to MCC, any funds not disbursed within 120 days after the compact ends would return to MCC for reprogramming.

As of December 2009, MCC had disbursed $66.3 million (approximately 22 percent) of compact funds, compared with the $215.1 million (70 percent) that it had planned to disburse as of that date.

Although it is not shown in the graphic, in addition to the above disbursements, $139.3 million has been committed under the compact for pending expenses as of December 2009.

Benin Compact Project Allocations

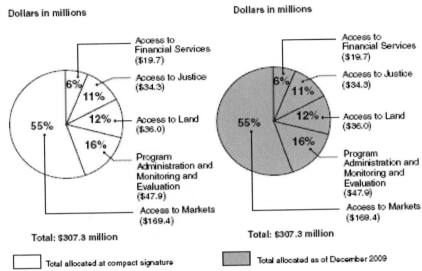

Source: GAO analysis of Millennium Challenge Corporation data.

Benin Compact Planned and Actual Disbursements

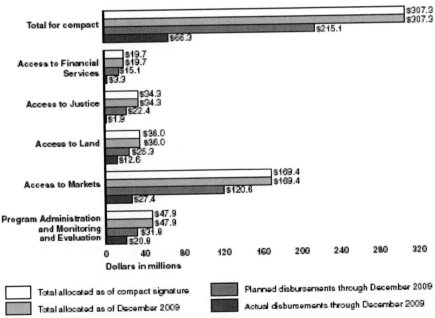

Source: GAO analysis of Millennium Challenge Corporation data.

Notes: We base planned disbursements on MCC's projections for the fiscal quarter ending December 2009. We assume that funds are disbursed evenly throughout each year. Actual disbursements by project may not add up to total disbursements because some disbursements are pending allocation to projects and are reflected in the total but not in the projects.

BURKINA FASO COMPACT FACT SHEET

Map of Burkina Faso

Source: Map Resources (map).

Key Events for Burkina Faso Compact

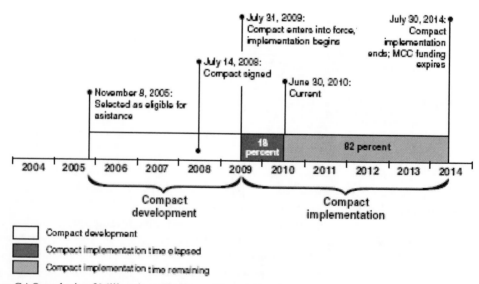

Source: GAO analysis of Millennium Challenge Corporation data.

MCC SELECTION CRITERIA

Burkina Faso GNI Per Capita

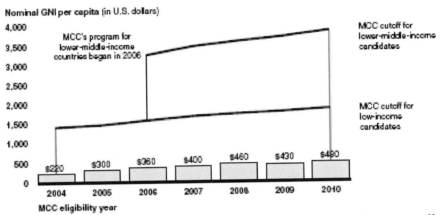

Source: GAO analysis of World Bank World Development Indicators and MCC income cutoffs.

Burkina Faso's Performance on MCC Eligibility Indicators

Indicator category		MCC eligibility year	2004	2005	2006	2007	2008	2009	2010
		MCC income group	Low	Low	Low	Low	Low	Low	Low
Ruling Justly		Political Rights	X	✓	X	X	X	X	X
		Civil Liberties	X	✓	✓	✓	✓	✓	✓
		Voice and Accountability	✓	✓	✓	✓	✓	✓	✓
		Government Effectiveness	✓	✓	✓	✓	✓	X	✓
		Rule of Law	✓	✓	✓	✓	✓	✓	✓
		Control of Corruption	✓	✓	✓	✓	✓	✓	✓
Investing in People		Girls' Primary Education Completion[a]	X	X	X	X	X	X	X
		Primary Education Expenditures	✓	✓	✓	✓	✓	✓	✓
		Health Expenditures	✓	✓	✓	✓	✓	✓	✓
		Immunization Rates	X	✓	✓	✓	✓	✓	X
		Natural Resource Management (2009-2010)						X	X	X
Economic Freedom		Country Credit Rating (2004-2005)	X	✓					
		Days to Start a Business (2004-2007)	X	X	✓	✓			
		Cost of Starting a Business (2006-2007)			X	X			
		Business Start-up (2008-2010)					✓	✓	✓
		Inflation	✓	✓	✓	✓	✓	✓	✓
		Fiscal Policy	X	X	X	X	✓	✓	✓
		Trade Policy	X	X	X	X	X	✓	✓
		Regulatory Quality	✓	✓	✓	✓	✓	✓	✓
		Land Rights and Access (2009-2010)						X	X	X
		Indicator performance results	Failed	Passed	Passed	Passed	Passed	Passed	Failed
		MCC eligibility determination	Not Eligible	Not Eligible	Eligible	Eligible	Eligible	NA[b]	NA[b]

✓ Passed (scored above the median)   X Failed (scored at the median or below)   ☐ NA for that year

Source: GAO analysis of Millennium Challenge Corporation data.

[a] In 2004, the indicator was "Primary Education Completion."

[b] In 2009, MCC stopped making an eligibility determination for countries with existing compacts.

MCC Candidate Criteria

Each fiscal year, MCC uses per capita gross national income (GNI) data to identify two pools of candidate countries—low-income and lower-middle-income—based on World Bank lending thresholds. Also, a candidate country must not be statutorily barred from receiving U.S. assistance. By law, MCC can use up to 25 percent of compact assistance each year for new compacts with lower-middleincome countries.

Burkina Faso was selected as eligible in fiscal year 2006 and has been classified as a low-income country ever since.

MCC Eligibility Criteria

MCC's board uses quantitative indicators to assess a candidate's policy performance. To meet MCC's criteria, a country must pass the control of corruption indicator and at least half of the indictors in each of three categories. To pass an indicator, a country must score above the median in its income group. However, the board may select a country as eligible even if it does not meet the criteria. Once MCC has signed a compact with a country, MCC continues to work with it—even if it fails the criteria—as long as its actions are not inconsistent with the criteria. If a country's policy performance declines, the board can suspend or terminate the compact.

Burkina Faso became eligible in 2006 and met MCC's eligibility criteria each year from 2006 through 2009. It did not meet the criteria in 2010 because it failed three of the five Investing in People indicators.

COMPACT SUMMARY

Compact Characteristics

MCC and the partner country determine the compact structure before the compact is signed. However, the structure of some compacts has been altered during implementation.

Burkina Faso's compact targets rural areas, which, according to MCC, are home to 95 percent of the country's poor. Many of the compact projects are focused in Boucle de Mouhoun, the third poorest of Burkina Faso's 13 regions. In addition, a small number of projects focus on the Comoé region. At compact signature, Burkina Faso was one of the poorest countries in the world.

Expected Results

This graphic presents MCC's expectations of selected compact results at compact signature and at the end of fiscal year 2009.

GAO has not independently verified the reliability of MCC's results projections for this compact. Previous GAO work has identified several problems with the methodology used to determine compact results. (See GAO-08-730 and GAO-07-909.)

Structure of Burkina Faso Compact, as of December 2009

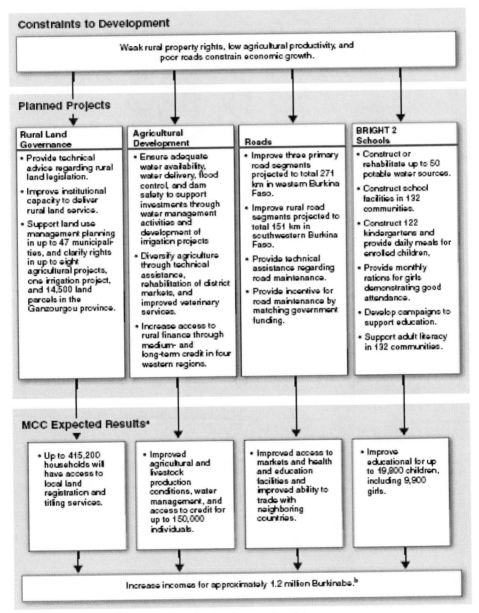

Source: GAO analysis of Millennium Challenge Corporation data.

[a] MCC expected results are reported as of compact signature, except the number of beneficiaries with increased incomes.

[b] In fiscal year 2009, MCC recalculated the number of expected beneficiaries using a standardized methodology. MCC did not publish a beneficiary estimate for Burkina Faso at compact signature.

COMPACT FUNDING

Burkina Faso Project Allocations

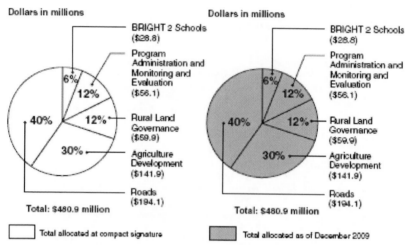

Source: GAO analysis of Millennium Challenge Corporation data.

Burkina Faso Planned and Actual Disbursements

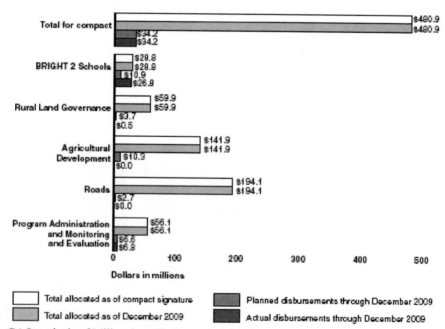

Source: GAO analysis of Millennium Challenge Corporation data.

Notes: We base planned disbursements on MCC's projections for the fiscal quarter ending December 2009. We assume that funds are disbursed evenly throughout each year. Actual disbursements by project may not add up to total disbursements because some disbursements are pending allocation to projects and are reflected in the total but not in the projects.

Compact Project Funding

MCC and the country may reallocate funds among projects during implementation. In some cases, MCC has also changed the overall compact obligation.

At signature (July 2008), MCC obligated $480.9 million for the Burkina Faso compact. As of December 2009, the overall obligation amount and project allocations had not changed.

Compact Disbursements

At compact signature, MCC develops a disbursement plan for the compact. MCC disburses funds as the country begins implementing projects. According to MCC, any funds not disbursed within 120 days after the compact ends would return to MCC for reprogramming.

As of December 2009, MCC had disbursed $34.2 million (approximately 7 percent) of compact funds, compared with the $34.2 million (approximately 7 percent) that it had planned to disburse as of that date.

Although it is not shown in the graphic, in addition to the above disbursements, $48.6 million has been committed under the compact for pending expenses as of December 2009.

CAPE VERDE COMPACT FACT SHEET

Map of Cape Verde

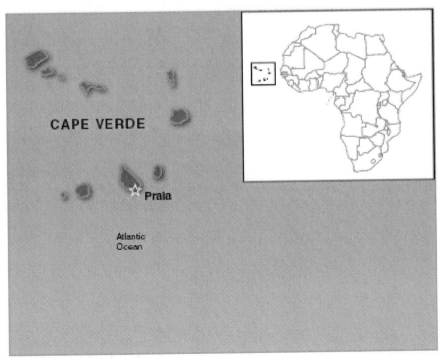

Source: Map Resources (map).

Key Events for Cape Verde Compact

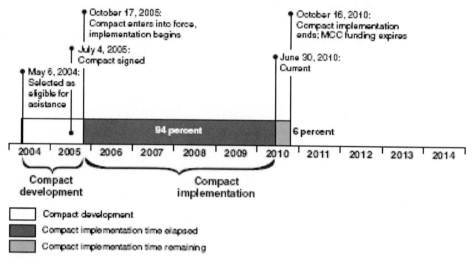

Source: GAO analysis of Millennium Challenge Corporation data.

Country Characteristics

Located off the coast of West Africa, Cape Verde is a group of 10 islands with a population of about 500,000. It is a lower-middle-income country. Its economy is heavily based on services, which constitute 74 percent of its gross domestic product (GDP); industry and agriculture constitute 17 and 9 percent of GDP, respectively. Its economy suffers from a poor natural resource base and relies heavily on foreign assistance and remittances. Cape Verde is considered one of Africa's most stable democracies and, despite its economic challenges, has experienced economic growth, a reduction of poverty, and increases in access to education and health care. Cape Verde is the first country eligible for a second MCC compact.

Compact Timeline

During compact development, MCC and an eligible country negotiate project proposals and the compact's terms. After the compact is signed, the country finalizes administrative requirements, such as procurement and disbursement agreements. When the compact enters into force, MCC obligates funds and compact implementation begins. MCC's statute limits compact implementation to 5 years.

Cape Verde was 1 of 16 countries that MCC selected as eligible in its first eligibility round. It was the third country to begin implementing a compact. As of June 30, 2010, 94 percent of the compact's 5-year period had elapsed.

MCC SELECTION CRITERIA

Cape Verde GNI Per Capita

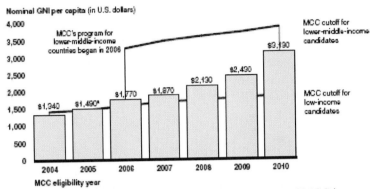

Source: GAO analysis of World Bank World Development Indicators and MCC income cutoffs.

[a] Cape Verde was not a candidate for assistance in 2005 because it surpassed the cut-off for low-income candidates.

Cape Verde's Performance on MCC Eligibility Indicators

Indicator category	MCC eligibility year	2004	2005	2006	2007	2008	2009	2010
	MCC income group	Low	Lower-middle	Lower-middle	Lower-middle	Lower-middle	Lower-middle	Lower-middle
Ruling Justly	Political Rights	✓		✓	✓	✓	✓	✓
Ruling Justly	Civil Liberties	✓		✓	✓	✓	✓	✓
Ruling Justly	Voice and Accountability	✓		✓	✓	✓	✓	✓
Ruling Justly	Government Effectiveness	✓		✓	✓	✓	✓	✓
Ruling Justly	Rule of Law	✓		✓	✓	✓	✓	✓
Ruling Justly	Control of Corruption	✓		✓	✓	✓	✓	✓
Investing in People	Girls' Primary Education Completion[a]	✓		✓	✓	X	X	X
Investing in People	Primary Education Expenditures	✓		✓	✓	✓	✓	✓
Investing in People	Health Expenditures	✓		✓	✓	X	✓	✓
Investing in People	Immunization Rates	✓		X	X	X	X	✓
Investing in People	Natural Resource Management (2009-2010)						X	X
Economic Freedom	Country Credit Rating (2004-2005)	✓						
Economic Freedom	Days to Start a Business (2004-2007)	X		X	X			
Economic Freedom	Cost of Starting a Business (2006-2007)			X	X			
Economic Freedom	Business Start-up (2008-2010)					X	X	✓
Economic Freedom	Inflation	✓		✓	✓	✓	✓	✓
Economic Freedom	Fiscal Policy	✓		X	X	X	X	X
Economic Freedom	Trade Policy	X		X	X	X	X	✓
Economic Freedom	Regulatory Quality			✓	✓	X	X	X
Economic Freedom	Land Rights and Access (2008-2010)					X	X	X
	Indicator performance results	Passed		Failed	Failed	Failed	Failed	Passed
	MCC eligibility determination	Eligible	Not Eligible	Eligible	Eligible	Not Eligible	NA[b]	NA[b]

Note: 2005 column — Cape Verde was not a candidate in 2005.

✓ Passed (scored above the median)   X Failed (scored at the median or below)   ☐ NA for that year

Source: GAO analysis of Millennium Challenge Corporation data.

[a] In 2004, the indicator was "Primary Education Completion."

[b] In 2009, MCC stopped making an eligibility determination for countries with existing compacts.

MCC Candidate Criteria

Each fiscal year, MCC uses per capita gross national income (GNI) data to identify two pools of candidate countries—low-income and lower-middle-income—based on World Bank lending thresholds. Also, candidate country must not be statutorily barred from receiving U.S. assistance. By law, MCC can use up to 25 percent of compact assistance each year for new compacts with lower-middleincome countries.

Cape Verde was a low-income country in 2004. It was not a candidate in 2005 because its GNI rose above the low-income cut-off. Since 2006, Cape Verde has been a lower-middle-income country.

MCC Eligibility Criteria

MCC's board uses quantitative indicators to assess a candidate's policy performance. To meet MCC's criteria, a country must pass the control of corruption indicator and at least half of the indictors in each of three categories. To pass an indicator, a country must score above the median in its income group. However, the board may select a country as eligible even if it does not meet the criteria. Once MCC has signed a compact with a country, MCC continues to work with it—even if it fails the criteria—as long as its actions are not inconsistent with the criteria. If a country's policy performance declines, the board can suspend or terminate the compact.

Cape Verde met MCC's eligibility criteria in 2004 as a low-income country. In 2005, it rose to lowermiddle-income status and was not a candidate. In 2006, it failed the indicators for its group and did not meet the criteria again until 2010.

COMPACT SUMMARY

Compact Characteristics

MCC and the partner country determine the compact structure before the compact is signed. However, the structure of some compacts has been altered during implementation.

At signature, Cape Verde's compact focused on water and infrastructure projects on four islands. Compact funds support the upgrade and expansion of the Port of Praia, which is Cape Verde's busiest port and handles half of the country's cargo. At signature, 10 percent of Cape Verde's land was arable, and agricultural productivity was low; approximately 85 percent of food was imported (70 percent in the form of food aid). In May 2008, MCC restructured the Cape Verde compact in response to project rescoping, increased input costs, and currency fluctuations.

Structure of Cape Verde Compact, as of December 2009

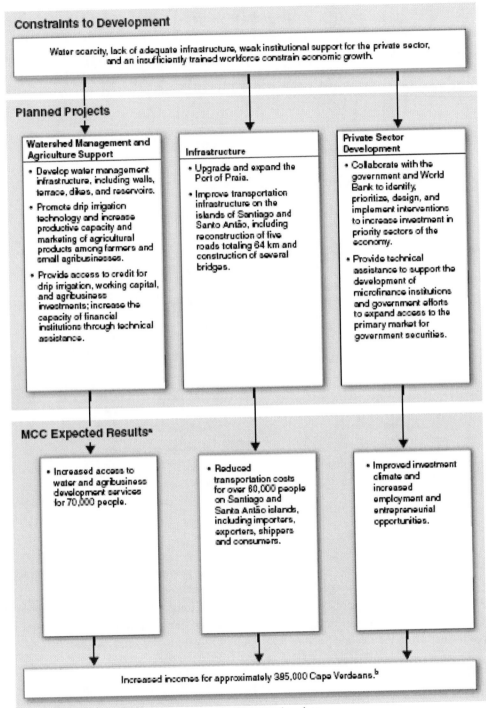

Constraints to Development

Water scarcity, lack of adequate infrastructure, weak institutional support for the private sector, and an insufficiently trained workforce constrain economic growth.

Planned Projects

Watershed Management and Agriculture Support
- Develop water management infrastructure, including walls, terrace, dikes, and reservoirs.
- Promote drip irrigation technology and increase productive capacity and marketing of agricultural products among farmers and small agribusinesses.
- Provide access to credit for drip irrigation, working capital, and agribusiness investments; increase the capacity of financial institutions through technical assistance.

Infrastructure
- Upgrade and expand the Port of Praia.
- Improve transportation infrastructure on the islands of Santiago and Santo Antão, including reconstruction of five roads totaling 64 km and construction of several bridges.

Private Sector Development
- Collaborate with the government and World Bank to identify, prioritize, design, and implement interventions to increase investment in priority sectors of the economy.
- Provide technical assistance to support the development of microfinance institutions and government efforts to expand access to the primary market for government securities.

MCC Expected Results[a]

- Increased access to water and agribusiness development services for 70,000 people.

- Reduced transportation costs for over 80,000 people on Santiago and Santo Antão islands, including importers, exporters, shippers and consumers.

- Improved investment climate and increased employment and entrepreneurial opportunities.

Increased incomes for approximately 385,000 Cape Verdeans.[b]

Source: GAO analysis of Millennium Challenge Corporation data.

[a] MCC expected results are reported as of compact signature, except the number of beneficiaries with increased incomes.

[b] In fiscal year 2009, MCC recalculated the number of expected beneficiaries using a standardized methodology. MCC did not publish a beneficiary estimate for Cape Verde at compact signature.

Expected Results

This graphic presents MCC's expectations of selected compact results at compact signature and at the end of fiscal year 2009.

GAO has not independently verified the reliability of MCC's results projections for this compact. Previous GAO work has identified several problems with the methodology used to determine compact results. (See GAO-08-730 and GAO-07-909.)

COMPACT FUNDING

Cape Verde Project Allocations

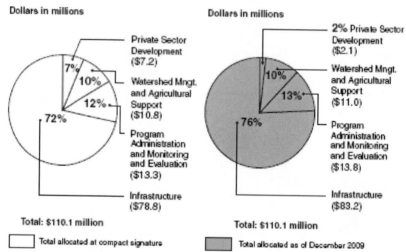

Source: GAO analysis of Millennium Challenge Corporation data.
Note: Project allocations in figures may not add up to 100 percent due to rounding.

Compact Project Funding

MCC and the country may reallocate funds among projects during implementation. In some cases, MCC has also changed the overall compact obligation.

At signature (July 2005), MCC obligated $110.1 million for the Cape Verde compact. As of December 2009, the overall obligation amount had not changed, however over $4 million was reallocated from the Private Sector Development Project to the Infrastructure Project.

Compact Disbursements

At compact signature, MCC develops a disbursement plan for the compact. MCC disburses funds as the country begins implementing projects. According to MCC, any funds not disbursed within 120 days after the compact ends would return to MCC for reprogramming.

As of December 2009, MCC had disbursed $69.1 million (approximately 63 percent) of compact funds, compared with the $92.6 million (approximately 84 percent) that it had planned to disburse as of that date.

Although it is not shown in the graphic, in addition to the above disbursements, $31.7 million has been committed under the compact for pending expenses as of December 2009.

Cape Verde Planned and Actual Disbursements

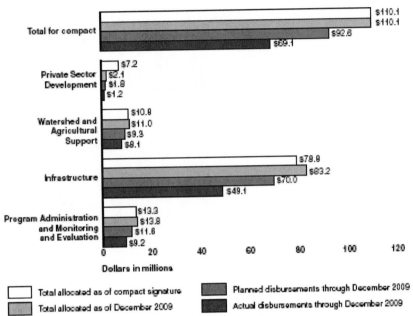

Source: GAO analysis of Millennium Challenge Corporation data.

Notes: We base planned disbursements on MCC's projections for the fiscal quarter ending December 2009. We assume that funds are disbursed evenly throughout each year. Actual disbursements by project may not add up to total disbursements because some disbursements are pending allocation to projects and are reflected in the total but not in the projects.

EL SALVADOR COMPACT FACT SHEET

Country Characteristics

Located in Central America, El Salvador has a population of about 6.1 million. It is a lower-middleincome country. Its economy is largely based on services, which constitute an estimated 61 percent of its gross domestic product (GDP) and employ about 58 percent of the labor force. Industry and agriculture constitute 28 and 11 percent of GDP, respectively. A 12-year civil war that ended in 1992 left nearly two-thirds of the country's population in poverty. During the war, public investment was deferred and deterioration of the natural resource base accelerated. Despite a strong record of economic reform, El Salvador's economic growth has been modest in recent years and contracted by 2.6 percent in 2009.

Map of El Salvador

Source: Map Resources (map).

Key Events for El Salvador Compact

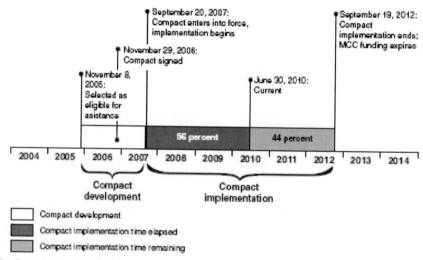

Source: GAO analysis of Millennium Challenge Corporation data.

Compact Timeline

During compact development, MCC and an eligible country negotiate project proposals and the compact's terms. After the compact is signed, the country finalizes administrative requirements, such as procurement and disbursement agreements.

When the compact enters into force, MCC obligates funds and compact implementation begins. MCC's statute limits compact implementation to 5 years.

El Salvador was one of two lowermiddle-income countries selected in the fiscal year 2006 eligibility round, the first year of MCC's program for lower-middle-income countries. El Salvador was the first lower-middleincome country to begin implementing a compact. As of June 30, 2010, 56 percent of the compact's 5-year period had elapsed.

MCC SELECTION CRITERIA

El Salvador GNI Per Capita

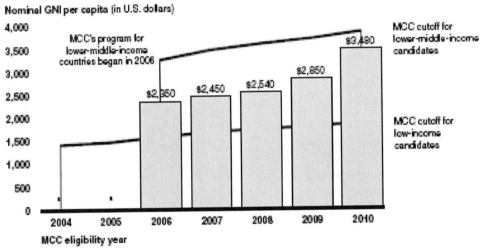

Source: GAO analysis of World Bank World Development Indicators and MCC income cutoffs.
[a] El Salvador was not a candidate in 2004 and 2005.

MCC Candidate Criteria

Each fiscal year, MCC uses per capita gross national income (GNI) data to identify two pools of candidate countries—low-income and lower-middle-income—based on World Bank lending thresholds. Also, a candidate country must not be statutorily barred from receiving U.S. assistance. By law, MCC can use up to 25 percent of compact assistance each year for new compacts with lower-middle-income countries.

El Salvador became a candidate for MCC assistance in 2006, the first year that MCC considered lowermiddle-income countries.

MCC Eligibility Criteria

MCC's board uses quantitative indicators to assess a candidate's policy performance. To meet MCC's criteria, a country must pass the control of corruption indicator and at least half of the indictors in each of three categories. To pass an indicator, a country must score above the median in its income group. However, the board may select a country as eligible even if it does not meet the criteria. Once MCC has signed a compact with a country, MCC continues to work with it—even if it fails the criteria—as long as its actions are not inconsistent with the criteria. If a country's policy performance declines, the board can suspend or terminate the compact.

El Salvador met MCC's eligibility criteria in 2006 and 2007. It did not meet the criteria in 2008, 2009, or 2010 because it failed three or more of the five Investing in People indicators.

El Salvador's Performance on MCC Eligibility Indicators

Indicator category	MCC eligibility year	2004	2005	2006	2007	2008	2009	2010
	MCC income group	Lower-middle	Lower-middle	Lower-middle	Lower-middle	Lower-middle	Lower-middle	Lower-middle
Ruling Justly	Political Rights			✓	✓	✓	✓	✓
Ruling Justly	Civil Liberties			X	✓	✓	✓	✓
Ruling Justly	Voice and Accountability			✓	✓	✓	✓	✓
Ruling Justly	Government Effectiveness			✓	X	X	✓	✓
Ruling Justly	Rule of Law			X	✓	X	X	X
Ruling Justly	Control of Corruption			✓	✓	✓	✓	✓
Investing in People	Girls' Primary Education Completion[a]			X	X	X	X	X
Investing in People	Primary Education Expenditures			X	X	X	X	X
Investing in People	Health Expenditures			✓	✓	X	✓	✓
Investing in People	Immunization Rates			✓	✓	✓	✓	✓
Investing in People	Natural Resource Management (2008-2010)	El Salvador was not a candidate in 2004.	El Salvador was not a candidate in 2005.			X	X	X
Economic Freedom	Country Credit Rating (2004-2005)							
Economic Freedom	Days to Start a Business (2004-2007)			X	✓			
Economic Freedom	Cost of Starting a Business (2006-2007)			X	X			
Economic Freedom	Business Start-up (2009-2010)					X	X	X
Economic Freedom	Inflation			✓	✓	✓	✓	✓
Economic Freedom	Fiscal Policy			X	X	X	X	X
Economic Freedom	Trade Policy			✓	✓	✓	✓	✓
Economic Freedom	Regulatory Quality			✓	✓	✓	✓	✓
Economic Freedom	Land Rights and Access (2008-2010)					X	X	X
	Indicator performance results			Passed	Passed	Failed	Failed	Failed
	MCC eligibility determination	Not Eligible	Not Eligible	Eligible	Eligible	Eligible	NA[b]	NA[b]

✓ Passed (scored above the median)   X Failed (scored at the median or below)   ☐ NA for that year

Source: GAO analysis of Millennium Challenge Corporation data.

[a] In 2004, the indicator was "Primary Education Completion."

[b] In 2009, MCC stopped making an eligibility determination for countries with existing compacts.

COMPACT SUMMARY

Structure of El Salvador Compact, as of December 2009

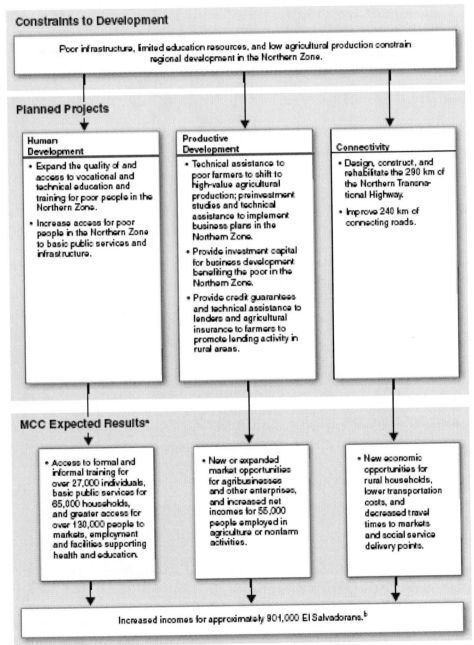

Constraints to Development

Poor infrastructure, limited education resources, and low agricultural production constrain regional development in the Northern Zone.

Planned Projects

Human Development
- Expand the quality of and access to vocational and technical education and training for poor people in the Northern Zone.
- Increase access for poor people in the Northern Zone to basic public services and infrastructure.

Productive Development
- Technical assistance to poor farmers to shift to high-value agricultural production; preinvestment studies and technical assistance to implement business plans in the Northern Zone.
- Provide investment capital for business development benefiting the poor in the Northern Zone.
- Provide credit guarantees and technical assistance to lenders and agricultural insurance to farmers to promote lending activity in rural areas.

Connectivity
- Design, construct, and rehabilitate the 290 km of the Northern Transnational Highway.
- Improve 240 km of connecting roads.

MCC Expected Results[a]

- Access to formal and informal training for over 27,000 individuals, basic public services for 65,000 households, and greater access for over 130,000 people to markets, employment and facilities supporting health and education.

- New or expanded market opportunities for agribusinesses and other enterprises, and increased net incomes for 55,000 people employed in agriculture or nonfarm activities.

- New economic opportunities for rural households, lower transportation costs, and decreased travel times to markets and social service delivery points.

Increased incomes for approximately 901,000 El Salvadorans.[b]

Source: GAO analysis of Millennium Challenge Corporation data.

[a] MCC expected results are reported as of compact signature, except the number of beneficiaries with increased incomes.

[b] In fiscal year 2009, MCC recalculated the number of expected beneficiaries using a standardized methodology. At compact signature, MCC reported the compact would benefit at least 1 million people.

Compact Characteristics

MCC and the partner country determine the compact structure before the compact is signed. However, the structure of some compacts has been altered during implementation.

At signature, El Salvador's compact focused on developing the economy of the country's Northern Zone, where, according to the MCC compact at signature, nearly 20 percent of El Salvador's poor lived. At that time, significant numbers of the poor lacked access to basic public services and less than 10 percent of children completed secondary school.

Expected Results

This graphic presents MCC's expectations of selected compact results at compact signature and at the end of fiscal year 2009.

The El Salvador compact is one of five compacts for which GAO has independently verified the reliability of MCC's results projections. In June 2008, GAO reported that MCC had made errors in its original projections of the impact of El Salvador's compact (GAO-08-730). MCC corrected these errors, reducing the expected impact on poverty and income. For example, MCC originally projected that beneficiaries' per capita income would increase by $148.0 but now projects an increase of $123.0.

COMPACT FUNDING

Compact Project Funding

MCC and the country may reallocate funds among projects during implementation. In some cases, MCC has also changed the overall compact obligation.

At signature (November 2006), MCC obligated $460.9 million for the El Salvador compact. As of December 2009, the overall obligation amount had not changed, however minor funding reallocations were made.

Compact Disbursements

At compact signature, MCC develops a disbursement plan for the compact. MCC disburses funds as the country begins implementing projects. According to MCC, any funds not disbursed within 120 days after the compact ends would return to MCC for reprogramming.

As of December 2009, MCC had disbursed $66.1 million (approximately 14 percent) of compact funds, compared with the $222.9 million (approximately 48 percent) that it had planned to disburse as of that date.

Although it is not shown in the graphic, in addition to the above disbursements, $135.4 million has been committed under the compact for pending expenses as of December 2009.

El Salvador Compact Project Allocations

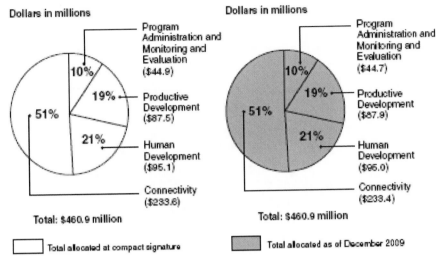

Source: GAO analysis of Millennium Challenge Corporation data.
Note: Project allocations in figures may not add up to 100 percent due to rounding.

El Salvador Compact Planned and Actual Disbursements

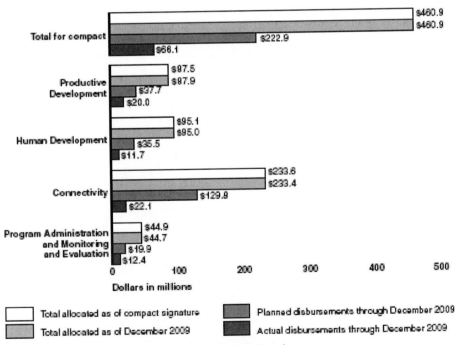

Source: GAO analysis of Millennium Challenge Corporation data.
Notes: We base planned disbursements on MCC's projections for the fiscal quarter ending December 2009. We assume that funds are disbursed evenly throughout each year. Actual disbursements by project may not add up to total disbursements because some disbursements are pending allocation to projects and are reflected in the total but not in the projects.

GEORGIA COMPACT FACT SHEET

Map of Georgia

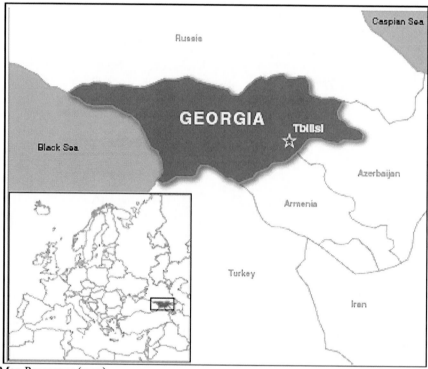

Source: Map Resources (map).

Key Events for Georgia Compact

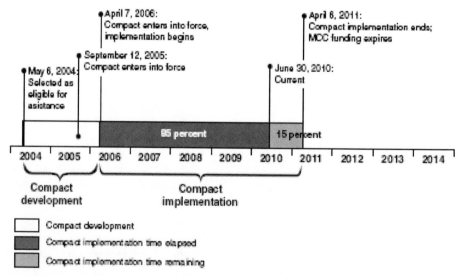

Source: GAO analysis of Millennium Challenge Corporation data.

Country Characteristics

Located in the Caucasus region of Asia on the southern border of Russia, Georgia has a population of about 4.4 million. It is a lower-middleincome country. Its economy is based on services and industry, which respectively constitute 62 and 26 percent of its gross domestic product (GDP). Agriculture constitutes 12 percent of GDP but employs 56 percent of the labor force. Other key economic activities include mining of manganese and copper. Following the "Rose Revolution"—widespread protests that led to its president's resignation—Georgia elected a new government in 2004 that focused on anticorruption efforts and other reforms. In August 2008, conflict erupted with Russia over regions in Georgia seeking independence. Although Georgia's GDP had been growing, the conflict and the global economic crisis negatively impacted its economy, which contracted by nearly 5 percent in 2009.

Compact Timeline

During compact development, MCC and an eligible country negotiate project proposals and the compact's terms. After the compact is signed, the country finalizes administrative requirements, such as procurement and disbursement agreements. When the compact enters into force, MCC obligates funds and compact implementation begins. MCC's statute limits compact implementation to 5 years.

Georgia was 1 of 16 countries that MCC selected as eligible in its first eligibility round. As of June 30, 2010, 85 percent of the compact's 5- year period had elapsed.

MCC SELECTION CRITERIA

Compact Characteristics

Each fiscal year, MCC uses per capita gross national income (GNI) data to identify two pools of candidate countries—low-income and lower-middle-income—based on World Bank lending thresholds. Also, a candidate country must not be statutorily barred from receiving U.S. assistance. By law, MCC can use up to 25 percent of compact assistance each year for new compacts with lower-middle-income countries. Georgia was a low-income candidate country from 2004 through 2008. In 2009, Georgia's rising GNI per capita lifted it to lower-middle-income status.

MCC Eligibility Criteria

MCC's board uses quantitative indicators to assess a candidate's policy performance. To meet MCC's criteria, a country must pass the control of corruption indicator and at least half of the indictors in each of three categories. To pass an indicator, a country must score above the median in its income group.

Georgia GNI Per Capita

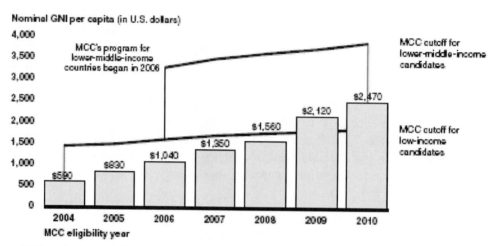

Source: GAO analysis of World Bank World Development Indicators and MCC income cutoffs.

Georgia's Performance on MCC Eligibility Indicators

Indicator category	MCC eligibility year	2004	2005	2006	2007	2008	2009	2010
	MCC income group	Low	Low	Low	Low	Low	Lower-middle	Lower-middle
Ruling Justly	Political Rights	X	✓	✓	✓	✓	X	X
	Civil Liberties	X	✓	✓	✓	✓	X	X
	Voice and Accountability	✓	✓	✓	✓	✓	X	✓
	Government Effectiveness	✓	✓	✓	✓	✓	✓	✓
	Rule of Law	X	X	X	✓	✓	✓	✓
	Control of Corruption	X	X	X	✓	✓	✓	✓
Investing in People	Girls' Primary Education Completion[a]	✓	✓	✓	✓	✓	X	X
	Primary Education Expenditures	X	X	X	X	X	X	X
	Health Expenditures	X	X	✓	X	X	X	X
	Immunization Rates	✓	X	✓	✓	✓	✓	✓
	Natural Resource Management (2008-2010)					✓	X	✓
Economic Freedom	Country Credit Rating (2004-2005)	X	✓					
	Days to Start a Business (2004-2007)	✓	✓	✓	✓			
	Cost of Starting a Business (2006-2007)			✓	✓			
	Business Start-up (2008-2010)					✓	✓	✓
	Inflation	✓	✓	✓	✓	✓	✓	✓
	Fiscal Policy	✓	✓	✓	✓	✓	X	X
	Trade Policy	X	X	✓	✓	✓	✓	✓
	Regulatory Quality	X	X	X	✓	✓	✓	✓
	Land Rights and Access (2008-2010)					✓	✓	✓
	Indicator performance results	Failed	Failed	Failed	Passed	Passed	Failed	Failed
	MCC eligibility determination	Eligible	Eligible	Eligible	Eligible	Eligible	NA[b]	NA[b]

✓ Passed (scored above the median)   X Failed (scored at the median or below)   ☐ NA for that year

[a] In 2004, the indicator was "Primary Education Completion."
[b] In 2009, MCC stopped making an eligibility determination for countries with existing compacts.

COMPACT SUMMARY

Structure of Georgia Compact, as of December 2009

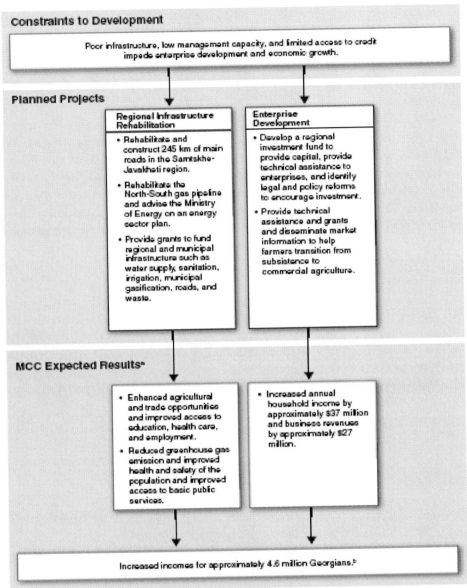

Constraints to Development

Poor infrastructure, low management capacity, and limited access to credit impede enterprise development and economic growth.

Planned Projects

Regional Infrastructure Rehabilitation

- Rehabilitate and construct 245 km of main roads in the Samtskhe-Javakheti region.
- Rehabilitate the North-South gas pipeline and advise the Ministry of Energy on an energy sector plan.
- Provide grants to fund regional and municipal infrastructure such as water supply, sanitation, irrigation, municipal gasification, roads, and waste.

Enterprise Development

- Develop a regional investment fund to provide capital, provide technical assistance to enterprises, and identify legal and policy reforms to encourage investment.
- Provide technical assistance and grants and disseminate market information to help farmers transition from subsistence to commercial agriculture.

MCC Expected Results[a]

- Enhanced agricultural and trade opportunities and improved access to education, health care, and employment.
- Reduced greenhouse gas emission and improved health and safety of the population and improved access to basic public services.

- Increased annual household income by approximately $37 million and business revenues by approximately $27 million.

Increased incomes for approximately 4.6 million Georgians.[b]

Source: GAO analysis of Millennium Challenge Corporation data.

[a] MCC expected results are reported as of compact signature, except the number of beneficiaries with increased incomes.

[b] In fiscal year 2009, MCC recalculated the number of expected beneficiaries using a standardized methodology. At compact signature, MCC reported the compact would benefit nearly 500,000 people.

However, the board may select a country as eligible even if it does not meet the criteria. Once MCC has signed a compact with a country, MCC continues to work with it—even if it fails the criteria—as long as its actions are not inconsistent with the criteria. If a country's policy performance declines, the board can suspend or terminate the compact. Georgia failed MCC's eligibility criteria in 2004, 2005, and 2006, in part because it failed the corruption indicator, but the MCC board deemed it eligible. It met the criteria in 2007 and 2008. In 2009, Georgia became lower-middle income and failed the criteria for that group that year and in 2010.

Compact Characteristics

MCC and the partner country determine the compact structure before the compact is signed. However, the structure of some compacts has been altered during implementation.

At signature, Georgia's compact aimed to stimulate growth in regions outside the capital, Tbilisi, with a particular emphasis on the Samtskhe-Javakheti region in southwestern Georgia. At that time, these regions were collectively home to more than 40 percent of the country's total population. The compact includes plans to rehabilitate key infrastructure. In addition, the compact includes plans to invest in, and provide technical assistance to, regional enterprises,

Expected Results

This graphic presents MCC's expectations of selected compact results at compact signature and at the end of fiscal year 2009.

GAO has not independently verified the reliability of MCC's results projections for this compact. Previous GAO work has identified several problems with the methodology used to determine compact projects' expected results. (See GAO-08-730 and GAO-07-909.)

COMPACT FUNDING

Compact Project Funding

MCC and the country may reallocate funds among projects during implementation. In some cases, MCC has also changed the overall compact obligation.

At signature (September 2005), MCC obligated $295.3 million for the Georgia compact. In addition to previous reallocations, MCC and Georgia amended the compact in November 2008, increasing the total compact amount to $395.3 million to complete works originally envisioned in the compact.

Compact Disbursements

At compact signature, MCC develops a disbursement plan for the compact. MCC disburses funds as the country begins implementing projects. According to MCC, any funds not disbursed within 120 days after the compact ends would return to MCC for reprogramming.

Georgia Project Allocations

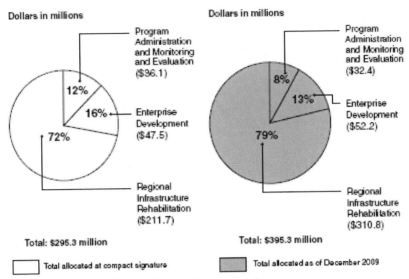

Source: GAO analysis of Millennium Challenge Corporation data.

Georgia Planned and Actual Disbursements

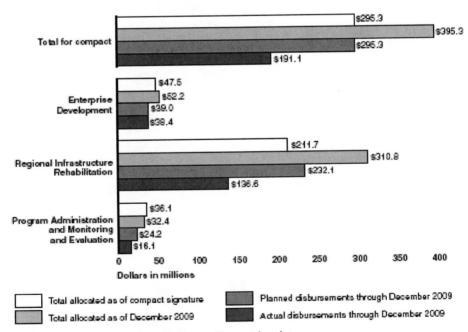

Source: GAO analysis of Millennium Challenge Corporation data.

Notes: We base planned disbursements on MCC's projections for the fiscal quarter ending December 2009. We assume that funds are disbursed evenly throughout each year. Actual disbursements by project may not add up to total disbursements because some disbursements are pending allocation to projects and are reflected in the total but not in the projects.

As of December 2009, MCC had disbursed $191.1 million (approximately 48 percent) of compact funds, compared with the $295.3 million (approximately 75 percent) that it had planned to disburse as of that date.

Although it is not shown in the graphic, in addition to the above disbursements, $143.3 million has been committed under the compact for pending expenses as of December 2009.

GHANA COMPACT FACT SHEET

Map of Ghana

Source: Map Resources (map).

Key Events for Ghana Compact

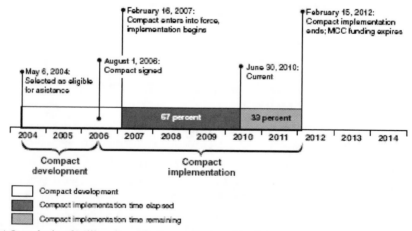

Source: GAO analysis of Millennium Challenge Corporation data.

Country Characteristics

Located in coastal West Africa, Ghana has a population of 23.9 million. It is a low-income country. Its economy is distributed among the services, agriculture, and industry sectors, which respectively account for 38, 37 and 25 percent of its gross domestic product (GDP). However, agriculture employs about 56 percent of the labor force. Despite an abundance of natural resources, Ghana remains heavily dependent on international financial and technical assistance. Ghana experienced consistent economic growth over the last decade, with real GDP growth rising from 3.7 percent in 2000 to 7.3 percent in 2008; GDP growth slowed to 4.7 percent in 2009.

Compact Timeline

During compact development, MCC and an eligible country negotiate project proposals and the compact's terms. After the compact is signed, the country finalizes administrative requirements, such as procurement and disbursement agreements. When the compact enters into force, MCC obligates funds and compact implementation begins. MCC's statute limits compact implementation to 5 years.

Ghana was 1 of 16 countries that MCC selected as eligible in its first eligibility round. As of June 30, 2010, 67 percent of the compact's 5- year period had elapsed.

MCC Candidate Criteria

Each fiscal year, MCC uses per capita gross national income (GNI) data to identify two pools of candidate countries—low-income and lower-middle-income—based on World Bank lending thresholds. Also, a candidate country must not be statutorily barred from receiving U.S. assistance. By law, MCC can use up to 25 percent of compact assistance each year for new compacts with lower-middle-income countries.

Ghana has been classified as a low-income candidate country every year since MCC began operations in 2004.

MCC Eligibility Criteria

MCC's board uses quantitative indicators to assess a candidate's policy performance. To meet MCC's criteria, a country must pass the control of corruption indicator and at least half of the indictors in each of three categories. To pass an indicator, a country must score above the median in its income group. However, the board may select a country as eligible even if it does not meet the criteria. Once MCC has signed a compact with a country, MCC continues to work with it—even if it fails the criteria—as long as its actions are not inconsistent with the criteria. If a country's policy performance declines, the board can suspend or terminate the compact.

Ghana has met MCC's eligibility criteria each year since 2004, except in 2007, when it failed four of six Economic Freedom indicators.

Ghana GNI Per Capita

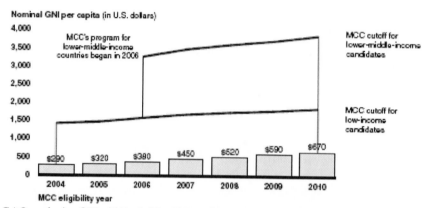

Source: GAO analysis of World Bank World Development Indicators and MCC income cutoffs.

Ghana's Performance on MCC Eligibility Indicators

Indicator category	MCC eligibility year	2004	2005	2006	2007	2008	2009	2010
	MCC income group	Low	Low	Low	Low	Low	Low	Low
Ruling Justly	Political Rights	✓	✓	✓	✓	✓	✓	✓
	Civil Liberties	✓	✓	✓	✓	✓	✓	✓
	Voice and Accountability	✓	✓	✓	✓	✓	✓	✓
	Government Effectiveness	✓	✓	✓	✓	✓	✓	✓
	Rule of Law	✓	✓	✓	✓	✓	✓	✓
	Control of Corruption	✓	✓	✓	✓	✓	✓	✓
Investing in People	Girls' Primary Education Completion[a]	✓	X	X	X	X	X	✓
	Primary Education Expenditures	✓	✓	✓	✓	✓	✓	✓
	Health Expenditures	✓	✓	✓	X	✓	✓	X
	Immunization Rates	✓	✓	✓	✓	✓	✓	✓
	Natural Resource Management (2009-2010)						✓	✓
Economic Freedom	Country Credit Rating (2004-2005)	✓	✓					
	Days to Start a Business (2004-2007)	X	X	X	X			
	Cost of Starting a Business (2006-2007)			✓	✓			
	Business Start-up (2008-2010)					✓	✓	✓
	Inflation	✓	✓	X	X	✓	✓	X
	Fiscal Policy	X	X	X	X	X	X	X
	Trade Policy	X	X	✓	X	X	X	X
	Regulatory Quality	✓	✓	✓	✓	✓	✓	✓
	Land Rights and Access (2009-2010)						✓	✓
	Indicator performance results	Passed	Passed	Passed	Failed	Passed	Passed	Passed
	MCC eligibility determination	Eligible	Eligible	Eligible	Eligible	Eligible	NA[b]	NA[b]

✓ Passed (scored above the median)   X Failed (scored at the median or below)   ☐ NA for that year

Source: GAO analysis of Millennium Challenge Corporation data.

[a]In 2004, the indicator was "Primary Education Completion."

[b]In 2009, MCC stopped making an eligibility determination for countries with existing compacts.

COMPACT SUMMARY

Structure of Ghana Compact, as of December 2009

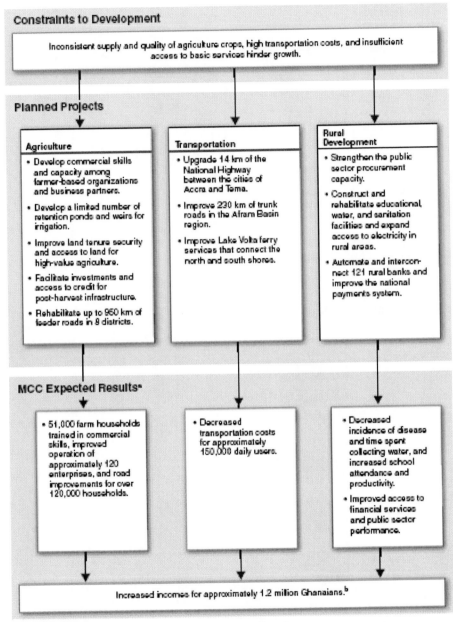

Constraints to Development

Inconsistent supply and quality of agriculture crops, high transportation costs, and insufficient access to basic services hinder growth.

Planned Projects

Agriculture
- Develop commercial skills and capacity among farmer-based organizations and business partners.
- Develop a limited number of retention ponds and weirs for irrigation.
- Improve land tenure security and access to land for high-value agriculture.
- Facilitate investments and access to credit for post-harvest infrastructure.
- Rehabilitate up to 950 km of feeder roads in 8 districts.

Transportation
- Upgrade 14 km of the National Highway between the cities of Accra and Tema.
- Improve 230 km of trunk roads in the Afram Basin region.
- Improve Lake Volta ferry services that connect the north and south shores.

Rural Development
- Strengthen the public sector procurement capacity.
- Construct and rehabilitate educational, water, and sanitation facilities and expand access to electricity in rural areas.
- Automate and interconnect 121 rural banks and improve the national payments system.

MCC Expected Results[a]

- 51,000 farm households trained in commercial skills, improved operation of approximately 120 enterprises, and road improvements for over 120,000 households.

- Decreased transportation costs for approximately 150,000 daily users.

- Decreased incidence of disease and time spent collecting water, and increased school attendance and productivity.
- Improved access to financial services and public sector performance.

Increased incomes for approximately 1.2 million Ghanaians.[b]

Source: GAO analysis of Millennium Challenge Corporation data.

[a] MCC expected results are reported as of compact signature, except the number of beneficiaries with increased incomes.

[b] In fiscal year 2009, MCC recalculated the number of expected beneficiaries using a standardized methodology. At compact signature, MCC reported the compact would benefit over 1 million people.

COMPACT FUNDING

Ghana Project Allocations

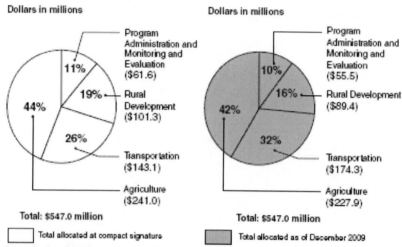

Source: GAO analysis of Millennium Challenge Corporation data.

Ghana Planned and Actual Disbursements

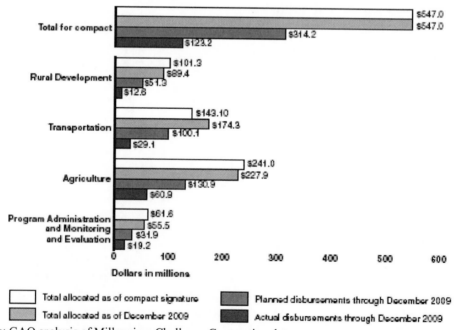

Source: GAO analysis of Millennium Challenge Corporation data.

Notes: We base planned disbursements on MCC's projections for the fiscal quarter ending December 2009. We assume that funds are disbursed evenly throughout each year. Actual disbursements by project may not add up to total disbursements because some disbursements are pending allocation to projects and are reflected in the total but not in the projects.

Compact Project Funding

MCC and the country may reallocate funds among projects during implementation. In some cases, MCC has also changed the overall compact obligation.

At signature (August 2006), MCC obligated $547.0 million for the Ghana compact. As of December 2009, the overall obligation amount had not changed, however funds were reallocated among the projects.

Compact Disbursements

At compact signature, MCC develops a disbursement plan for the compact. MCC disburses funds as the country begins implementing projects. According to MCC, any funds not disbursed within 120 days after the compact ends would return to MCC for reprogramming.

As of December 2009, MCC had disbursed $123.2 million (approximately 23 percent) of compact funds, compared with the $314.2 million (approximately 57 percent) that it had planned to disburse as of that date.

Although it is not shown in the graphic, in addition to the above disbursements, $216.7 million has been committed under the compact for pending expenses as of December 2009.

HONDURAS COMPACT FACT SHEET

Country Characteristics

Located in Central America, Honduras has a population of about 7.2 million. It is a low-income country. Its economy is based on services, which constitute 58 percent of its gross domestic product (GDP) and employ about 40 percent of the labor force. Industry and agriculture constitute 28 and 14 percent of GDP, respectively. Honduras's real GDP contracted in 2009 by 3.1 percent. In June 2009, Honduran President Zelaya was ousted from office after attempting to change the constitution to allow for his reelection, which the Honduran congress and judiciary strongly opposed. As a result of this situation, MCC has partially terminated assistance under its compact with Honduras.

Compact Timeline

During compact development, MCC and an eligible country negotiate project proposals and the compact's terms. After the compact is signed, the country finalizes administrative requirements, such as procurement and disbursement agreements. When the compact enters into force, MCC obligates funds and compact implementation begins. MCC's statute limits compact implementation to 5 years.

Honduras was 1 of 16 countries that MCC selected as eligible in its first eligibility round. Honduras was the second country to begin implementing a compact with MCC. As of June 30, 2010, 95 percent of the compact's 5-year period had elapsed.

Map of Honduras

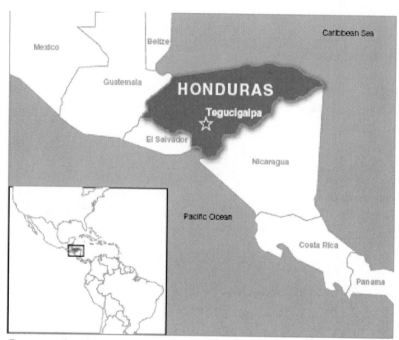

Source: Map Resources (map).

Key Events for Honduras Compact

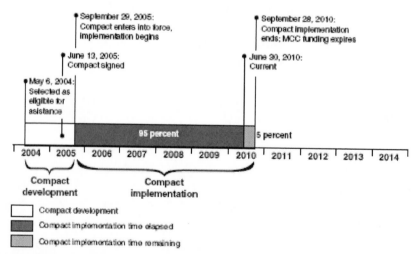

Source: GAO analysis of Millennium Challenge Corporation data.

MCC SELECTION CRITERIA

Honduras GNI Per Capita

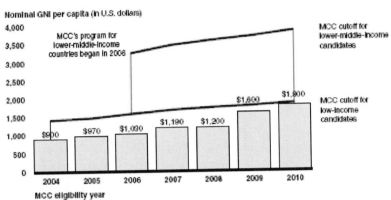

Source: GAO analysis of World Bank World Development Indicators and MCC income cutoffs.

Honduras' Performance on MCC Eligibility Indicators

Indicator category	MCC eligibility year	2004	2005	2006	2007	2008	2009	2010
	MCC income group	Low	Low	Low	Low	Low	Low	Low
Ruling Justly	Political Rights	✓	✓	✓	✓	✓	✓	✓
	Civil Liberties	✓	✓	✓	✓	✓	✓	✓
	Voice and Accountability	✓	✓	✓	✓	✓	✓	✓
	Government Effectiveness	✓	✓	✓	✓	✓	✓	✓
	Rule of Law	X	X	✓	✓	X	X	X
	Control of Corruption	✓	✓	✓	✓	X	✓	X
Investing In People	Girls' Primary Education Completion[a]	✓	✓	X	✓	✓	✓	✓
	Primary Education Expenditures	✓	✓	✓	✓	✓	✓	✓
	Health Expenditures	✓	✓	✓	✓	✓	✓	✓
	Immunization Rates	✓	✓	✓	✓	✓	✓	✓
	Natural Resource Management (2009-2010)						✓	✓
Economic Freedom	Country Credit Rating (2004-2005)	✓	✓					
	Days to Start a Business (2004-2007)	X	X	X	X			
	Cost of Starting a Business (2006-2007)			✓	✓			
	Business Start-up (2008-2010)					✓	✓	✓
	Inflation	✓	✓	✓	✓	✓	✓	✓
	Fiscal Policy	X	X	X	X	X	X	X
	Trade Policy	✓	✓	✓	✓	✓	✓	✓
	Regulatory Quality	✓	✓	✓	✓	✓	✓	✓
	Land Rights and Access (2009-2010)						✓	✓
	Indicator performance results	Passed	Passed	Passed	Passed	Failed	Passed	Failed
	MCC eligibility determination	Eligible	Eligible	Eligible	Eligible	Eligible	NA[b]	NA[b]

✓ Passed (scored above the median)   X Failed (scored at the median or below)   ☐ NA for that year

Source: GAO analysis of Millennium Challenge Corporation data.

[a] In 2004, the indicator was "Primary Education Completion."

[b] In 2009, MCC stopped making and eligibility determination for countries with existing compacts.

Candidate Criteria

Each fiscal year, MCC uses per capita gross national income (GNI) data to identify two pools of candidate countries—low-income and lower-middle-income—based on World Bank lending thresholds. Also, a candidate country must not be statutorily barred from receiving U.S. assistance. By law, MCC can use up to 25 percent of compact assistance each year for new compacts with lower-middle-income countries.

Honduras has been classified as a low-income country every year since MCC began operations in 2004.

MCC Eligibility Criteria

MCC's board uses quantitative indicators to assess a candidate's policy performance. To meet MCC's criteria, a country must pass the control of corruption indicator and at least half of the indictors in each of three categories. To pass an indicator, a country must score above the median in its income group. However, the Board may select a country as eligible even if it does not meet the criteria. Once MCC has signed a compact with a country, MCC continues to work with it—even if it fails the criteria—as long as its actions are not inconsistent with the criteria. If a country's policy performance declines, the Board can suspend or terminate the compact.

Honduras met MCC's eligibility criteria most years since 2004. It did not meet the criteria in 2008 and 2010 because it failed the corruption indicator.

COMPACT SUMMARY

Compact Characteristics

MCC and the partner country determine the compact structure before the compact is signed. However, the structure of some compacts has been altered during implementation.

At signature, the Honduras compact aimed to generate economic growth in rural areas. In September 2009, MCC partially terminated assistance under its compact with Honduras, ceasing to fund parts of the Transportation and Rural Development Projects. MCC also placed a hold on funding for a section of the CA-5 Highway Activity, under the Transportation Project; the hold on funding was lifted in early 2010. MCC acted in response to the Honduran president's removal and the failure to reestablish democratic order, which were inconsistent with MCC's eligibility criteria.

Expected Results

The graphic presents MCC's expectations of selected compact results at compact signature and at the end of fiscal year 2009.

GAO has not independently verified the reliability of MCC's results projections for this compact. Previous GAO work has identified several problems with the methodology used to determine compact results. (See GAO-08-730 and GAO-07-909.)

MCC has modified the Honduras compact but only partially recalculated the expected results.

Structure of Honduras Compact, as of December 2009

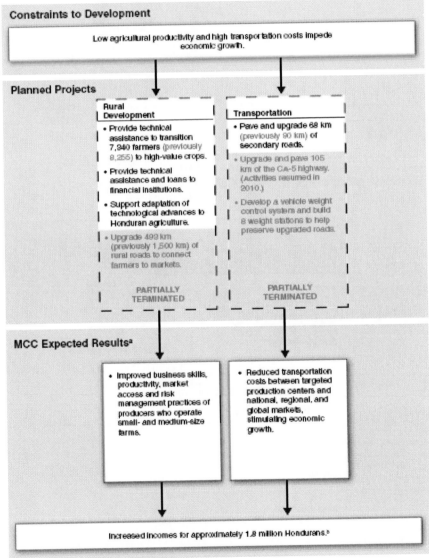

Source: GAO analysis of Millennium Challenge Corporation data.

[a] MCC expected results are reported as of compact signature, except the number of beneficiaries with increased incomes. The partial termination of the two projects may affect results.

[b] In fiscal year 2009, MCC recalculated the number of expected beneficiaries using a standardized methodology. MCC did not publish a beneficiary estimate for Honduras at compact signature.

COMPACT STATUS

Honduras Compact Funding

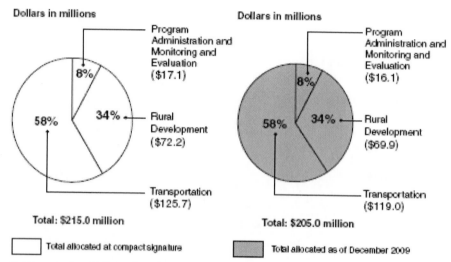

Source: GAO analysis of Millennium Challenge Corporation data.

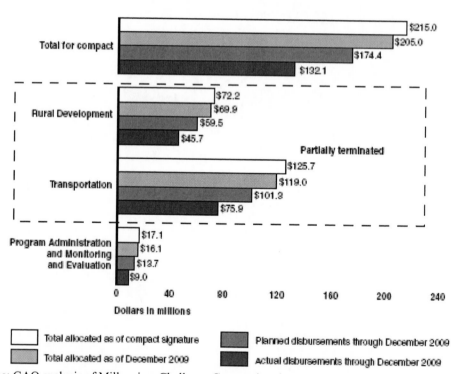

Source: GAO analysis of Millennium Challenge Corporation data.

Notes: We base planned disbursements on MCC's projections for the fiscal quarter ending December 2009. We assume that funds are disbursed evenly throughout each year. Actual disbursements by project may not add up to total disbursements because some disbursements are pending allocation to projects and are reflected in the total but not in the projects.

Compact Project Funding

MCC and the country may reallocate funds among projects during implementation. In some cases, MCC has also changed the overall compact obligation.

At signature (June 2005), MCC obligated $215.0 million for the Honduras compact. In September 2009, MCC terminated part of the compact assistance, representing about $10.0 million, and put a hold on funding for another part of the compact. As of December 2009, the overall obligation had decreased to $205.0 million.

Compact Disbursements

At compact signature, MCC develops a disbursement plan for the compact. MCC disburses funds as the country begins implementing projects. According to MCC, any funds not disbursed within 120 days after the compact ends would return to MCC for reprogramming.

As of December 2009, MCC had disbursed $132.1 million (approximately 65 percent) of compact funds, compared with the $174.4 million (approximately 85 percent) that it had planned to disburse as of that date.

Although it is not shown in the graphic, in addition to the above disbursements, $60.4 million has been committed under the compact for pending expenses as of December 2009.

LESOTHO COMPACT FACT SHEET

Country Characteristics

Located in southern Africa, Lesotho is a landlocked country, surrounded by South Africa, with a population of about 2.0 million. It is considered a low-income country. Its economy is based on industry and services, which respectively account for 45 and 39 percent of Lesotho's gross domestic product (GDP).

Agriculture accounts for 16 percent of GDP but employs 86 percent of the labor force. However, about 35 percent of Lesotho's male wage earners work in South Africa. In recent years, the government of Lesotho has embarked on major reforms to remove impediments to private sector growth, improve access to credit, and increase the participation of women in the economy. Lesotho's real GDP growth rate averaged 3.3 percent in 1991 through 2007, but the growth rate has been erratic, ranging from less than 1 percent in 2005 to more than 8 percent in 2006. In 2009, real GDP contracted by 0.9 percent.

Compact Timeline

During compact development, MCC and an eligible country negotiate project proposals and the compact's terms. After the compact is signed, the country finalizes administrative requirements, such as procurement and disbursement agreements. When the compact enters into force, MCC obligates funds and compact implementation begins. MCC's statute limits compact implementation to 5 years.

Lesotho was 1 of 16 countries that MCC selected as eligible in its first eligibility round. As of June 30, 2010, 36 percent of the compact's 5- year period had elapsed.

Map of Lesotho

Source: Map Resources (map).

Key Events for Lesotho Compact

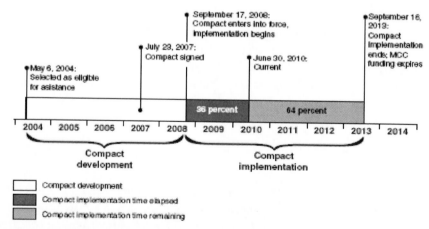

Source: GAO analysis of Millennium Challenge Corporation data.

MCC SELECTION CRITERIA

Lesotho GNI Per Capita

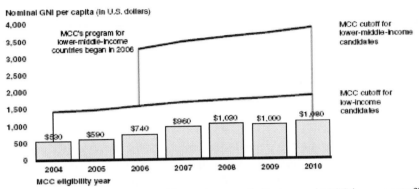

Source: GAO analysis of World Bank World Development Indicators and MCC income cutoffs.

Lesotho's Performance on MCC Eligibility Indicators

Indicator category	MCC eligibility year	2004	2005	2006	2007	2008	2009	2010
	MCC Income group	Low	Low	Low	Low	Low	Low	Low
Ruling Justly	Political Rights	✓	✓	✓	✓	✓	✓	✓
	Civil Liberties	✓	✓	✓	✓	✓	✓	✓
	Voice and Accountability	✓	✓	✓	✓	✓	✓	✓
	Government Effectiveness	✓	✓	✓	✓	✓	✓	✓
	Rule of Law	✓	✓	✓	✓	✓	✓	✓
	Control of Corruption	✓	✓	✓	✓	✓	✓	✓
Investing in People	Girls' Primary Education Completion[a]	✓	✓	✓	✓	✓	✓	✓
	Primary Education Expenditures	✓	✓	✓	✓	✓	✓	✓
	Health Expenditures	✓	✓	✓	✓	✓	✓	✓
	Immunization Rates	X	X	X	✓	X	✓	✓
	Natural Resource Management (2009-2010)						✓	X	X
Economic Freedom	Country Credit Rating (2004-2005)	✓	✓					
	Days to Start a Business (2004-2007)	X	X	X	X			
	Cost of Starting a Business (2006-2007)			✓	✓			
	Business Start-up (2008-2010)					✓	✓	✓
	Inflation	✓	✓	✓	✓	✓	✓	✓
	Fiscal Policy	✓	✓	✓	✓	✓	✓	✓
	Trade Policy	X	X	✓	✓	X	X	X
	Regulatory Quality	X	✓	✓	✓	✓	✓	✓
	Land Rights and Access (2009-2010)					X	✓	✓
	Indicator performance results	Passed	Passed	Passed	Passed	Passed	Passed	Passed
	MCC eligibility determination	Eligible	Eligible	Eligible	Eligible	Eligible	NA[b]	NA[b]

✓ Passed (scored above the median)   X Failed (scored at the median or below)   ☐ NA for that year

Source: GAO analysis of Millennium Challenge Corporation data.

[a] In 2004, the indicator was "Primary Education Completion."

[b] In 2009, MCC stopped making an eligibility determination for countries with existing compacts.

MCC Candidate Criteria

Each fiscal year, MCC uses per capita gross national income (GNI) data to identify two pools of candidate countries—low-income and lower-middle-income—based on World Bank lending thresholds. Also, a candidate country must not be statutorily barred from receiving U.S. assistance. By law, MCC can use up to 25 percent of compact assistance each year for new compacts with lower-middle-income countries.

Lesotho has been classified as a low-income country every year since MCC began operations in 2004.

MCC Eligibility Criteria

MCC's board uses quantitative indicators to assess a candidate's policy performance. To meet MCC's criteria, a country must pass the control of corruption indicator and at least half of the indictors in each of three categories. To pass an indicator, a country must score above the median in its income group. However, the board may select a country as eligible even if it does not meet the criteria. Once MCC has signed a compact with a country, MCC continues to work with it—even if it fails the criteria—as long as its actions are not inconsistent with the criteria. If a country's policy performance declines, the board can suspend or terminate the compact.

Lesotho has met MCC's eligibility criteria each year since 2004.

COMPACT SUMMARY

Compact Characteristics

MCC and the partner country determine the compact structure before the compact is signed. However, the structure of some compacts has been altered during implementation.

At signature, Lesotho's compact focused on sectors that affect most of the population, such as health care and potable water production. The compact aimed to strengthen the country's health care infrastructure to improve health outcomes, improve the water supply for industrial and domestic needs, and remove barriers to foreign and local private sector investment. At signature, nearly 25 percent of 15- to 49-year-old adults in Lesotho were HIV/AIDS-positive, the third highest prevalence rate in the world.

Expected Results

This graphic presents MCC's expectations of selected compact results at compact signature and at the end of fiscal year 2009.

The Lesotho compact is one of five compacts for which GAO has independently verified the reliability of MCC's results projections. In June 2008, GAO reported that it was unable to assess MCC's compact-level impact projections for Lesotho because MCC based them on a prior World Bank economic growth model (GAO-08-730).

Structure of Lesotho Compact, as of December 2009

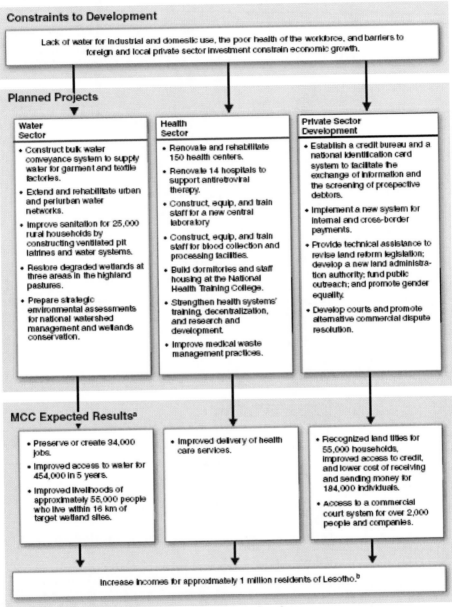

Source: GAO analysis of Millennium Challenge Corporation data.

[a] MCC expected results are reported as of compact signature, except the number of beneficiaries with increased incomes.

[b] In fiscal year 2009, MCC recalculated the number of expected beneficiaries using a standardized methodology. MCC did not publish a beneficiary estimate for Lesotho at compact signature.

COMPACT STATUS

Lesotho Compact Funding

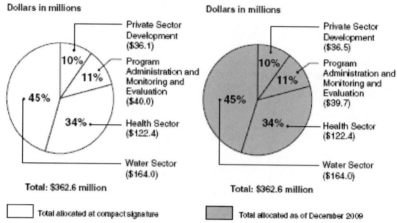

Source: GAO analysis of Millennium Challenge Corporation data.

Lesotho Compact Planned and Actual Disbursements

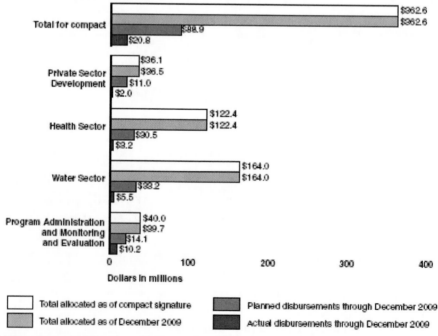

Source: GAO analysis of Millennium Challenge Corporation data.

Notes: We base planned disbursements on MCC's projections for the fiscal quarter ending December 2009. We assume that funds are disbursed evenly throughout each year. Actual disbursements by project may not add up to total disbursements because some disbursements are pending allocation to projects and are reflected in the total but not in the projects.

Compact Project Funding

MCC and the country may reallocate funds among projects during implementation. In some cases, MCC has also changed the overall compact obligation.

At signature (July 2007), MCC obligated $362.6 million for the Lesotho compact. As of December 2009, the overall obligation amount had not changed, however minor reallocations of funds were made among projects.

Compact Disbursements

At compact signature, MCC develops a disbursement plan for the compact. MCC disburses funds as the country begins implementing projects. According to MCC, any funds not disbursed within 120 days after the compact ends would return to MCC for reprogramming.

As of December 2009, MCC had disbursed $20.8 million (approximately 6 percent) of compact funds, compared with the $88.9 million (approximately 25 percent) that it had planned to disburse as of that date.

Although it is not shown in the graphic, in addition to the above disbursements, $59.1 million has been committed under the compact for pending expenses as of December 2009.

MALI COMPACT FACT SHEET

Country Characteristics

Located in West Africa, Mali has a population of about 12.7 million. It is a low-income country. Its economy is based on agriculture, which accounts for 45 percent of its gross domestic product (GDP) and employs about 80 percent of its labor force. Services and industry account for 38 and 17 percent of GDP, respectively. Despite its low income, Mali has experienced favorable economic growth in recent years; in 2009, Mali's real GDP grew by 3 percent. Mali is considered to be one of the strongest democracies in Africa, and its government has pursued economic reforms to encourage growth.

Compact Timeline

During compact development, MCC and an eligible country negotiate project proposals and the compact's terms. After the compact is signed, the country finalizes administrative requirements, such as procurement and disbursement agreements. When the compact enters into force, MCC obligates funds and compact implementation begins. MCC's statute limits compact implementation to 5 years.

Mali was 1 of 16 countries that MCC selected as eligible in its first eligibility round. As of June 30, 2010, 56 percent of the compact's 5- year period had elapsed.

Map of Mali

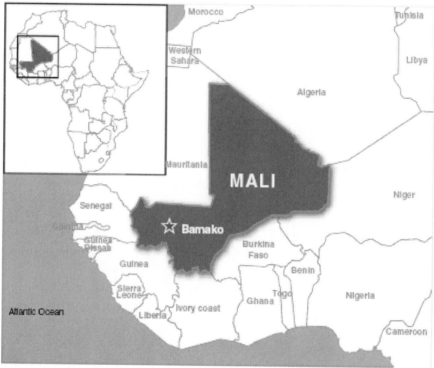

Source: Map Resources (map).

Key Events for Mali Compact

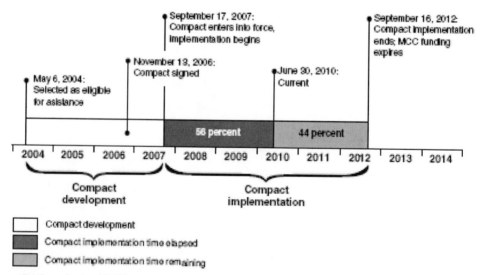

Source: GAO analysis of Millennium Challenge Corporation data.

MCC SELECTION CRITERIA

Mali GNI Per Capita

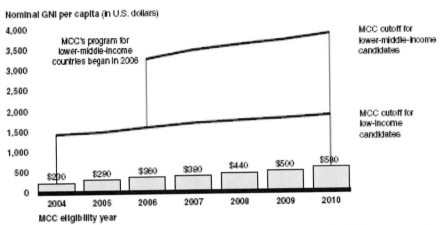

Source: GAO analysis of World Bank World Development Indicators and MCC income cutoffs.

Mali's Performance on MCC Eligibility Indicators

Indicator category	MCC eligibility year	2004	2005	2006	2007	2008	2009	2010
	MCC Income group	Low	Low	Low	Low	Low	Low	Low
Ruling Justly	Political Rights	✓	✓	✓	✓	✓	✓	✓
	Civil Liberties	✓	✓	✓	✓	✓	✓	✓
	Voice and Accountability	✓	✓	✓	✓	✓	✓	✓
	Government Effectiveness	X	X	✓	✓	✓	✓	✓
	Rule of Law	✓	✓	✓	✓	✓	✓	✓
	Control of Corruption	✓	✓	✓	✓	✓	✓	✓
Investing in People	Girls' Primary Education Completion[a]	X	X	X	X	X	X	X
	Primary Education Expenditures	✓	✓	✓	✓	X	✓	✓
	Health Expenditures	✓	✓	✓	✓	✓	✓	✓
	Immunization Rates	X	X	X	✓	✓	X	X
	Natural Resource Management (2008-2010)					X	X	X
Economic Freedom	Country Credit Rating (2004-2005)	✓	✓					
	Days to Start a Business (2004-2007)	✓	✓	✓	✓			
	Cost of Starting a Business (2006-2007)			X	X			
	Business Start-up (2008-2010)					X	X	X
	Inflation	✓	✓	✓	✓	✓	✓	✓
	Fiscal Policy	X	✓	X	✓	✓	✓	✓
	Trade Policy	✓	✓	✓	X	✓	✓	✓
	Regulatory Quality	✓	✓	✓	✓	✓	✓	✓
	Land Rights and Access (2009-2010)					X	X	X
	Indicator performance results	Passed	Passed	Passed	Passed	Failed	Failed	Failed
	MCC eligibility determination	Eligible	Eligible	Eligible	Eligible	Eligible	NA[b]	NA[b]

✓ Passed (scored above the median)   X Failed (scored at the median or below)   ☐ NA for that year

resultsSource: GAO analysis of Millennium Challenge Corporation data.

[a] In 2004, the indicator was "Primary Education Completion."

[b] In 2009, MCC stopped making an eligibility determination for countries with existing compacts.

MCC Candidate Criteria

Each fiscal year, MCC uses per capita gross national income (GNI) data to identify two pools of candidate countries—low-income and lower-middle-income—based on World Bank lending thresholds. Also, a candidate country must not be statutorily barred from receiving U.S. assistance. By law, MCC can use up to 25 percent of compact assistance each year for new compacts with lower-middle-income countries.

Mali has been classified as a low-income country each year since MCC began operations in 2004.

MCC Eligibility Criteria

MCC's board uses quantitative indicators to assess a candidate's policy performance. To meet MCC's criteria, a country must pass the control of corruption indicator and at least half of the indictors in each of three categories. To pass an indicator, a country must score above the median in its income group. However, the board may select a country as eligible even if it does not meet the criteria. Once MCC has signed a compact with a country, MCC continues to work with it—even if it fails the criteria—as long as its actions are not inconsistent with the criteria. If a country's policy performance declines, the board can suspend or terminate the compact.

Mali met MCC's eligibility criteria from 2004 through 2007. It did not meet the criteria in 2008 through 2010, because it failed three of five Investing in People indicators.

COMPACT SUMMARY

Compact Characteristics

MCC and the partner country determine the compact structure before the compact is signed. However, the structure of some compacts has been altered during implementation.

At signature, Mali's compact aimed to improve agricultural production and productivity in one of the poorest areas of central Mali. At that time, 64 percent of Malians were poor and one-third of poor Malians lived in extreme poverty. In 2008, MCC restructured the Mali compact because of escalating global construction costs, currency fluctuations, and operational issues. Funds formerly designated to the Industrial Park Project were reallocated to the Airport Project.

Expected Results

This graphic presents MCC's expectations of selected compact results at compact signature and at the end of fiscal year 2009.

GAO has not independently verified the reliability of MCC's results projections for this compact. Previous GAO work has identified several problems with the methodology used to determine compact projects' expected results. (See GAO-08-730 and GAO-07-909.)

Structure of Mali Compact, as of December 2009

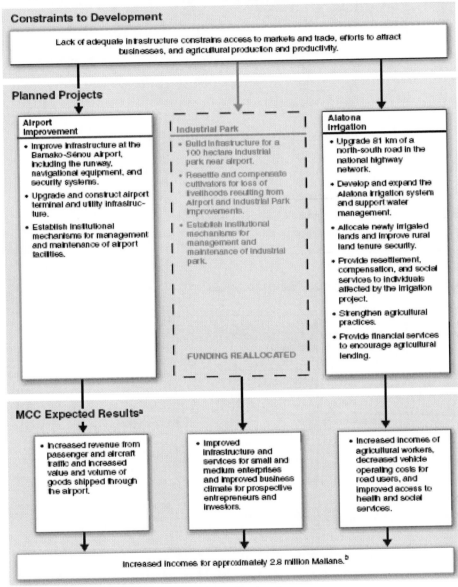

aSource: GAO analysis of Millennium Challenge Corporation data.

[a] MCC expected results are reported as of compact signature, except the number of beneficiaries with increased incomes. The reallocation of funds from the Industrial Park Project to the Airport Improvement Project may affect results.

[b] In fiscal year 2009, MCC recalculated the number of expected beneficiaries using a standardized methodology. MCC did not publish a beneficiary estimate for Mali at compact signature.

COMPACT FUNDING

Mali Project Allocations

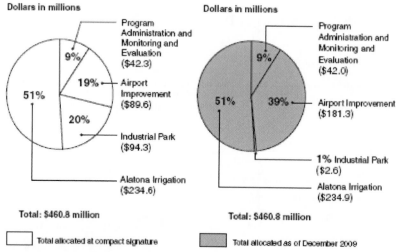

Source: GAO analysis of Millennium Challenge Corporation data
Note: Project allocations in figures may not add up to 100 percent due to rounding.

Mali Planned and Actual Disbursements

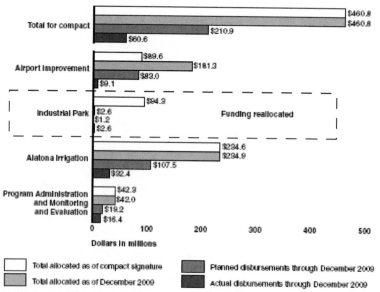

Source: GAO analysis of Millennium Challenge Corporation data.
Notes: We base planned disbursements on MCC's projections for the fiscal quarter ending December 2009. We assume that funds are disbursed evenly throughout each year. Actual disbursements by project may not add up to total disbursements because some disbursements are pending allocation to projects and are reflected in the total but not in the projects.

Compact Project Funding

MCC and the country may reallocate funds among projects during implementation. In some cases, MCC has also changed the overall compact obligation.

At signature (November 2006), MCC obligated $460.8 million for the Mali compact. In September 2008, MCC and Mali amended the compact, removing the Industrial Park Project and reallocating funds to the Airport Project. As of December 2009, the overall obligation amount had not changed.

Compact Disbursements

At compact signature, MCC develops a disbursement plan for the compact. MCC disburses funds as the country begins implementing projects. According to MCC, any funds not disbursed within 120 days after the compact ends would return to MCC for reprogramming.

As of December 2009, MCC had disbursed $60.6 million (approximately 13 percent) of compact funds, compared with the $210.9 million (approximately 46 percent) that it had planned to disburse as of that date.

Although it is not shown in the graphic, in addition to the above disbursements, $110.2 million has been committed under the compact for pending expenses as of December 2009.

MONGOLIA COMPACT FACT SHEET

Map of Mongolia

Source: Map Resources (map).

Key Events for Mongolia Compact

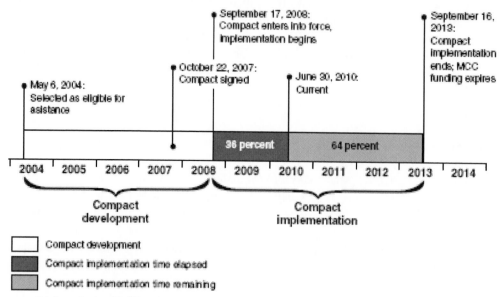

Source: GAO analysis of Millennium Challenge Corporation data.

Country Characteristics

Located in Asia between Russia and China, Mongolia has a population of approximately 2.6 million. It is a low-income country. Its economy is based on services, which account for 49 percent of its gross domestic product (GDP) and employ 61 percent of the labor force. Industry and agriculture account for 30 and 21 percent of GDP, respectively. Mongolia's economy struggled during the 1990s following the dissolution of the Soviet Union, which had provided up to one-third of Mongolia's annual GDP in foreign assistance. In the mid-2000s, Mongolia's economy grew by nearly 9 percent each year owing largely to its copper and gold mining industries, although it has been negatively affected by the global financial crisis.

Compact Timeline

During compact development, MCC and an eligible country negotiate project proposals and the compact's terms. After the compact is signed, the country finalizes administrative requirements, such as procurement and disbursement agreements. When the compact enters into force, MCC obligates funds and compact implementation begins. MCC's statute limits compact implementation to 5 years.

Mongolia was 1 of 16 countries that MCC selected as eligible in its first eligibility round. As of June 30, 2010, 36 percent of the compact's 5- year period had elapsed.

MCC SELECTION CRITERIA

MCC Candidate Criteria

Each fiscal year, MCC uses per capita gross national income (GNI) data to identify two pools of candidate countries—low-income and lower-middle-income—based on World Bank lending thresholds. Also, a candidate country must not be statutorily barred from receiving U.S. assistance. By law, MCC can use up to 25 percent of compact assistance each year for new compacts with lower-middleincome countries.

Mongolia has been classified as a low-income country every year since MCC began operations in 2004.

MCC Eligibility Criteria

MCC's board uses quantitative indicators to assess a candidate's policy performance. To meet MCC's criteria, a country must pass the control of corruption indicator and at least half of the indictors in each of three categories. To pass an indicator, a country must score above the median in its income group. However, the board may select a country as eligible even if it does not meet the criteria. Once MCC has signed a compact with a country, MCC continues to work with it—even if it fails the criteria—as long as its actions are not inconsistent with the criteria. If a country's policy performance declines, the board can suspend or terminate the compact.

Mongolia has met MCC's eligibility criteria each year since 2004.

Mongolia GNI Per Capita

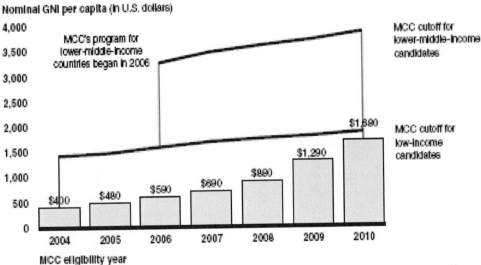

Source: GAO analysis of World Bank World Development Indicators and MCC income cutoffs.

Mongolia's Performance on MCC Eligibility Indicators

Indicator category	MCC eligibility year	2004	2005	2006	2007	2008	2009	2010
	MCC income group	Low	Low	Low	Low	Low	Low	Low
Ruling Justly	Political Rights	✓	✓	✓	✓	✓	✓	✓
	Civil Liberties	✓	✓	✓	✓	✓	✓	✓
	Voice and Accountability	✓	✓	✓	✓	✓	✓	✓
	Government Effectiveness	✓	✓	✓	✓	✓	✓	✓
	Rule of Law	✓	✓	✓	✓	✓	✓	✓
	Control of Corruption	✓	✓	✓	✓	✓	✓	✓
Investing in People	Girls' Primary Education Completion[a]	✓	✓	✓	✓	✓	✓	✓
	Primary Education Expenditures	✓	✓	✓	X	X	X	X
	Health Expenditures	✓	✓	✓	✓	✓	✓	✓
	Immunization Rates	✓	✓	✓	✓	✓	✓	✓
	Natural Resource Management (2008-2010)					✓	✓	✓
Economic Freedom	Country Credit Rating (2004-2005)	✓	✓					
	Days to Start a Business (2004-2007)	✓	✓	✓	✓			
	Cost of Starting a Business (2006-2007)			✓	✓			
	Business Start-up (2008-2010)					✓	✓	✓
	Inflation	✓	✓	X	✓	✓	✓	X
	Fiscal Policy	X	X	X	✓	✓	✓	✓
	Trade Policy	✓	✓	✓	✓	✓	✓	✓
	Regulatory Quality	✓	✓	✓	✓	✓	✓	✓
	Land Rights and Access (2008-2010)					✓	✓	✓
	Indicator performance results	Passed	Passed	Passed	Passed	Passed	Passed	Passed
	MCC eligibility determination	Eligible	Eligible	Eligible	Eligible	Eligible	NA[b]	NA[b]

✓ Passed (scored above the median)   X Failed (scored at the median or below)   ☐ NA for that year

Source: GAO analysis of Millennium Challenge Corporation data.

[a] In 2004, the indicator was "Primary Education Completion."

[b] In 2009, MCC stopped making an eligibility determination for countries with existing compacts.

COMPACT SUMMARY

Compact Characteristics

MCC and the partner country determine the compact structure before the compact is signed. However, the structure of some compacts has been altered during implementation.

At signature, Mongolia's compact focused on improving the country's human, institutional, and physical resources. In April 2009, the government of Mongolia withdrew the Rail Project of the compact. In September 2009, MCC approved the reallocation of $50.0 million from the $188.4 million Rail Project to expand and modify three existing compact projects—Health, Vocational Education, and the periurban component of the Property Rights Project. In December 2009, MCC approved the reallocation of the remaining funds from the Rail Project to two new projects—the Energy and Environment and the North-South Road Projects—as well as a contingency fund. The reallocations went into effect in January 2010.

Structure of Mongolia Compact, as of December 2009

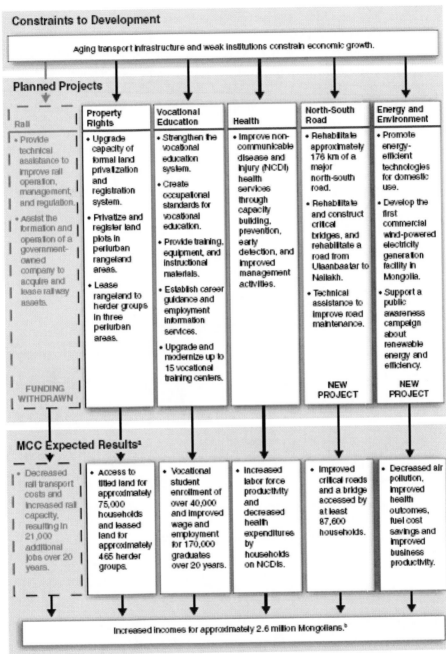

Source: GAO analysis of Millennium Challenge Corporation data.

[a] MCC expected results are reported as of compact signature, but reflect the two new projects.

[b] In fiscal year 2009, MCC recalculated the number of expected beneficiaries with increased income using a standardized methodology. At compact signature, MCC reported the compact would benefit approximately 3.1 million people by 2028.

Expected Results

This graphic presents MCC's expectations of selected compact results at compact signature and at the end of fiscal year 2009.

GAO has not independently verified the reliability of MCC's results projections for this compact. Previous GAO work has identified several problems with the methodology used to determine compact results. (See GAO-08-730 and GAO-07-909.)

MCC has modified the Mongolia compact but only partially recalculated the expected results.

COMPACT FUNDING

Mongolia Project Allocations

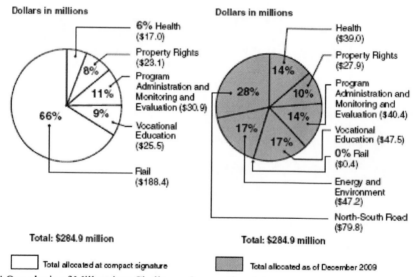

Total: $284.9 million   Total: $284.9 million

☐ Total allocated at compact signature   ▨ Total allocated as of December 2009

Source: GAO analysis of Millennium Challenge Corporation data.
Note: The reallocation of Rail Project funds went into effect in January 2010.

Compact Project Funding

MCC and the country may reallocate funds among projects during implementation. In some cases, MCC has also changed the overall compact obligation.

At signature (October 2007), MCC obligated $284.9 million for the Mongolia compact. In September 2009, due to Mongolia's request to withdraw the $188.4 million Rail Project, MCC approved the reallocation of $50.0 million to the three remaining projects. In December 2009, MCC approved the reallocation of the remaining Rail Project funds to two new projects— Energy and Environment and the North-South Road—and a contingency fund. The reallocations went into effect in January 2010. As of December 2009, the overall obligation remained $284.9 million.

Compact Disbursements

At compact signature, MCC develops a disbursement plan for the compact. MCC disburses funds as the country begins implementing projects. According to MCC, any funds not disbursed within 120 days after the compact ends would return to MCC for reprogramming.

As of December 2009, MCC had disbursed $9.8 million (approximately 4 percent) of compact funds, compared with the $64.5 million (approximately 23 percent) that it had planned to disburse as of that date.

Although it is not shown in the graphic, in addition to the above disbursements, $6.7 million has been committed under the compact for pending expenses as of December 2009.

Rail Project reallocations went into effect in January 2010.

Mongolia Planned and Actual Disbursements

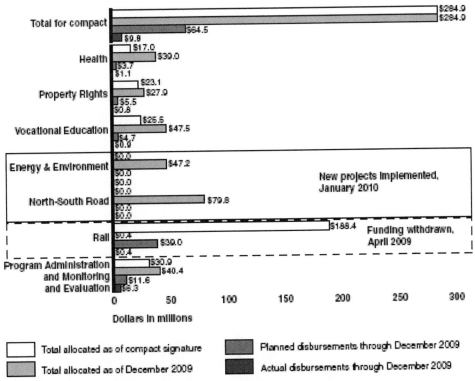

Source: GAO analysis of Millennium Challenge Corporation data.

Notes: We base planned disbursements on MCC's projections for the fiscal quarter ending December 2009. We assume that funds are disbursed evenly throughout each year. Planned disbursements for Mongolia do not reflect Rail Project reallocations because reallocations did not go into effect until January 2010. Actual disbursements by project may not add up to total disbursements because some disbursements are pending allocation to projects and are reflected in the total but not in the projects.

Morocco Compact Fact Sheet

Map of Morocco

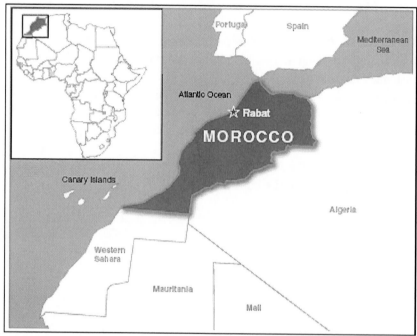

Source: Map Resources (map).

Key Events for Morocco Compact

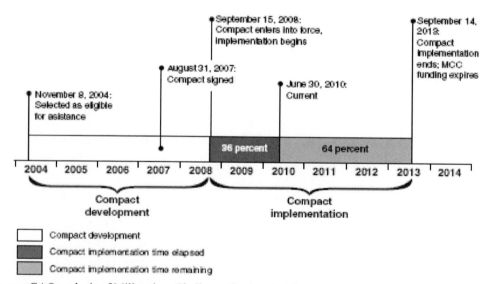

Source: GAO analysis of Millennium Challenge Corporation data

Country Characteristics

Located in northern Africa, bordering both the Atlantic Ocean and Mediterranean Sea, Morocco has a population of about 31.2 million. It is a lower-middle-income country. Its economy is based largely on services and industry, which respectively account for 49 and 33 percent of the country's gross domestic product (GDP). Agriculture accounts for 19 percent of GDP but 45 percent of the labor force. Morocco's economic policies have brought macroeconomic stability to the country, with generally low inflation, improved financial sector performance, and steady development of the services and industrial sectors. Morocco's primary economic challenge is to accelerate and sustain growth in order to reduce high levels of unemployment and underemployment. Morocco's GDP grew by 5.1 percent in 2009.

Compact Timeline

During compact development, MCC and an eligible country negotiate project proposals and the compact's terms. After the compact is signed, the country finalizes administrative requirements, such as procurement and disbursement agreements. When the compact enters into force, MCC obligates funds and compact implementation begins. MCC's statute limits compact implementation to 5 years.

Morocco was the only country to be newly selected as eligible in fiscal year 2005, MCC's second eligibility round. As of June 30, 2010, 36 percent of the compact's 5-year period had elapsed.

MCC SELECTION CRITERIA

Morocco GNI Per Capita

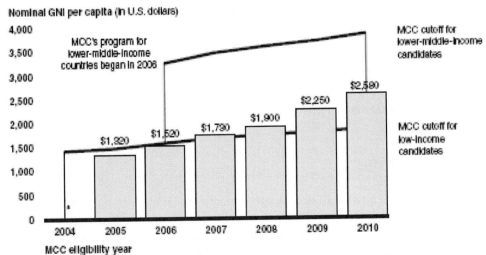

Source: GAO analysis of World Bank World Development Indicators and MCC income cutoffs.

[a] Morocco was not a candidate in 2004.

Morocco's Performance on MCC Eligibility Indicators

Indicator category	MCC eligibility year	2004	2005	2006	2007	2008	2009	2010
	MCC income group	Low	Low	Low	Lower-middle	Lower-middle	Lower-middle	Lower-middle
Ruling Justly	Political Rights	Morocco was not a candidate in 2004.	X	X	X	X	X	X
	Civil Liberties		X	✓	X	X	X	X
	Voice and Accountability		✓	✓	X	X	X	X
	Government Effectiveness		✓	✓	X	✓	✓	✓
	Rule of Law		✓	✓	✓	✓	✓	✓
	Control of Corruption		✓	✓	✓	✓	✓	✓
Investing in People	Girls' Primary Education Completion[a]		✓	✓	X	X	X	X
	Primary Education Expenditures		✓	✓	✓	✓	X	X
	Health Expenditures		X	X	X	X	X	X
	Immunization Rates		✓	✓	✓	✓	X	✓
	Natural Resource Management (2008-2010)					✓	✓	X
Economic Freedom	Country Credit Rating (2004-2005)		✓					
	Days to Start a Business (2004-2007)		✓	✓	✓			
	Cost of Starting a Business (2006-2007)			✓	✓			
	Business Start-up (2008-2010)					✓	✓	✓
	Inflation		✓	✓	✓	✓	✓	✓
	Fiscal Policy		X	X	X	X	X	✓
	Trade Policy		X	X	X	X	✓	X
	Regulatory Quality		✓	✓	X	X	✓	✓
	Land Rights and Access (2008-2010)					X	✓	✓
	Indicator performance results		Passed	Passed	Failed	Failed	Failed	Failed
	MCC eligibility determination	NA	Eligible	Eligible	Not Eligible	Eligible	NA[b]	NA[b]

✓ Passed (scored above the median) X Failed (scored at the median or below) ☐ NA for that year

Source: GAO analysis of Millennium Challenge Corporation data.

[a] In 2004, the indicator was "Primary Education Completion."

[b] In 2009, MCC stopped making an eligibility determination for countries with existing compacts.

MCC Candidate Criteria

Each fiscal year, MCC uses per capita gross national income (GNI) data to identify two pools of candidate countries—low-income and lower-middle-income—based on World Bank lending thresholds. Also, a candidate country must not be statutorily barred from receiving U.S. assistance. By law, MCC can use up to 25 percent of compact assistance each year for new compacts with lower-middle-income countries.

Morocco was selected as eligible in fiscal year 2005 as a low-income country. In 2007, Morocco's rising GNI per capita lifted it to lower-middle-income status.

MCC Eligibility Criteria

MCC's Board uses quantitative indicators to assess a candidate's policy performance. To meet MCC's criteria, a country must pass the control of corruption indicator and at least half of the indictors in each of three categories. To pass an indicator, a country must score above the median in its income group. However, the board may select a country as eligible even if it does not meet the criteria. Once MCC has signed a compact with a country, MCC continues to work with it—even if it fails the criteria—as long as its actions are not inconsistent with the criteria. If a country's policy performance declines, the board can suspend or terminate the compact.

Morocco met MCC's eligibility criteria in 2005 and 2006 but has failed each year since.

COMPACT SUMMARY

Structure of Morocco Compact, as of December 2009

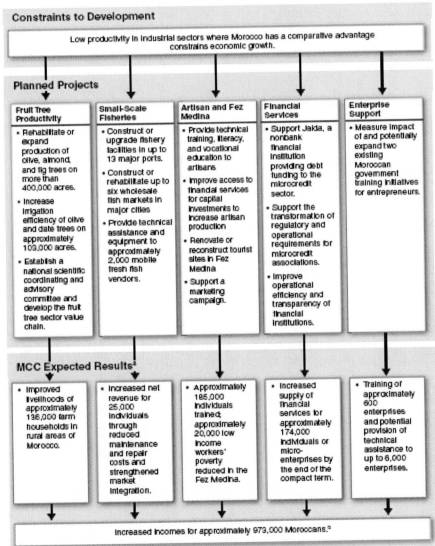

Constraints to Development

Low productivity in industrial sectors where Morocco has a comparative advantage constrains economic growth.

Planned Projects

Fruit Tree Productivity	Small-Scale Fisheries	Artisan and Fez Medina	Financial Services	Enterprise Support
• Rehabilitate or expand production of olive, almond, and fig trees on more than 400,000 acres. • Increase irrigation efficiency of olive and date trees on approximately 103,000 acres. • Establish a national scientific coordinating and advisory committee and develop the fruit tree sector value chain.	• Construct or upgrade fishery facilities in up to 13 major ports. • Construct or rehabilitate up to six wholesale fish markets in major cities • Provide technical assistance and equipment to approximately 2,000 mobile fresh fish vendors.	• Provide technical training, literacy, and vocational education to artisans • Improve access to financial services for capital investments to increase artisan production • Renovate or reconstruct tourist sites in Fez Medina • Support a marketing campaign.	• Support Jaida, a nonbank financial institution providing debt funding to the microcredit sector. • Support the transformation of regulatory and operational requirements for microcredit associations. • Improve operational efficiency and transparency of financial institutions.	• Measure impact of and potentially expand two existing Moroccan government training initiatives for entrepreneurs.

MCC Expected Results[a]

• Improved livelihoods of approximately 136,000 farm households in rural areas of Morocco.	• Increased net revenue for 25,000 individuals through reduced maintenance and repair costs and strengthened market integration.	• Approximately 185,000 individuals trained; approximately 20,000 low income workers' poverty reduced in the Fez Medina.	• Increased supply of financial services for approximately 174,000 individuals or micro-enterprises by the end of the compact term.	• Training of approximately 600 enterprises and potential provision of technical assistance to up to 6,000 enterprises.

Increased incomes for approximately 973,000 Moroccans.[b]

Source: GAO analysis of Millennium Challenge Corporation data.

[a] MCC expected results are reported as of compact signature, except the number of beneficiaries with increased incomes.

[b] In fiscal year 2009, MCC recalculated the number of expected beneficiaries using a standardized methodology. At compact signature, MCC reported the compact would directly benefit 600,000 people over the compact term.

Compact Characteristics

MCC and the partner country determine the compact structure before the compact is signed. However, the structure of some compacts has been altered during implementation.

At signature, Morocco's compact aimed to stimulate economic growth by increasing productivity and improving employment in sectors of the economy that the Kingdom of Morocco has identified as having high potential for growth, such as agribusiness, fishing, and artisan crafts. The compact also focused on supporting small business creation and growth by investments in financial services and enterprise support. At signature, 11 percent of Moroccans lived in extreme poverty

Expected Results

This graphic presents MCC's expectations of selected compact results at compact signature and at the end of fiscal year 2009.

GAO has not independently verified the reliability of MCC's results projections for this compact. Previous GAO work has identified several problems with the methodology used to determine compact projects' expected results. (See GAO-08-730 and GAO-07-909.)

COMPACT FUNDING

Morocco Project Allocations

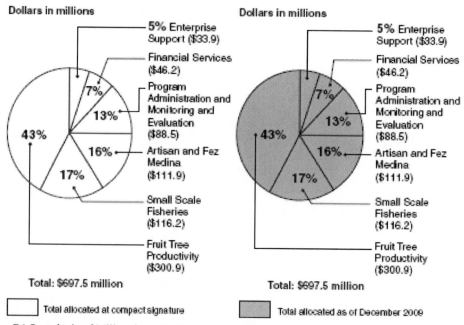

Source: GAO analysis of Millennium Challenge Corporation data.

Note: Project allocations in figures may not add up to 100 percent due to rounding.

Morocco Planned and Actual Disbursements

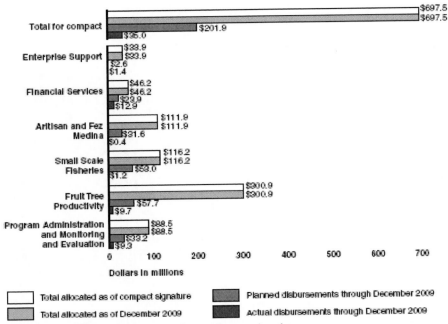

Source: GAO analysis of Millennium Challenge Corporation data.

Notes: We base planned disbursements on MCC's projections for the fiscal quarter ending December 2009. We assume that funds are disbursed evenly throughout each year. Actual disbursements by project may not add up to total disbursements because some disbursements are pending allocation to projects and are reflected in the total but not in the projects.

Compact Project Funding

MCC and the country may reallocate funds among projects during implementation. In some cases, MCC has also changed the overall compact obligation.

At signature (August 2007), MCC obligated $697.5 million for the Morocco compact. As of December 2009, the overall obligation amount and project allocations had not changed.

Compact Disbursements

At compact signature, MCC develops a disbursement plan for the compact. MCC disburses funds as the country begins implementing projects. According to MCC, any funds not disbursed within 120 days after the compact ends would return to MCC for reprogramming.

As of December 2009, MCC had disbursed $35.0 million (5 percent) of compact funds, compared with the $201.9 million (29 percent) that it had planned to disburse as of that date.

Although it is not shown in the graphic, in addition to the above disbursements, $115.2 million has been committed under the compact for pending expenses as of December 2009.

Mozambique Compact Fact Sheet

Map of Mozambique

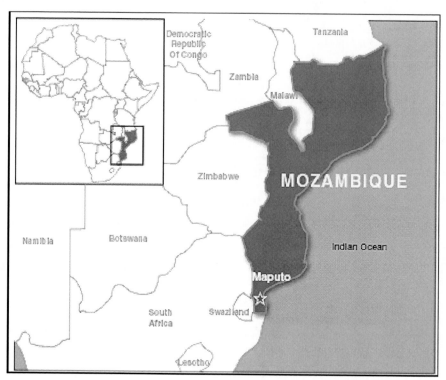

Source: Map Resources (map).

Key Events for Mozambique Compact

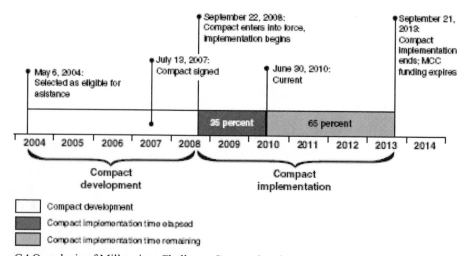

Source: GAO analysis of Millennium Challenge Corporation data.

Country Characteristics

Located on the Indian Ocean coast of southern Africa, Mozambique has a population of about 21.8 million.

It is a low-income country. Its economy is based on services and industry, which respectively account for 45 and 31 percent of the country's gross domestic product (GDP). Agriculture accounts for 24 percent of GDP but employs about 81 percent of the labor force. Mozambique is considered a strong economic performer in Africa and experienced an average of 8 percent growth from 1994 to 2007, although growth has slowed in more recent years. Macroeconomic reforms by the government, starting in the late 1980s, have contributed to the country's economic growth. However, Mozambique's government is still heavily reliant on foreign aid, which comprises more than half of its budget.

Compact Timeline

During compact development, MCC and an eligible country negotiate project proposals and the compact's terms. After the compact is signed, the country finalizes administrative requirements, such as procurement and disbursement agreements. When the compact enters into force, MCC obligates funds and compact implementation begins. MCC's statute limits compact implementation to 5 years.

Mozambique was 1 of 16 countries that MCC selected as eligible in its first eligibility round. As of June 30, 2010, 35 percent of the compact's 5-year period had elapsed.

MCC SELECTION CRITERIA

Mozambique GNI Per Capita

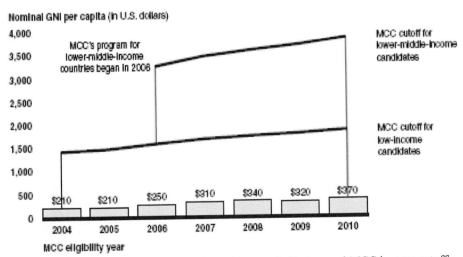

Source: GAO analysis of World Bank World Development Indicators and MCC income cutoffs.

Mozambique's Performance on MCC Eligibility Indicators

Indicator category		MCC eligibility year	2004	2005	2006	2007	2008	2009	2010
		MCC income group	Low	Low	Low	Low	Low	Low	Low
Ruling Justly		Political Rights	✓	✓	✓	✓	✓	✓	✓
		Civil Liberties	X	✓	✓	✓	✓	✓	✓
		Voice and Accountability	✓	✓	✓	✓	✓	✓	✓
		Government Effectiveness	✓	✓	✓	✓	✓	✓	✓
		Rule of Law	✓	✓	✓	✓	✓	✓	✓
		Control of Corruption	X	X	✓	✓	✓	✓	✓
Investing in People		Girls' Primary Education Completion[a]	X	X	X	X	X	X	X
		Primary Education Expenditures	X	X	✓	✓	✓	✓	✓
		Health Expenditures	X	X	✓	✓	✓	✓	✓
		Immunization Rates	X	X	X	X	X	X	X
		Natural Resource Management (2009-2010)					X	X	X
Economic Freedom		Country Credit Rating (2004-2005)	✓	✓					
		Days to Start a Business (2004-2007)	X	X	X	X			
		Cost of Starting a Business (2006-2007)			X	X			
		Business Start-up (2008-2010)					✓	✓	✓
		Inflation	✓	✓	✓	✓	✓	✓	✓
		Fiscal Policy	X	X	X	X	X	X	X
		Trade Policy	X	X	✓	✓	✓	✓	✓
		Regulatory Quality	✓	✓	✓	✓	✓	✓	✓
		Land Rights and Access (2009-2010)					✓	✓	✓
		Indicator performance results	Failed	Failed	Passed	Passed	Failed	Failed	Failed
		MCC eligibility determination	Eligible	Eligible	Eligible	Eligible	Eligible	NA[b]	NA[b]

✓ Passed (scored above the median)   X Failed (scored at the median or below)   ☐ NA for that year

Source: GAO analysis of Millennium Challenge Corporation data.

[a] In 2004, the indicator was "Primary Education Completion."

[b] In 2009, MCC stopped making an eligibility determination for countries with existing compacts.

MCC Candidate Criteria

Each fiscal year, MCC uses per capita gross national income (GNI) data to identify two pools of candidate countries—low-income and lower-middle-income—based on World Bank lending thresholds. Also, a candidate country must not be statutorily barred from receiving U.S. assistance. By law, MCC can use up to 25 percent of compact assistance each year for new compacts with lower-middle-income.

Mozambique has been classified as a low-income country every year since MCC began operations in 2004.

MCC Eligibility Criteria

MCC's board uses quantitative indicators to assess a candidate 's policy performance. To meet MCC's criteria, a country must pass the control of corruption indicator and at least half of the indictors in each of three categories. To pass an indicator, a country must score above the median in its income group. However, the board may select a country as eligible even if it does not meet the criteria. Once MCC has signed a compact with a country, MCC continues to work with it—even if it fails the criteria—as long as its actions are not inconsistent with the criteria. If a country's policy performance declines, the board can suspend or terminate the compact.

Mozambique failed MCC's criteria in 2004 and 2005, but the MCC board deemed it eligible. It met the criteria in 2006 and 2007. Since 2008, when MCC added a fifth Investing in People indicator, Mozambique again failed the criteria.

COMPACT SUMMARY

Compact Characteristics

MCC and the partner country determine the compact structure before the compact is signed. However, the structure of some compacts has been altered during implementation.

At signature, Mozambique's compact targeted four northern provinces: Cabo Delgado, Nampula, Niassa, and Zambézia. The compact aims to increase the productive capacity of the population in the targeted areas. At that time, these provinces were home to more than 10 million people.

Expected Results

This graphic presents MCC's expectations of selected compact results at compact signature and at the end of fiscal year 2009.

The Mozambique compact is one of five compacts for which GAO has independently verified the reliability of MCC's results projections. In June 2008, GAO reported that MCC had made errors in its original projections of the impact of Mozambique's compact (GAO-08-730). MCC corrected these errors, reducing the expected impact on poverty. For example, MCC originally expected to lift 270,000 people out of poverty by 2015 but revised that projection to 56,000 people.

Structure of Mozambique Compact, as of December 2009

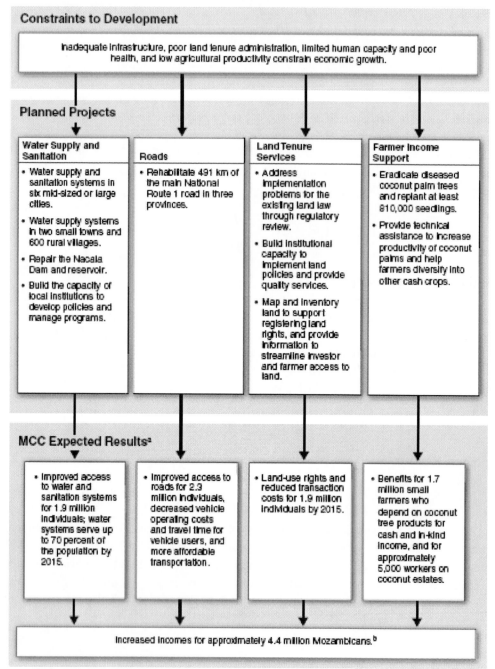

Source: GAO analysis of Millennium Challenge Corporation data.

[a] MCC expected results are reported as of compact signature, except the number of beneficiaries with increased incomes.

[b] In fiscal year 2009, MCC recalculated the number of expected beneficiaries using a standardized methodology. At compact signature, MCC reported the compact would benefit approximately 5 million people over the compact term.

COMPACT FUNDING

Mozambique Project Allocations

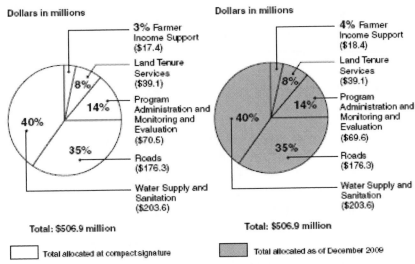

Source: GAO analysis of Millennium Challenge Corporation data.
Note: Project allocations in figures may not add up to 100 percent due to rounding.

Mozambique Planned and Actual Disbursements

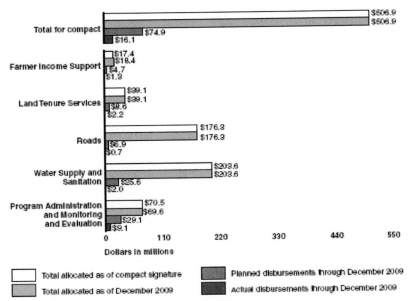

Source: GAO analysis of Millennium Challenge Corporation data.
Notes: We base planned disbursements on MCC's projections for the fiscal quarter ending December 2009. We assume that funds are disbursed evenly throughout each year. Actual disbursements by project may not add up to total disbursements because some disbursements are pending allocation to projects and are reflected in the total but not in the projects.

Compact Project Funding

MCC and the country may reallocate funds among projects during implementation. In some cases, MCC has also changed the overall compact obligation.

At signature (July 2007), MCC obligated $506.9 million for the Mozambique compact. As of December 2009, the overall obligation amount had not changed, however minor reallocations of funds were made among projects.

Compact Disbursements

At compact signature, MCC develops a disbursement plan for the compact. MCC disburses funds as the country begins implementing projects. According to MCC, any funds not disbursed within 120 days after the compact ends would return to MCC for reprogramming.

As of December 2009, MCC had disbursed $16.1 million (approximately 3 percent) of compact funds, compared with the $74.9 million (approximately 15 percent) that it had planned to disburse as of that date.

Although it is not shown in the graphic, in addition to the above disbursements, $57.0 million has been committed under the compact for pending expenses as of December 2009.

NAMIBIA COMPACT FACT SHEET

Map of Namibia

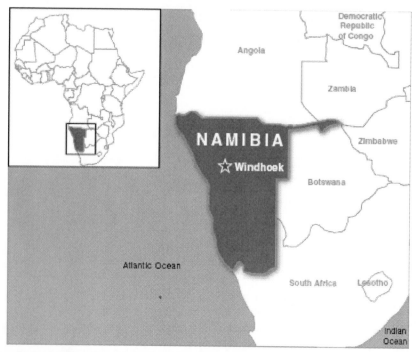

Source: Map Resources (map).

Key Events for Namibia Compact

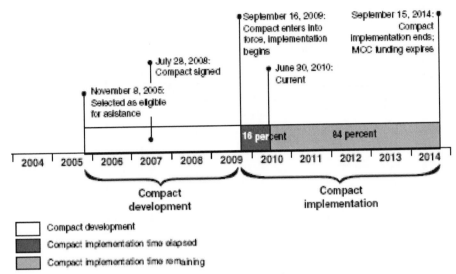

Source: GAO analysis of Millennium Challenge Corporation data.

Country Characteristics

Located on the Atlantic coast of southern Africa, Namibia has a population of about 2.1 million. It is an upper-middle-income country. Its economy is based on services and industry, which respectively account for 56 and 35 percent of the country's gross domestic product (GDP); the extraction and processing of minerals is an important economic activity. Agriculture accounts for 9 percent of GDP but employs 47 percent of the labor force. Namibia's annual economic growth since independence from South Africa in 1990 has averaged 4.5 percent but has slowed in recent years. According to the World Bank, Namibia has a strong democracy with sound economic management, good governance, basic civic freedoms, and respect for human rights. However, the social and economic imbalances of apartheid still affect Namibia.

Compact Timeline

During compact development, MCC and an eligible country negotiate project proposals and the compact's terms. After the compact is signed, the country finalizes administrative requirements, such as procurement and disbursement agreements. When the compact enters into force, MCC obligates funds and compact implementation begins. MCC's statute limits compact implementation to 5 years.

Namibia was one of two lowermiddle-income countries selected in the fiscal year 2006 eligibility round, the first year of MCC's program for lower-middle-income countries. As of June 30, 2010, 16 percent of the compact's 5-year period had elapsed.

MCC Selection Criteria

Namibia GNI Per Capita

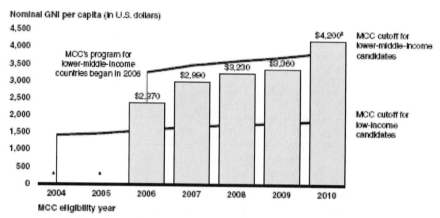

Nominal GNI per capita (in U.S. dollars)

MCC's program for lower-middle-income countries began in 2006

$2,370 $2,990 $3,230 $3,360 $4,200[a]

MCC cutoff for lower-middle-income candidates

MCC cutoff for low-income candidates

MCC eligibility year: 2004, 2005, 2006, 2007, 2008, 2009, 2010

Source: GAO analysis of World Bank World Development Indicators and MCC income cutoffs.

[a] Namibia was not a candidate in 2004 and 2005.

[b] Because Namibia rose to upper-middle-income status, it was not a candidate for assistance in 2010. However its existing compact with MCC was not affected.

Namibia Performance on MCC Eligibility Indicators

Indicator category	MCC eligibility year	2004	2005	2006	2007	2008	2009	2010
	MCC income group	Lower-middle	Lower-middle	Lower-middle	Lower-middle	Lower-middle	Lower-middle	Upper-middle
Ruling Justly	Political Rights			✓	✓	✓	✓	
Ruling Justly	Civil Liberties			X	✓	✓	✓	
Ruling Justly	Voice and Accountability			✓	✓	✓	✓	
Ruling Justly	Government Effectiveness			✓	✓	✓	✓	
Ruling Justly	Rule of Law			✓	✓	✓	✓	
Ruling Justly	Control of Corruption			✓	✓	✓	✓	
Investing in People	Girls' Primary Education Completion[a]			X	X	X	X	
Investing in People	Primary Education Expenditures			✓	✓	✓	✓	
Investing in People	Health Expenditures			✓	✓	✓	X	
Investing in People	Immunization Rates			X	X	X	X	
Investing in People	Natural Resource Management (2009-2010)						X	X
Economic Freedom	Country Credit Rating (2004-2005)							
Economic Freedom	Days to Start a Business (2004-2007)			X	X			
Economic Freedom	Cost of Starting a Business (2006-2007)			✓	✓			
Economic Freedom	Business Start-up (2008-2010)					X	X	
Economic Freedom	Inflation			✓	✓	✓	✓	
Economic Freedom	Fiscal Policy			X	X	X	✓	
Economic Freedom	Trade Policy			✓	✓	✓	✓	
Economic Freedom	Regulatory Quality			✓	✓	✓	✓	
Economic Freedom	Land Rights and Access (2008-2010)					X	X	
	Indicator performance results			Passed	Passed	Failed	Failed	
	MCC eligibility determination	NA	NA	Eligible	Eligible	Eligible	NA[b]	NA[b]

(2004: Namibia was not a candidate in 2004. 2005: Namibia was not a candidate in 2005. 2010: MCC did not create a scorecard for Namibia in 2010 because it rose to upper-middle-income status.)

Legend: ✓ Passed (scored above the median)   X Failed (scored at the median or below)   ☐ NA for that year

Source: GAO analysis of Millennium Challenge Corporation data.

[a] In 2004, the indicator was "Primary Education Completion."

[b] In 2009, MCC stopped making an eligibility determination for countries with existing compacts.

MCC Candidate Criteria

Each fiscal year, MCC uses per capita gross national income (GNI) data to identify two pools of candidate countries—low-income and lower-middle-income—based on World Bank lending thresholds. Also, a candidate country must not be statutorily barred from receiving U.S. assistance. By law, MCC can use up to 25 percent of compact assistance each year for new compacts with lower-middle-income countries.

Namibia was selected as eligible in fiscal year 2006 and was classified as a lower-middle-income country until 2009. In 2010, Namibia's rising GNI per capita lifted it to uppermiddle-income status.

MCC Eligibility Criteria

MCC's board uses quantitative indicators to assess a candidate's policy performance. To meet MCC's criteria, a country must pass the control of corruption indicator and at least half of the indictors in each of three categories. To pass an indicator, a country must score above the median in its income group. However, the board may select a country as eligible even if it does not meet the criteria. Once MCC has signed a compact with a country, MCC continues to work with it—even if it fails the criteria—as long as its actions are not inconsistent with the criteria. If a country's policy performance declines, the board can suspend or terminate the compact.

Namibia met MCC's eligibility criteria in 2006 and 2007 but not in 2008 and 2009 because it failed more than half of the Investing in People indicators. MCC did not create a scorecard for Namibia in 2010 because it became an uppermiddle-income country.

COMPACT SUMMARY

Compact Characteristics

MCC and the partner country determine the compact structure before the compact is signed. However, the structure of some compacts has been altered during implementation.

At signature, Namibia's compact focused on improving the quality of education for the rural poor, primarily in the northern part of the country, and diversifying Namibia's economy with an emphasis on its growing agriculture and tourism sectors. At that time, Namibia had high unemployment, extreme disparity in wealth and income between the rich and poor, and an HIV prevalence rate of nearly 20 percent.

Expected Results

This graphic presents MCC's expectations of selected compact results at compact signature and at the end of fiscal year 2009.

GAO has not independently verified the reliability of MCC's results projections for this compact. Previous GAO work has identified several problems with the methodology used to determine compact projects' expected results. (See GAO-08-730 and GAO-07-909.)

Structure of Namibia Compact, as of December 2009

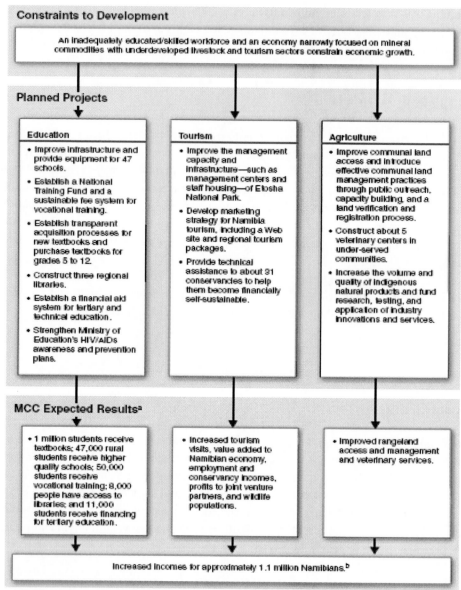

Source: GAO analysis of Millennium Challenge Corporation data.

[a] MCC expected results are reported as of compact signature, except the number of beneficiaries with increased incomes.

[b] In fiscal year 2009, MCC recalculated the number of expected beneficiaries using a standardized methodology. At compact signature, MCC reported the compact would benefit approximately 1.5 million people.

COMPACT FUNDING

Namibia Project Allocations

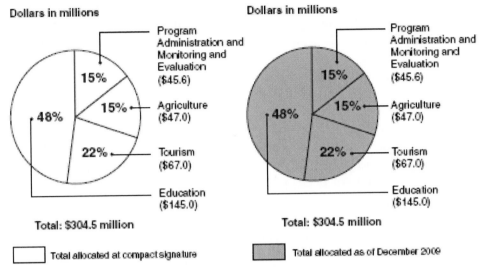

Source: GAO analysis of Millennium Challenge Corporation data.

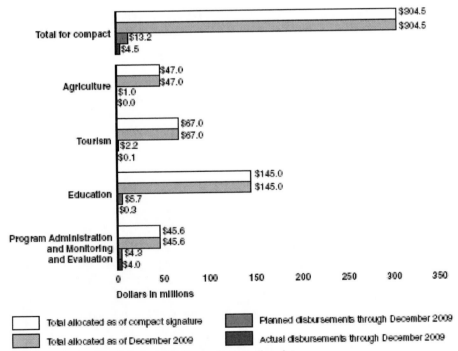

Source: GAO analysis of Millennium Challenge Corporation data.

Notes: We base planned disbursements on MCC's projections for the fiscal quarter ending December 2009. We assume that funds are disbursed evenly throughout each year. Actual disbursements by project may not add up to total disbursements because some disbursements are pending allocation to projects and are reflected in the total but not in the projects.

Compact Project Funding

MCC and the country may reallocate funds among projects during implementation. In some cases, MCC has also changed the overall compact obligation.

At signature (July 2008), MCC obligated $304.5 million for the Namibia compact. As of December 2009, the overall obligation amount and project allocations had not changed.

Compact Disbursements

At compact signature, MCC develops a disbursement plan for the compact. MCC disburses funds as the country begins

implementing projects. According to MCC, any funds not disbursed within 120 days after the compact ends would return to MCC for reprogramming.

As of December 2009, MCC had disbursed $4.5 million (approximately 2 percent) of compact funds, compared with the $13.2 million (approximately 5 percent) that it had planned to disburse as of that date.

Although it is not shown in the graphic, in addition to the above disbursements, $5.9 million has been committed under the compact for pending expenses as of December 2009.

NICARAGUA COMPACT FACT SHEET

Map of Nicaragua

Source: Map Resources (map).

Key Events for Nicaragua Compact

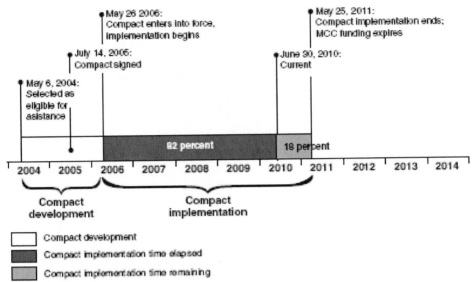

Source: GAO analysis of Millennium Challenge Corporation data.

Country Characteristics

Located in Central America, Nicaragua has a population of 5.7 million. It is a low-income country. Its economy is based primarily on services, which account for 57 percent of the country's gross domestic product (GDP) and employ 52 percent of the labor force. Industry and agriculture account for 26 and 18 percent of GDP, respectively. Nicaragua's real GDP contracted by about 3 percent in 2009. In November 2008, Nicaragua held municipal elections, the credibility of which was questioned by the U.S. government. Subsequently, the MCC partially terminated its compact with Nicaragua on the grounds that the government had engaged in actions inconsistent with MCC eligibility criteria.

Compact Timeline

During compact development, MCC and an eligible country negotiate project proposals and the compact's terms. After the compact is signed, the country finalizes administrative requirements, such as procurement and disbursement agreements. When the compact enters into force, MCC obligates funds and compact implementation begins. MCC's statute limits compact implementation to 5 years.

Nicaragua was 1 of 16 countries that MCC selected as eligible in its first eligibility round. As of June 30, 2010, 82 percent of the compact's 5- year period had elapsed.

MCC Selection Criteria

MCC Candidate Criteria

Each fiscal year, MCC uses per capita gross national income (GNI) data to identify two pools of candidate countries—low-income and lower-middle-income—based on World Bank lending thresholds. Also, a candidate country must not be statutorily barred from receiving U.S. assistance. By law, MCC can use up to 25 percent of compact assistance each year for new compacts with lower-middleincome countries.

Nicaragua has been classified as a low-income country every year since MCC began operations in 2004.

MCC Eligibility Criteria

MCC's board uses quantitative indicators to assess a candidate's policy performance. To meet MCC's criteria, a country must pass the control of corruption indicator and at least half of the indictors in each of three categories. To pass an indicator, a country must score above the median in its income group. However, the board may select a country as eligible even if it does not meet the criteria. Once MCC has signed a compact with a country, MCC continues to work with it—even if it fails the criteria—as long as its actions are not inconsistent with the criteria. If a country's policy performance declines, the board can suspend or terminate the compact.

Nicaragua has met MCC's eligibility criteria each year from 2004 through 2008. It did not meet the criteria in 2009 and 2010 because it failed the corruption indicator.

Nicaragua GNI Per Capita

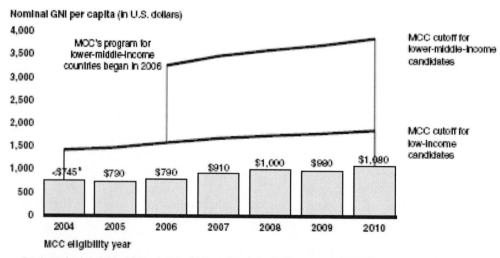

Source: GAO analysis of World Bank World Development Indicators and MCC income cutoffs.
[a]Nicaragua did not have a confirmed GNI for 2004. The World Bank estimated it at <$745.

Nicaragua's Performance on MCC Eligibility Indicators

Indicator category	MCC eligibility year	2004	2005	2006	2007	2008	2009	2010
	MCC income group	Low	Low	Low	Low	Low	Low	Low
Ruling Justly	Political Rights	✓	✓	✓	✓	✓	✓	✓
	Civil Liberties	✓	✓	✓	✓	✓	✓	✓
	Voice and Accountability	✓	✓	✓	✓	✓	✓	✓
	Government Effectiveness	X	X	✓	✓	X	X	X
	Rule of Law	✓	✓	✓	✓	✓	✓	✓
	Control of Corruption	✓	✓	✓	✓	✓	X	X
Investing in People	Girls' Primary Education Completion*	✓	✓	✓	✓	✓	✓	✓
	Primary Education Expenditures	X	X	X	X	X	X	✓
	Health Expenditures	✓	✓	✓	✓	✓	✓	✓
	Immunization Rates	✓	✓	✓	✓	✓	✓	✓
	Natural Resource Management (2009-2010)					✓	✓	✓
Economic Freedom	Country Credit Rating (2004-2005)	X	✓					
	Days to Start a Business (2004-2007)	✓	✓	✓	✓			
	Cost of Starting a Business (2006-2007)			X	X			
	Business Start-up (2008-2010)					X	X	X
	Inflation	✓	✓	✓	✓	✓	✓	✓
	Fiscal Policy	X	X	X	✓	✓	✓	✓
	Trade Policy	✓	✓	✓	✓	✓	✓	✓
	Regulatory Quality	✓	✓	✓	✓	✓	✓	✓
	Land Rights and Access (2009-2010)					X	X	✓
	Indicator performance results	Passed	Passed	Passed	Passed	Passed	Failed	Failed
	MCC eligibility determination	Eligible	Eligible	Eligible	Eligible	Eligible	NAᵇ	NAᵇ

✓ Passed (scored above the median)   X Failed (scored at the median or below)   ☐ NA for that year

Source: GAO analysis of Millennium Challenge Corporation data.
ᵃ In 2004, the indicator was "Primary Education Completion."
ᵇ In 2009, MCC stopped making an eligibility determination for countries with existing compacts.

COMPACT STRUCTURE

Compact Characteristics

MCC and the partner country determine the compact structure before the compact is signed. However, the structure of some compacts has been altered during implementation.

At signature, Nicaragua's compact aimed to build productive capacity in León and Chinandega, two regions in the northwest, where 70 percent of the rural population was poor. In June 2009, MCC partially terminated the Nicaragua compact, ceasing to fund the Property Regularization Project and activities not yet contracted under the Transportation Project. MCC acted in response to actions by the government of Nicaragua inconsistent with MCC's eligibility criteria: electoral irregularities were reported surrounding the November 2008 municipal elections. MCC will continue to upgrade 20 km of the Pacific Corridor highway and 54 km of rural secondary roads under the compact.

Structure of Nicaragua Compact, as of December 2009

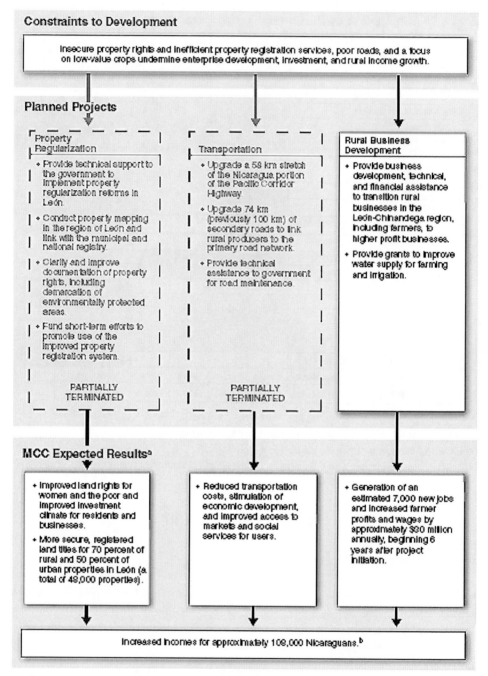

Constraints to Development

Insecure property rights and inefficient property registration services, poor roads, and a focus on low-value crops undermine enterprise development, investment, and rural income growth.

Planned Projects

Property Regularization
- Provide technical support to the government to implement property regularization reforms in León.
- Conduct property mapping in the region of León and link with the municipal and national registry.
- Clarify and improve documentation of property rights, including demarcation of environmentally protected areas.
- Fund short-term efforts to promote use of the improved property registration system.

PARTIALLY TERMINATED

Transportation
- Upgrade a 58 km stretch of the Nicaragua portion of the Pacific Corridor Highway.
- Upgrade 74 km (previously 100 km) of secondary roads to link rural producers to the primary road network.
- Provide technical assistance to government for road maintenance.

PARTIALLY TERMINATED

Rural Business Development
- Provide business development, technical, and financial assistance to transition rural businesses in the León-Chinandega region, including farmers, to higher profit businesses.
- Provide grants to improve water supply for farming and irrigation.

MCC Expected Results[a]

- Improved land rights for women and the poor and improved investment climate for residents and businesses.
- More secure, registered land titles for 70 percent of rural and 50 percent of urban properties in León (a total of 43,000 properties).

- Reduced transportation costs, stimulation of economic development, and improved access to markets and social services for users.

- Generation of an estimated 7,000 new jobs and increased farmer profits and wages by approximately $30 million annually, beginning 6 years after project initiation.

Increased incomes for approximately 109,000 Nicaraguans.[b]

Source: GAO analysis of Millennium Challenge Corporation data.

[a] MCC expected results are reported as of compact signature, except the number of beneficiaries with increased incomes. The termination of two projects may affect results.

[b] In fiscal year 2009, MCC recalculated the number of expected beneficiaries using a standardized methodology. MCC did not publish a beneficiary estimate for Nicaragua at compact signature.

Expected Results

This graphic presents MCC's expectations of selected compact results at compact signature and at the end of fiscal year 2009.

GAO has not independently verified the reliability of MCC's results projections for this compact. Previous GAO work has identified several problems with the methodology used to determine compact results. (See GAO-08-730 and GAO-07-909.)

MCC has modified the Nicaragua compact but only partially recalculated the expected results.

COMPACT FUNDING

Nicaragua Project Allocations

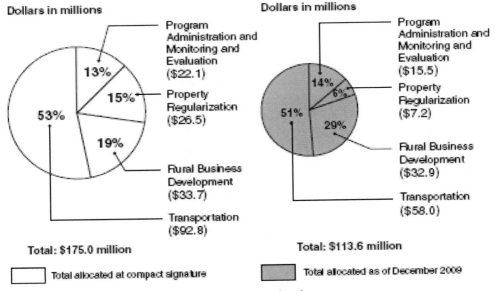

Total: $175.0 million   Total: $113.6 million

☐ Total allocated at compact signature   ▨ Total allocated as of December 2009

Source: GAO analysis of Millennium Challenge Corporation data.

Compact Project Funding

MCC and the country may reallocate funds among projects during implementation. In some cases, MCC has also changed the overall compact obligation.

At signature (July 2005), MCC obligated $175.0 million for the Nicaragua compact. In June 2009, MCC partially terminated assistance under the Nicaragua compact ceasing to fund the Property Regularization Project and activities not already contracted under the Transportation Project. As of December 2009, the overall obligation had decreased to $113.6 million.

Nicaragua Planned and Actual Disbursements

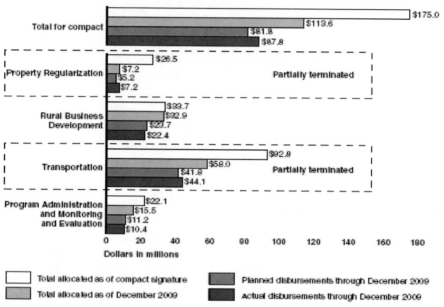

Source: GAO analysis of Millennium Challenge Corporation data.

Notes: We base planned disbursements on MCC's projections for the fiscal quarter ending December 2009. We assume that funds are disbursed evenly throughout each year. Actual disbursements by project may not add up to total disbursements because some disbursements are pending allocation to projects and are reflected in the total but not in the projects.

Compact Disbursements

At compact signature, MCC develops a disbursement plan for the compact. MCC disburses funds as the country begins implementing projects. According to MCC, any funds not disbursed within 120 days after the compact ends would return to MCC for reprogramming.

As of December 2009, MCC had disbursed $87.8 million (approximately 77 percent) of compact funds, compared with the $81.8 million (72 percent) that it had planned to disburse as of that date.

Although it is not shown in the graphic, in addition to the above disbursements, $15.3 million has been committed under the compact for pending expenses as of December 2009.

TANZANIA COMPACT FACT SHEET

Country Characteristics

Located in eastern Africa, Tanzania—including the islands of Zanzibar—has a population of about 42.5 million. It is a low-income country. Its economy is based primarily on services, which account for 51 percent of the country's gross domestic product (GDP).

Industry accounts for 23 percent of GDP, with gold and mineral mining growing in importance. Agriculture accounts for 27 percent of GDP but employs 80 percent of the labor force. Tanzania has experienced several years of real GDP growth—more than 7 percent in 2007 and 2008— although it slowed to about 4.5 percent in 2009.

Compact Timeline

During compact development, MCC and an eligible country negotiate project proposals and the compact's terms. After the compact is signed, the country finalizes administrative requirements, such as procurement and disbursement agreements. When the compact enters into force, MCC obligates funds and compact implementation begins. MCC's statute limits compact implementation to 5 years.

Tanzania was first selected as eligible in MCC's third eligibility round for low-income countries. As of June 30, 2010, 36 percent of the compact's 5-year period had elapsed.

MAP OF TANZANIA

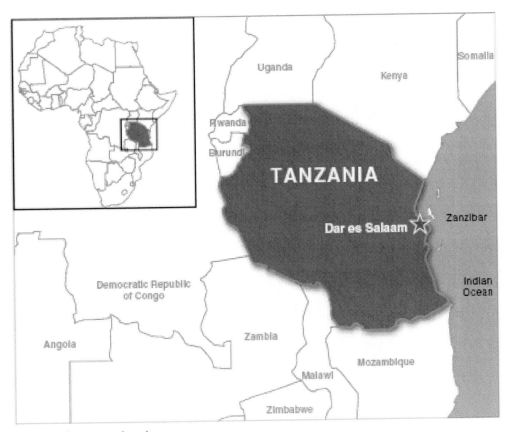

Source: Map Resources (map).

Key Events for Tanzania Compact

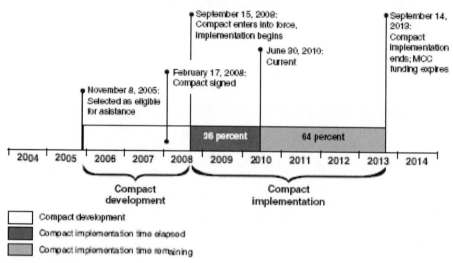

Source: GAO analysis of Millennium Challenge Corporation data.

MCC SELECTION CRITERIA

MCC Candidate Criteria

Each fiscal year, MCC uses per capita gross national income (GNI) data to identify two pools of candidate countries—low-income and lower-middle-income—based on World Bank lending thresholds. Also, a candidate country must not be statutorily barred from receiving U.S. assistance. By law, MCC can use up to 25 percent of compact assistance each year for new compacts with lower-middle-income countries.

Tanzania was selected as eligible in fiscal year 2006 and has been classified as a low-income country ever since

MCC Eligibility Criteria

MCC's board uses quantitative indicators to assess a candidate's policy performance. To meet MCC's criteria, a country must pass the control of corruption indicator and at least half of the indictors in each of three categories. To pass an indicator, a country must score above the median in its income group. However, the board may select a country as eligible even if it does not meet the criteria. Once MCC has signed a compact with a country, MCC continues to work with it—even if it fails the criteria—as long as its actions are not inconsistent with the criteria. If a country's policy performance declines, the board can suspend or terminate the compact.

Tanzania has met MCC's eligibility indicator criteria each year since it was first deemed eligible in 2006.

Tanzania GNI Per Capita

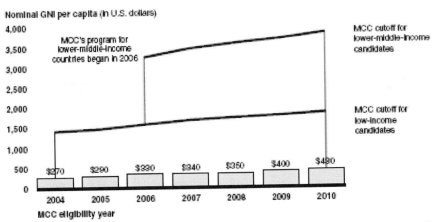

Source: GAO analysis of World Bank World Development Indicators and MCC income cutoffs.

Tanzania's Performance on MCC Eligibility Indicators

Indicator category		MCC eligibility year	2004	2005	2006	2007	2008	2009	2010
		MCC income group	Low	Low	Low	Low	Low	Low	Low
Ruling Justly		Political Rights	X	✓	✓	✓	✓	✓	✓
		Civil Liberties	✓	✓	✓	✓	✓	✓	✓
		Voice and Accountability	✓	✓	✓	✓	✓	✓	✓
		Government Effectiveness	✓	✓	✓	✓	✓	✓	✓
		Rule of Law	✓	✓	✓	✓	✓	✓	✓
		Control of Corruption	X	X	✓	✓	✓	✓	✓
Investing in People		Girls' Primary Education Completion[a]	X	X	X	X	✓	✓	✓
		Primary Education Expenditures	✓	✓	✓	✓	✓	✓	✓
		Health Expenditures	✓	✓	X	X	X	✓	✓
		Immunization Rates	✓	✓	✓	✓	✓	✓	✓
		Natural Resource Management (2009-2010)					✓	X	✓
Economic Freedom		Country Credit Rating (2004-2005)	✓	✓					
		Days to Start a Business (2004-2007)	✓	✓	✓	✓			
		Cost of Starting a Business (2006-2007)			X	X			
		Business Start-up (2008-2010)					✓	✓	✓
		Inflation	✓	✓	✓	✓	✓	✓	✓
		Fiscal Policy	✓	✓	✓	✓	X	X	X
		Trade Policy	X	X	X	✓	✓	✓	✓
		Regulatory Quality	✓	✓	✓	✓	✓	✓	✓
		Land Rights and Access (2009-2010)					✓	✓	✓
		Indicator performance results	Failed	Failed	Passed	Passed	Passed	Passed	Passed
		MCC eligibility determination	Not Eligible	Not Eligible	Eligible	Eligible	Eligible	NA[b]	NA[b]

✓ Passed (scored above the median)   X Failed (scored at the median or below)   ☐ NA for that year

Source: GAO analysis of Millennium Challenge Corporation data.
[a] In 2004, the indicator was "Primary Education Completion."
[b] In 2009, MCC stopped making an eligibility determination for countries with existing compacts.

COMPACT STRUCTURE

Structure of Tanzania Compact, as of December 2009

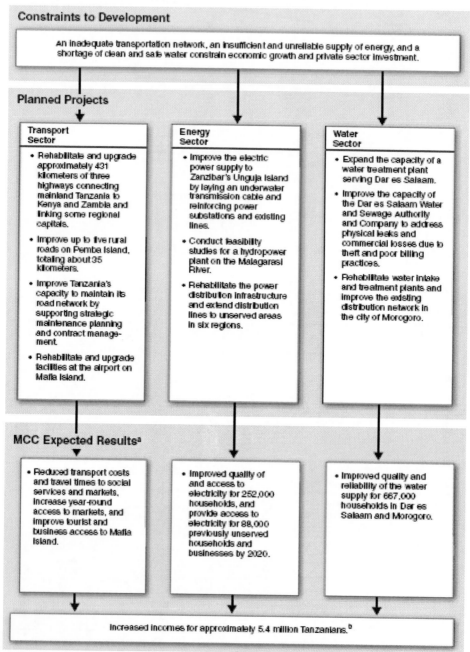

Source: GAO analysis of Millennium Challenge Corporation data.

[a] MCC expected results are reported as of compact signature, except the number of beneficiaries with increased incomes.

[b] In fiscal year 2009, MCC recalculated the number of expected beneficiaries using a standardized methodology. At compact signature, MCC reported the compact would benefit approximately 4.8 million people.

Compact Characteristics

MCC and the partner country determine the compact structure before the compact is signed. However, the structure of some compacts has been altered during implementation.

At signature, Tanzania's compact focused on rehabilitating road networks, improving and extending electricity service and coverage, and increasing the quantity and reliability of clean and safe water for domestic and commercial use. At that time, approximately 35 percent of the mainland and nearly 50 percent of the Zanzibar region's populations lived below the national poverty line.

Expected Results

This graphic presents MCC's expectations of selected compact results at compact signature and at the end of fiscal year 2009.

GAO has not independently verified the reliability of MCC's results projections for this compact. Previous GAO work has identified several problems with the methodology used to determine compact projects' expected results. (See GAO-08-730 and GAO-07-909.)

COMPACT FUNDING

Tanzania Project Allocations

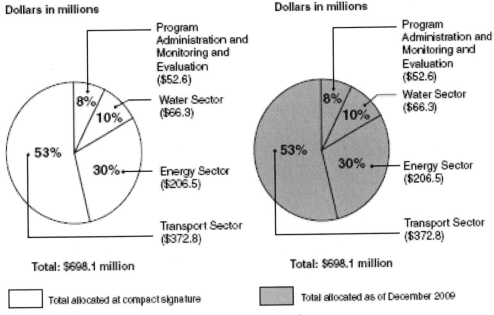

Source: GAO analysis of Millennium Challenge Corporation data.

Tanzania Planned and Actual Disbursements

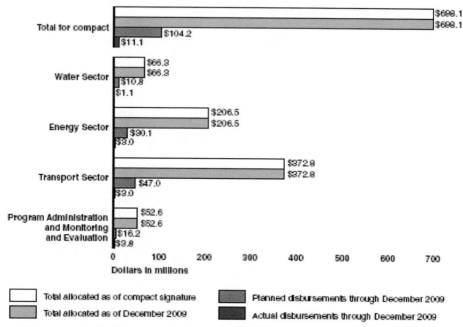

Source: GAO analysis of Millennium Challenge Corporation data.

Notes: We base planned disbursements on MCC's projections for the fiscal quarter ending December 2009. We assume that funds are disbursed evenly throughout each year. Actual disbursements by project may not add up to total disbursements because some disbursements are pending allocation to projects and are reflected in the total but not in the projects.

Compact Funding

MCC and the country may reallocate funds among projects during implementation. In some cases, MCC has also changed the overall compact obligation.

At signature (February 2008), MCC obligated $698.1 million for the Tanzania compact. As of December 2009, the overall obligation amount and project allocations had not changed.

Compact Disbursements

At compact signature, MCC develops a disbursement plan for the compact. MCC disburses funds as the country begins implementing projects. According to MCC, any funds not disbursed within 120 days after the compact ends would return to MCC for reprogramming.

As of December 2009, MCC had disbursed $11.1 million (approximately 2 percent) of compact funds, compared with the $104.2 million (approximately 15 percent) that it had planned to disburse as of that date.

Although it is not shown in the graphic, in addition to the above disbursements, $85.7 million has been committed under the compact for pending expenses as of December 2009.

VANUATU COMPACT FACT SHEET

Map of Vanuatu

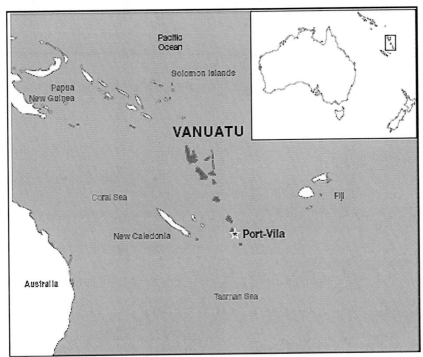

Source: Map Resources (map).

Key Events for Vanuatu Compact

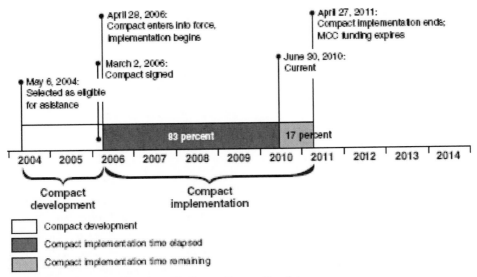

Source: GAO analysis of Millennium Challenge Corporation data.

Country Characteristics

Located in the South Pacific about 1,300 miles northeast of Sydney, Australia, Vanuatu consists of 83 islands and has a population of about 200,000. It is a lower-middleincome country. Its economy is based primarily on services, which account for about 62 percent of its gross domestic product (GDP). Agriculture accounts for 26 percent of GDP but employs 65 percent of the labor force. Industry accounts for 12 percent of GDP. Fishing, offshore financial services, and tourism are important economic activities. Vanuatu has experienced several years of real GDP growth— more than 6 percent in 2007 and 2008—although it slowed to about 3.8 percent in 2009.

Compact Timeline

During compact development, MCC and an eligible country negotiate project proposals and the compact's terms. After the compact is signed, the country finalizes administrative requirements, such as procurement and disbursement agreements. When the compact enters into force, MCC obligates funds and compact implementation begins. MCC's statute limits compact implementation to 5 years.

Vanuatu was 1 of 16 countries that MCC selected as eligible in its first eligibility round. As of June 30, 2010, 83 percent of the compact's 5- year period had elapsed.

MCC SELECTION CRITERIA

MCC Candidate Criteria

Each fiscal year, MCC uses per capita gross national income (GNI) data to identify two pools of candidate countries—low-income and lower-middle-income—based on World Bank lending thresholds. In addition, a candidate country must not be statutorily barred from receiving U.S. assistance. By law, MCC can use up to 25 percent of compact assistance each year for new compacts with lower-middle-income countries.

Vanuatu was a low-income country from 2004, the year that MCC began operations, through 2008. In 2009 Vanuatu's rising GNI per capita lifted it to lower-middle-income status.

MCC Eligibility Criteria

MCC's board uses quantitative indicators to assess a candidate's policy performance. To meet MCC's criteria, a country must pass the control of corruption indicator and at least half of the indictors in each of three categories. To pass an indicator, a country must score above the median in its income group. However, the board may select a country as eligible even if it does not meet the criteria. Once MCC has signed a compact with a country, MCC continues to work with it—even if it fails the criteria—as long as its actions are not inconsistent with the criteria. If a country's policy performance declines, the board can suspend or terminate the compact.

Vanuatu met MCC's eligibility criteria each year from 2004 through 2008. In 2009, Vanuatu rose to lower-middle-income status and failed the indicator criteria for that group.

Vanuatu GNI Pe

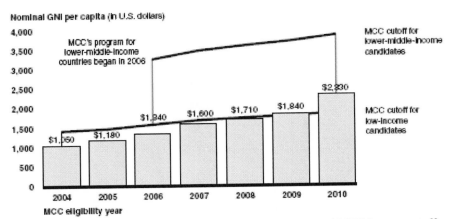

Source: GAO analysis of World Bank World Development Indicators and MCC income cutoffs.

Vanuatu's Performance on MCC Eligibility Indicators

Indicator category	MCC eligibility year	2004	2005	2006	2007	2008	2009	2010
	MCC income group	Low	Low	Low	Low	Low	Lower-middle	Lower-middle
Ruling Justly	Political Rights	✓	✓	✓	✓	✓	✓	✓
	Civil Liberties	✓	✓	✓	✓	✓	✓	✓
	Voice and Accountability	✓	✓	✓	✓	✓	✓	✓
	Government Effectiveness	✓	✓	✓	✓	✓	✓	✓
	Rule of Law	✓	✓	✓	✓	✓	✓	✓
	Control of Corruption	✓	✓	✓	✓	✓	✓	✓
Investing in People	Girls' Primary Education Completion[a]	✓	✓	✓	✓	✓	X	X
	Primary Education Expenditures	✓	✓	✓	✓	✓	✓	✓
	Health Expenditures	✓	✓	✓	✓	✓	X	✓
	Immunization Rates	X	X	X	X	✓	X	X
	Natural Resource Management (2008-2010)					X	X	X
Economic Freedom	Country Credit Rating (2004-2005)	✓	✓					
	Days to Start a Business (2004-2007)	✓	✓	✓	✓			
	Cost of Starting a Business (2006-2007)			✓	✓			
	Business Start-up (2008-2010)					✓	X	X
	Inflation	✓	✓	✓	✓	✓	✓	✓
	Fiscal Policy	✓	✓	✓	✓	✓	✓	✓
	Trade Policy	X	X	X	X	X	X	X
	Regulatory Quality	X	X	✓	✓	✓	X	X
	Land Rights and Access (2009-2010)					X	X	X
	Indicator performance results	Passed	Passed	Passed	Passed	Passed	Failed	Failed
	MCC eligibility determination	Eligible	Eligible	Eligible	Eligible	Eligible	NA[b]	NA[a]

✓ Passed (scored above the median)   X Failed (scored at the median or below)   ☐ NA for that year

Source: GAO analysis of Millennium Challenge Corporation data.
[a] In 2004, the indicator was "Primary Education Completion."
[b] In 2009, MCC stopped making an eligibility determination for countries with existing compacts.

COMPACT SUMMARY

Structure of Vanuatu's Compact, as of December 2009

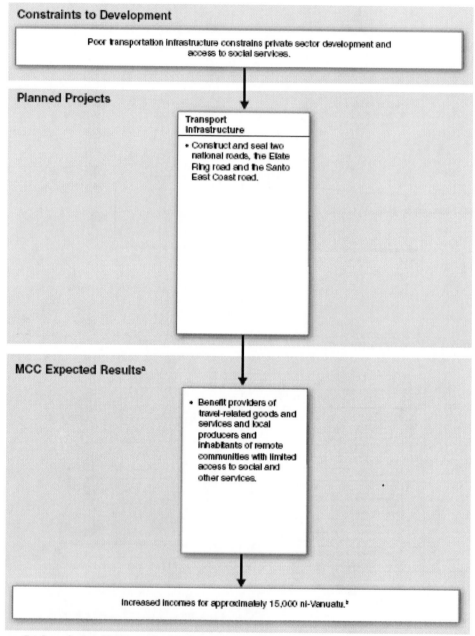

Source: GAO analysis of Millennium Challenge Corporation data.

[a] MCC expected results are reported as of compact signature, except the number of beneficiaries with increased incomes.

[b] In fiscal year 2009, MCC recalculated the number of expected beneficiaries using a standardized methodology. At compact signature, MCC reported the compact would benefit approximately 65,000 people.

Compact Characteristics

MCC and the partner country determine the compact structure before the compact is signed. However, the structure of some compacts has been altered during implementation.

At signature, Vanuatu's compact aimed to benefit poor, rural, agricultural producers and providers of tourism-related goods and services by reducing transportation costs and improving the reliability of access to transportation services. At signature, 80 percent of the population lived in rural areas and 51 percent of rural residents lived in hardship. The compact was rescoped in early 2008 due to several circumstances, including escalating global construction costs and currency fluctuations, and the scope of the Transport Infrastructure Project was reduced.

Expected Results

This graphic presents MCC's expectations of selected compact results at compact signature and at the end of fiscal year 2009.

The Vanuatu compact is one of five compacts for which GAO has independently verified the reliability of MCC's results projections. In July 2007, GAO reported that MCC had overstated the expected results of its Vanuatu compact; GAO also identified additional risks that could affect compact results (GAO-07-909).

COMPACT FUNDING

Compact Project Funding

MCC and the country may reallocate funds among projects during implementation. In some cases, MCC has also changed the overall compact obligation.

At signature (March 2006), MCC obligated $65.7 million for the Vanuatu compact. As of December 2009, the overall obligation amount had not changed, however funds were reallocated from Transport Infrastructure project to the Program Administration and Monitoring and Evaluation.

Compact Disbursements

At compact signature, MCC develops a disbursement plan for the compact. MCC disburses funds as the country begins implementing projects. According to MCC, any funds not disbursed within 120 days after the compact ends would return to MCC for reprogramming.

As of December 2009, MCC had disbursed $45.2 million (approximately 69 percent) of compact funds, compared with the $63.2 million (approximately 96 percent) that it had planned to disburse as of that date.

Although it is not shown in the graphic, in addition to the above disbursements, $18.4 million has been committed under the compact for pending expenses as of December 2009.

Vanuatu Project Allocations

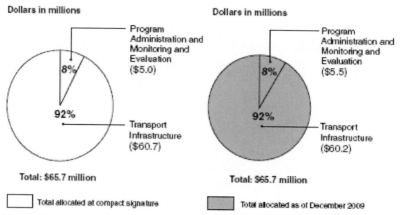

Source: GAO analysis of Millennium Challenge Corporation data.

Vanuatu Planned and Actual Disbursements

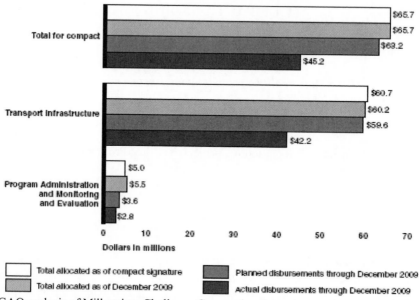

Source: GAO analysis of Millennium Challenge Corporation data.

Notes: We base planned disbursements on MCC's projections for the fiscal quarter ending December 2009. We assume that funds are disbursed evenly throughout each year. Actual disbursements by project may not add up to total disbursements because some disbursements are pending allocation to projects and are reflected in the total but not in the projects.

End Notes

[1] We have not included a fact sheet on the Madagascar compact because, as the result of an undemocratic transfer of power in Madagascar in March 2009, MCC formally terminated the compact effective August 31, 2009.

[2] The data within the fact sheets reflect the most recent information available on compact modifications and take into account MCC's ongoing planning and disbursement processes. As a result, key compact events are reported as of the end of the third quarter of fiscal year 2010 (June 2010); compact project allocations are reported as of the end of the first quarter of fiscal year 2010 (December 2009); planned actual compact fund disbursements are reported through the end of the first quarter of fiscal year 2010 (December 2009).

[3] MCC compact funds are committed up front when compacts are signed with the partner country and obligated after a compact enters into force. MCC defines allocations as compact funds assigned to a specific compact project, which may be reallocated among projects during compact implementation. Disbursements are payments from MCC compact funds, usually directly to a vendor. These funds are authorized for expenditure on a quarterly basis for costs associated with program implementation. The agency defines contract commitments as the forecasted value of any contract (or recurring expense outside of a contract such as salaries or utilities), and on the project level, these forecasts are often listed as "commitments."

[4] Previous GAO work examined the methodology used by MCC to determine compact projects' results. See GAO, Millennium Challenge Corporation: Vanuatu Compact Overstates Projected Program Impact, GAO-07-909 (Washington, D.C.: July 11, 2007) and Millennium Challenge Corporation: Independent Reviews and Consistent Approaches Will Strengthen Projections of Program Impact, GAO-08-730 (Washington D.C.: June 17, 2008).

In: Millenium Challenge Corporation
Editor: Lautaro B. Rojas

ISBN: 978-1-62100-584-1
© 2012 Nova Science Publishers, Inc.

Chapter 3

COMPACTS IN CAPE VERDE AND HONDURAS ACHIEVED REDUCED TARGETS[*]

United States Government Accountability Office

WHY GAO DID THIS STUDY

The Millennium Challenge Corporation (MCC) was established in 2004 to help developing countries reduce poverty and stimulate economic growth through multiyear compact agreements. As of June 2011, MCC had signed compacts with 23 countries totaling approximately $8.2 billion in assistance. MCC asks countries to develop compacts with a focus on results and effective monitoring and evaluation. MCC sets targets, which may be revised, to measure the compact results. In late 2010, the Cape Verde and Honduras compacts reached the end of the 5-year implementation period. This report, prepared in response to a congressional mandate to review compact results, examines the extent to which MCC has (1) achieved performance targets and sustainability for projects in Cape Verde and Honduras and (2) assessed progress toward the goal of income growth and poverty reduction. GAO analyzed MCC documents and interviewed MCC officials and stakeholders in Washington, D.C., Cape Verde, and Honduras.

WHAT GAO RECOMMENDS

GAO recommends that MCC (1) work with countries to make decisions that reduce long-term maintenance needs, (2) ensure updated economic analyses are documented and consistent with monitoring targets, and (3) develop guidance for updating economic analyses following compact completion. MCC agreed with the intent of all three recommendations.

---

[*] This is an edited, reformatted and augmented version of theUnited States Government Accountability Office publication GAO-11-728, dated July 2011.

WHAT GAO FOUND

In its first two completed compacts, Cape Verde and Honduras, MCC met some key original targets and many final targets, but the sustainability of some activities is uncertain. In Cape Verde, MCC altered the scope of its three projects, meeting some key original targets and many final targets by the compact's end. For example, an activity to upgrade and expand a major port in Cape Verde, which represented almost 50 percent of the $110.1 million compact at signature, faced inaccurate early planning assumptions and increased costs. As a result, MCC split the port activity into two phases, funding the completion of the first phase—which covered about one-third of total expected costs for the port activity. In Honduras, MCC met a key original target and most final targets by the end of the $205 million compact. For example, MCC constructed approximately half of the planned highway and all rescoped secondary roads. In addition, several compact activities in Cape Verde and Honduras face challenges to long-term sustainability. Although MCC took steps to provide for sustainability, the governments of both Cape Verde and Honduras may have difficulty maintaining the infrastructure projects in the long term due to lack of funding, among other challenges. For example, MCC included privatization of port operations and road maintenance funding as conditions of the Cape Verde compact. However, the government has had difficulty meeting these requirements, calling into question the long-term sustainability of some projects. In Honduras, both uncertain government funding for road maintenance and design decisions on construction projects may jeopardize the sustainability of MCC-funded roads.

MCC impact evaluations for the Cape Verde and Honduras compacts are ongoing but delayed, and updated economic rate of return (ERR) analyses of the largest compact projects have not been well documented or linked to revised targets. MCC has taken steps to modify impact evaluation designs in response to implementation challenges and delays. For example, challenges in implementing the original evaluation design for the farmer training and development activity in Honduras led MCC to enhance the methodology by adding a supplemental design. Furthermore, updated ERR analyses of projects representing over 50 percent of compact funds have not been well documented or supported. For example, MCC updated its ERR analysis for the Honduras transportation project, but documentation for the underlying quantitative analysis supporting the updated ERR is not available. Additionally, ERR analyses updated in response to rescoping compact activities were not consistently linked to revised targets and indicators. For example, MCC updated the ERR analysis for the watershed management and agricultural support project in Cape Verde, but the analysis does not reflect the values and numerical ranges of key revised targets. In addition, although original ERRs are estimated for a 20-year period, MCC has not developed guidance for updating ERRs following compact completion. Re-estimated end-of-compact ERRs will likely be lower than predicted at compact signature.

ABBREVIATIONS

CABEI   Central American Bank for Economic Integration
CEO   chief executive officer

ERR	economic rate of return
IRI	International Roughness Index
ISO	International Organization for Standardization
MCA	Millennium Challenge Account
MCC	Millennium Challenge Corporation
MFI	microfinance institution

July 25, 2011

The Honorable Patrick Leahy Chairman
The Honorable Lindsey Graham Ranking Member
Subcommittee on the Department of State,
Foreign Operations,
and Related Programs
Committee on Appropriations
United States Senate

The Honorable Kay Granger
Chairwoman

The Honorable Nita Lowey
Ranking Member
Subcommittee on State, Foreign Operations,
and Related Programs
Committee on Appropriations
House of Representatives

The Millennium Challenge Corporation (MCC) was established in 2004 to provide aid to developing countries that have demonstrated a commitment to ruling justly, encouraging economic freedom, and investing in people. MCC provides assistance to eligible countries through multiyear compact agreements to fund specific programs targeted at reducing poverty and stimulating economic growth. MCC compacts may not be longer than 5 years.[1] As of June 2011, MCC had signed compacts with 23 countries, committing a total of approximately $8.2 billion.[2] The President has requested approximately $1.1 billion in additional funds for MCC for fiscal year 2012.

Cape Verde and Honduras were among the first countries selected by MCC for a compact. In the fiscal year 2008 Consolidated Appropriations Act, Congress directed GAO to review the results achieved by MCC compacts.[3] In late 2010, the compacts for Cape Verde and Honduras were the first to reach the end of the 5-year implementation period.[4] This report examines the extent to which MCC has (1) achieved performance targets and longer-term sustainability for projects in the Cape Verde and Honduras compacts and (2) assessed progress toward the two compacts' goals of income growth and poverty reduction.

To assess the results achieved by MCC's compacts in Cape Verde and Honduras, we analyzed U.S. agency documents, interviewed MCC officials and stakeholders, and observed project results in both countries. We reviewed MCC guidance and policy documents, as well as the compacts and monitoring and evaluation plans for each country, to identify criteria for our assessment. We interviewed MCC officials in Washington, D.C., as well as MCC and Millennium Challenge Account (MCA) officials in Cape Verde and Honduras, regarding the results of each compact activity, including the quality and sustainability of the projects. We also visited compact projects in both countries and met with contractors, construction supervisors, grantees, and beneficiaries.

We focused our review more heavily on activities that represent a higher proportion of compact funds in both countries. In assessing and reporting MCC's results, we compared actual results achieved at the end of the compact for select performance indicators to both the original and, in some cases, revised targets associated with each indicator. We considered the original target to be that which was first documented for each performance indicator, and the final target to be the target last documented in MCC monitoring documents. Given that MCC tracked several performance indicators for each compact project, we reported on key indicators that most closely represented the goal of each compact activity and also considered which indicators MCC reports in its public communications. Additionally, we reviewed the monitoring information collected by MCC and MCA and interviewed officials and contractors about the quality of the data. In reviewing the extent to which MCC has assessed progress toward the compacts' goals, we reviewed planned evaluation designs and interviewed officials from MCC and MCA, as well as impact evaluators. MCC enters into a legal relationship with partner country governments, which vest responsibility for day-to-day management of compact project implementation to the MCA, including monitoring and evaluation activities such as setting and revising targets, but such MCA actions require MCC's direct oversight and approval. Therefore, throughout this report, we attribute all decisions related to project rescoping and compact targets to MCC. (See app. I for further details of our objectives, scope, and methodology.)

We conducted this performance audit from September 2010 to July 2011 in accordance with generally accepted government auditing standards. Those standards require that we plan and perform the audit to obtain sufficient, appropriate evidence to provide a reasonable basis for our findings and conclusions based on our audit objectives. We believe the evidence obtained provides a reasonable basis for our findings and conclusions based on our audit objectives.

BACKGROUND

Management of MCC Programs

MCC, a government corporation, is managed by a chief executive officer (CEO), whom the President appoints with the advice and consent of the Senate, and is overseen by a Board of Directors. The Secretary of State serves as board chair, and the Secretary of the Treasury serves as vicechair.[5] MCC's model is based on a set of core principles deemed essential for effective development assistance, including good governance, country ownership, focus on results, and transparency. According to MCC, country ownership of an MCC compact occurs when a country's national government controls the prioritization process during compact development, is responsible for implementation, and is accountable to its domestic stakeholders for both decision making and results.

In keeping with the MCC principle of country ownership, MCC enters into a legal relationship with partner country governments. During the 5-year compact implementation period the partner government vests responsibility for day-to-day management, including monitoring and evaluation of the progress of compact projects, to accountable entities in recipient countries (the entities' name is usually formed from "MCA" plus the country's name—for example, MCA-Cape Verde). MCC provides the frameworks and guidance for compact implementation, monitoring, and evaluation that MCAs are to use in implementing compact projects.

To promote transparency, MCC makes information available on its Web site throughout the life of a compact, such as project budgets and descriptions, projected outcomes, and quarterly updates on financial and program progress. This transparency enables stakeholders to review the information that contributed to MCC investment decisions, track program progress against targets, and, once programs reach completion, see clearly which programs did or did not achieve their goals.

MCC Compacts in Cape Verde and Honduras

The Cape Verde and Honduras compacts were among the first countries that MCC selected as eligible for assistance and the first to reach the end of the 5-year implementation period. The two compacts varied in the type and size of projects funded, but each devoted more than half of compact funds to infrastructure projects such as roads and ports. Each compact also included a smaller agricultural development project such as farmer training or construction of agricultural infrastructure.

Cape Verde Compact
MCC and the government of Cape Verde signed a 5-year compact in July 2005, which entered into force in October 2005 and ended in October 2010. The compact, for which MCC committed $110.1 million in funding at compact signature, consisted of three projects. Figure 1 shows Cape Verde compact funding by project at signature and compact end.

Honduras Compact
MCC and the government of Honduras signed a 5-year compact in June 2005, which entered into force in September 2005 and ended in September 2010. The compact, for which MCC committed $215 million in funding at compact signature, consisted of two projects. Figure 2 shows Honduras compact funding by project at signature and compact end.

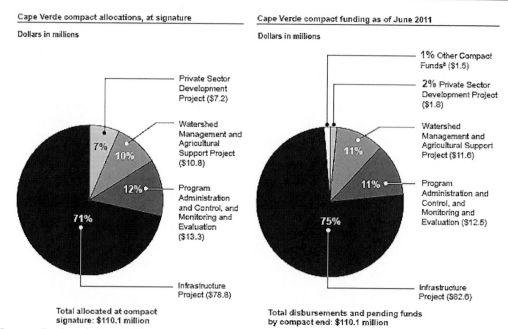

Cape Verde compact allocations, at signature

Dollars in millions

Cape Verde compact funding as of June 2011

Dollars in millions

Private Sector Development Project ($7.2)

Watershed Management and Agricultural Support Project ($10.8)

Program Administration and Control, and Monitoring and Evaluation ($13.3)

Infrastructure Project ($78.8)

Total allocated at compact signature: $110.1 million

1% Other Compact Funds[a] ($1.5)

2% Private Sector Development Project ($1.8)

Watershed Management and Agricultural Support Project ($11.6)

Program Administration and Control, and Monitoring and Evaluation ($12.5)

Infrastructure Project ($82.6)

Total disbursements and pending funds by compact end: $110.1 million

Source: GAO analysis of Millennium Challenge Corporation data.

[a] According to MCC, approximately $1.5 million of compact funds were not disbursed, and following final payments and audits the remaining compact funds will be deobligated.

Figure 1. Cape Verde Compact Funding at Signature and Compact End.

Table 1 shows the Cape Verde projects' planned activities and funding allocations at compact signature.

Table 1. Cape Verde Compact Structure and Funding, at Signature (Dollars in millions)

Planned projects and activities	Funding allocation
Infrastructure project	78.8
Port activity	53.7
Roads and bridges activity	25.0
Watershed management and agricultural support project	**10.8**
Water management and soil conservation activity	6.8
Agribusiness development services activity	3.6
Access to credit activity	0.5
Private sector development project	**7.2**
Partnership to mobilize investment activity	5.0
Financial sector reform activity	2.2
Program administration and monitoring and evaluation	**13.3**
Program administration	8.4
Monitoring and evaluation	4.9
Compact total	**110.1**

Source: GAO analysis of Millennium Challenge Corporation data.

Note: The sum of activity funding may not equal total project funding due to rounding.

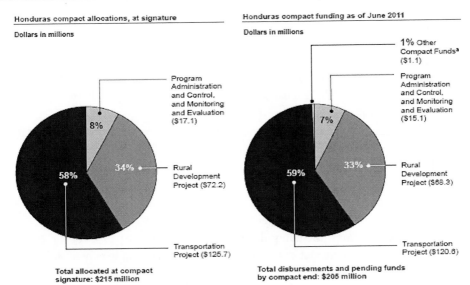

Source: GAO analysis of Millennium Challenge Corporation data.

aAccording to MCC, approximately $1.1 million of compact funds were not disbursed, and following final payments and audits the remaining compact funds will be deobligated.

Figure 2. Honduras Compact Funding at Signature and Compact End.

Table 2 shows the Honduras projects' planned activities and funding allocations at compact signature.

Table 2. Honduras Compact Structure and Funding, at Signature
(Dollars in millions)

Planned projects and activities	Funding allocation
Transportation project	125.7
Highway CA-5 activity	96.4
Secondary road activity	21.3
Weight control system activity	4.7
Transportation project manager	3.3
Rural development project	**72.2**
Farmer training and development activity	27.4
Farm–to-market roads activity	21.5
Farmer access to credit activity	13.8
Agricultural public goods grant facility activity	8.0
Rural development project manager	1.5
Program administration and monitoring and evaluation	**17.1**
Program administration	12.1
Monitoring and evaluation	5.0
Compact total	**215.0**

Source: GAO analysis of Millennium Challenge Corporation data.

Note: The sum of activity funding may not equal total project funding due to rounding.

MCC Compact Development

Each fiscal year, MCC identifies countries that are candidates for assistance. MCC uses per capita income data to identify two pools of candidate countries: low-income and lower-middle-income countries.[6] MCC's Board of Directors then uses quantitative indicators to assess a candidate country's policy performance to determine eligibility.[7] If the policy performance of a country declines during implementation of a compact, the board can suspend or terminate the compact.

After MCC selects a country as eligible, the country begins a four-phase process that can lead to a compact's entry into force: (1) the eligible country develops and submits a compact proposal; (2) MCC conducts a due diligence review of the proposed projects; (3) MCC and the country negotiate and sign the compact after MCC board approval; (4) MCC and the country complete preparations, including developing disbursement plans, for the compact to enter into force. After the compact enters into force, compact implementation begins, and funds are obligated and disbursed. Following MCC's internal reorganization in October 2007,

MCC revamped its compact development process to include greater initial engagement with eligible countries and assistance to countries in conducting needed studies and establishing management structures.[8]

Sustainability

MCC compacts are to be designed so that projects are sustainable over 20 years. During the compact development process, MCC is to assess the mechanisms in place to enhance sustainability, including the policies and practices that will enable MCC investments to continue to provide benefits. For instance, as part of compact proposals submitted to MCC, partner countries are required to identify risks to project sustainability and describe measures needed to ensure that project benefits can be sustained beyond the period of MCC financing. Partner countries are to consider a number of issues affecting sustainability, including environmental sustainability; institutional capacity for operations and maintenance; and for proposed infrastructure projects, recent funding, performance, and expected expenses for operations and maintenance. Furthermore, during compact implementation, MCC tracks progress against key policy reforms and institutional improvements that were included in the compact to enhance project impact and sustainability.

MCC Monitoring and Evaluation Framework and Economic Rate of Return Analysis

For each compact, countries are required to create a monitoring and evaluation plan, which is one aspect of MCC's efforts to assess a compact's results. MCC developed guidelines in 2006 to assist eligible countries in the preparation of the monitoring and evaluation plan and issued an updated policy in 2009. According to MCC's 2009 monitoring and evaluation policy, the policy applies to new or revised monitoring and evaluation plans developed after issuance of the policy in May 2009.

Monitoring

According to MCC's 2006 guidelines for monitoring and evaluation plans, performance monitoring helps track progress toward compact goals and objectives, as well as serves as a management tool. In addition, according to MCC's 2009 monitoring and evaluation policy, the plan's monitoring component outlines the performance indicators by which compact results will be measured.[9] The plan's monitoring component also establishes a performance target for each indicator and the expected time the target will be achieved.[10] For example, the number of kilometers completed may be an indicator for road construction projects and a numeric target is set to be completed by compact end.

Revisions to Compact Projects, Indicators, and Targets

In response to MCC's experiences with early compacts, MCC has learned that plans may change during compact implementation and that it may be necessary to modify programs after the execution of a compact agreement. Recognizing that MCC has a responsibility to ensure that program modifications are promptly and transparently assessed based on adequate due diligence and consultation, in August 2010, MCC adopted a policy to establish a single process for evaluating and approving such modifications. The agency updated this policy in March 2011.

A rescoped compact project or activity refers to any change in the scope or substance of a compact program, including the modification, addition or elimination of a project, activity or subactivity that may entail potential alterations to the intended beneficiary group. In response to such changes, MCC allows for modifications to associated indicators and targets. According to MCC policy issued in 2009, indicators in the monitoring and evaluation plan can be modified by (1) adding a new indicator, (2) removing an existing indicator, or (3) changing a descriptive quality of an existing indicator. The policy also outlines several reasons for adding or changing indicators. For instance, an indicator may be removed because a change to the project renders the indicator irrelevant or the cost of collecting data for an indicator outweighs its usefulness. End-of-compact targets associated with these indicators can also be changed, including increasing or decreasing targets. MCC's 2009 policy also outlines specific circumstances under which targets may be changed, including changes in scope of the activity or exogenous factors such as natural disasters or political turmoil. Ultimately, the justification for deleting or modifying an indicator or target must be adequately documented in revised monitoring and evaluation plans.

Figure 3 shows a timeline of the MCC monitoring and evaluation plans for the Cape Verde and Honduras compacts. For both countries, only final monitoring and evaluation plans, issued in October and December 2010 for Cape Verde and Honduras, respectively, were subject to MCC's 2009 monitoring and evaluation policy.

Impact Evaluation

MCC hires independent researchers to evaluate the impact of compact projects, and the monitoring and evaluation plan outlines aspects of planned impact evaluations, including questions, methodologies, and data collection.[11] These analyses compare projects' final results with an estimate of what would have happened without the project, measuring changes in individual, household, or community income and well-being that result from a particular project.[12]

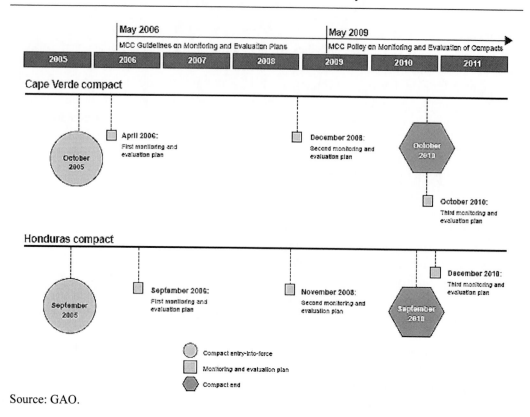

Source: GAO.

Figure 3. Timeline of Monitoring and Evaluation Plans for Cape Verde and Honduras Compacts.

MCC Economic Analyses

During its due diligence review of each compact proposal,[13] MCC analyzes proposed projects' estimated impact on the country's economic growth and poverty reduction. Specifically, MCC calculates a projected economic rate of return (ERR)—that is, the expected annual average return to the country's firms, individuals, or sectors for each dollar that MCC spends on the project. In calculating project ERRs, MCC uses information such as MCC's expected annual expenditures for the project and the projected annual benefits to the country. In calculating expected project benefits, MCC projects the sustainability of investments over a relatively long term, typically 20 years, and includes assumptions about the probability that necessary maintenance will be completed. MCC establishes a minimum acceptable ERR, referred to as a hurdle rate, that compact projects should achieve to be eligible for funding. It uses this, as well as other information gathered during the due diligence process, to inform its internal decisions to fund proposed projects and compacts.[14]

According to MCC's 2006 guidelines for monitoring and evaluation plans, the economic analysis links to the development of indicators and targets for monitoring compact results.[15] Furthermore, according to MCC's 2009 policy on monitoring and evaluation of compacts, monitoring and evaluation plans should be directly linked to economic analyses. The variables from the ERR analysis of benefit streams should be used as performance indicators and targets in the monitoring and evaluation plan. MCC's 2009 policy also states that when MCC is considering changes to targets that are linked to the ERR analysis, modified targets should be analyzed to assess whether they maintain the integrity of the original ERR. If the new ERR is below the minimum acceptable ERR for the compact, the target change will require additional MCC approval.[16]

MCC's Project Management and Quality Assurance Framework for Infrastructure Projects

MCC's implementation process for infrastructure contracts and projects requires that the MCAs have individual project directors—for example, a roads director—who oversee the activities of outside implementing entities, project management consultants, design engineers, independent construction supervisors, and project construction contractors.[17] In general, MCAs deliver infrastructure projects through a design-bid-build approach in which a design engineer[18] develops technical plans and specifications that are used by a construction contractor, hired under a separate MCA procurement action, to build the works.

Independent construction supervisors contracted by the MCA conduct oversight of day-to-day construction and the activities of the project construction contractors to ensure compliance with contract requirements. Independent construction supervisors play an important role in ensuring construction quality[19] by performing such tasks as approving construction materials, overseeing testing,[20] and inspecting completed work. In addition to MCA's independent construction supervisor, MCC employs its own independent engineering consultants to monitor progress of the construction works as managed by the MCA and to assess its quality.

PERFORMANCE TARGETS
AND SUSTAINABILITY ISSUES

MCC met some key original targets and many of its final targets for the Cape Verde and Honduras compacts. Additionally, MCC took steps to provide for the sustainability of the projects, but the governments of both Cape Verde and Honduras may have difficulty maintaining the infrastructure projects in the long term due to the lack of funding, among other challenges.

Cape Verde: MCC Altered the Scope of Its Three Projects, Meeting Some Key Original Targets and Many Final Targets

MCC rescoped each of the three projects under the Cape Verde compact, reducing some key targets. MCC met or exceeded some key original targets and met many final targets by the compact's end. Table 3 shows the performance results for key indicators for the Cape Verde compact projects. For more detail on the Cape Verde compact results, see appendix II.

Table 3. Key Performance Results for the Cape Verde Compact Activities

Activity	Amount disbursed (dollars in millions)	Indicator	Original target	Final target	Final result	Percentage of origina target met	Percenta ge of final target met
Port	54.9	Phase 1 port works—percent complete[a]	100% by year 3	100% by year 5	100% by year 5[b]	Not determined	100
		Phase 2 port works—percent complete[c]	100%	Activity eliminated			
Roads and bridgesd	27.7	Kilometers of road rehabilitate[d] (km)	63	39.3	40.6[e]	64	103
Water management and soil conservation	6.0	Reservoirs constructed	28	28	28	100	100
		Volume of available water (m3)[f]	875,355	465,8 00	352,9 78	40	76
Agribusiness development services	5.0	Hectares under improved or new irrigation[g]	121	111	13.4	11	12
Access to credit	0.6	Value of agricultural and rural loans	$600,000	$600, 000	$617, 000	103	103
Partnership to mobilize investment	0.4	Value added in priority sectors above current trends	none set	Activity eliminated[h]			
Financial sector reform	1.4	Microfinance institutions operationally self-sufficient	4 of 8	4 of 5	5 of 5	125	125

Source: GAO analysis of Millennium Challenge Corporation data

Notes: We considered the original target to be that which was first documented for each performance indicator, in either the 2006, 2008, or 2010 monitoring and evaluation plan, and the final target to be that which was documented in the 2010 monitoring and evaluation plan. In addition, the final results in this table reflect the results achieved by compact completion, although some activities continued after the compact completion and continue to achieve results.

[a]MCC originally had three separate indicators for sections of the port activity that it combined into one indicator for phase 1 port works.

[b]At the end of the compact, a small amount of phase 1 work remained undone, with its completion contingent upon the completion of other work that is part of a contract funded by another source.

[c]MCC originally had two separate indicators—one showing related work to be 100 percent complete by year 3 and the other showing related work to be 100 percent complete by year 5—for sections of the port activity that it combined into one indicator for phase 2 port works. This indicator was eliminated when the port project was rescoped and phase 2 works were funded by another source.

[d]MCC did not have an associated indicator for tracking the number of bridges built.

[e]The length of rehabilitated roads consists of 39.6 kilometers along three road segments on Santiago Island and a 1-kilometer road associated with bridge construction on Santo Antão Island. Four bridges were constructed on Santo Antão Island as initially planned.

[f]MCC revised and reduced the target for the volume of water available to 627,500 cubic meters to reflect a new indicator definition in its 2008 monitoring and evaluation plan. In its 2010 monitoring and evaluation plan, the agency again revised and reduced the final target to reflect a calculation error related to spring-fed reservoirs.

[g]MCC reduced the target to 111 hectares to reflect project changes in its 2008 monitoring and evaluation plan. MCC renamed the original indicator "area irrigated with drip irrigation" to reflect a modified definition in its 2010 monitoring and evaluation plan.

[h]All components of this activity were eliminated, except the establishment of a private credit bureau, which did not have an associated indicator.

Cape Verde Infrastructure Project: MCC Rescoped Port Construction and Road Rehabilitation Activities, Meeting Final Targets

Port of Praia. MCC disbursed $54.9 million to fund reconstruction of a wharf, a new container yard, and a new access road. MCC and MCA-Cape Verde reduced the activity's original scope as a result of inaccurate early planning concerning design details and construction materials that led to cost increases and implementation delays.[21] They split the activity into two phases, with MCC funding the first and the Cape Verde government funding the second. The first phase of construction represents about one-third of the total expected cost of both phases of port construction, and nearly 100 percent of the works for phase 1 were completed by compact end.[22] MCA-Cape Verde established a management structure consistent with MCC's requirements to ensure work met quality standards and functions as intended. The Cape Verde government is funding construction of the second phase— expansion of another wharf and construction of a new breakwater.[23] Figure 4 shows the locations and photographs of the two phases of the port activity.

Roads and bridges. MCC disbursed $27.7 million to fund the rehabilitation of three roads and construction of four bridges. MCC's original targets included the rehabilitation of five roads totaling 63 kilometers and four bridges. However, MCA-Cape Verde found that the World Bank-funded designs were of poor quality and decided to revise them to a higher standard, which led to increased costs. As a result of the increased costs, MCC and MCA-Cape Verde reduced the scope of the activity, and MCC exceeded the final target of 39.3 kilometers of road rehabilitated. MCA-Cape Verde established a management structure consistent with MCC's requirements to ensure work met quality standards and functions as intended.

Cape Verde Watershed Management and Agricultural Support Project: MCC Rescoped Certain Activities and Met Some Key Original and Final Targets

Water management and soil conservation. MCC disbursed $6 million to build water management infrastructure in three watersheds. MCC met its original key target of constructing 28 reservoirs, and 40 percent of its key original target and 76 percent of its final target for the volume of water available. When environmental concerns were identified during implementation, MCC rescoped the activity from a combination of wells and reservoirs to reservoirs only.[24] According to MCC officials and stakeholders, rescoping and implementation delays reduced the amount of water available by compact end.

Agribusiness development services. MCC disbursed $5 million for the agribusiness development services activity. Midway through the compact implementation period, MCA-Cape Verde determined that the Cape Verde agricultural ministry lacked the capacity to train farmers. It hired a contractor to train ministry staff, delaying implementation of the activity. By the compact's end, MCC achieved about 13 hectares under improved or new irrigation, or 11 percent of the original target of 121 hectares and 12 percent of the final target of 111 hectares.

Access to credit. MCC disbursed $600,000 to make a credit line available to microfinance institutions (MFI) for agricultural loans in the three watersheds. The MFIs provided $617,000 in loans, or 103 percent, of the key original and final target of $600,000.

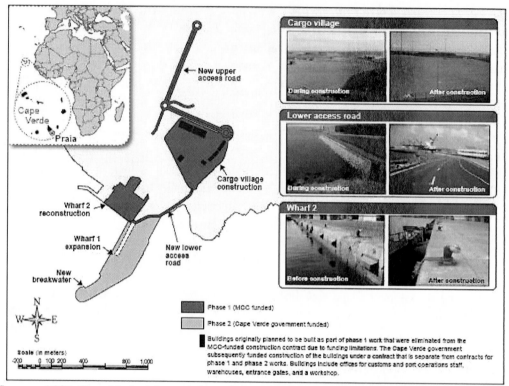

Sources: MCA-Cape Verde (photographs and map details); Map Resources (base map); and GAO (synthesis of information).

Figure 4. Phases 1 and 2 of Port Activity, Cape Verde Infrastructure Project.

Cape Verde Private Sector Development Project: MCC Eliminated Most Funding and Targets, but Exceeded the Remaining Original and Final Target

Partnership to mobilize investment. MCC disbursed about $400,000 to fund the creation of a credit bureau during the compact closeout period in January 2011. However, MCC had initially allocated $5 million for this activity but eliminated some funding and associated indicators when MCC, the World Bank, and the government of Cape Verde were unable to agree on the sectors that should receive investment.

Financial sector reform. MCC disbursed $1.4 million to fund technical assistance to MFIs and support financial sector policy reforms, and exceeded its key original and final target.

Honduras: MCC Rescoped Some Activities under the Honduras Compact, Meeting Few Key Original Targets and Most Final Targets

MCC rescoped some activities under the Honduras compact, reducing certain key targets. MCC met a key original target for the Honduras compact, and met or exceeded most of its final targets by the compact's end. Table 4 shows the performance results for key indicators for the Honduras compact projects. For more detail on the Honduras compact results, see appendix III.

Table 4. Key Performance Results for the Honduras Compact Activities

Activity	Amount disbursed (dollars in millions)	Indicator	Original target	Final target	Final result	Percentage of original target met	Percentage of final target met
CA-5 highway	90.3	Kilometers of highway upgraded (km)	109	109	49.5	45	45
Secondary roads	27.7	Kilometers of secondary road upgraded (km)	91	65.5	65.5	72	100
Weight control system	0.09	Number of weight stations built	8			Activity eliminated	
Farmer training and development	26.6	Program farmers harvesting high-value horticulture crops	7,340[a]	6,000	6,029	82	100
Farm-to-market roads	20.1	Kilometers of farm-to-market road upgraded (km)	1,500	499	495	33	99
Farmer access to credit	12.8	Value of loans disbursed to the horticulture industry (millions of U.S. dollars)	28.8[b]	6	10.7[c]	37	178
Access to public goods grant facility	8.8	Number of farmers connected to irrigation system	392	392	967	247	247

Source: GAO analysis of Millennium Challenge Corporation data.

Notes: We considered the original target to be that which was first documented for each performance indicator, in either the 2006, 2008, or 2010 monitoring and evaluation plan, and the final target to be that which was documented in the 2010 monitoring and evaluation plan. In addition, the final results in this table reflect the results achieved by compact completion, although some activities continue after the compact completion and continue to achieve results.

[a]This indicator was originally set with a higher target of 8,255 that was meant to be achieved 1 year after compact completion. As a result, this target represents the target that was originally scheduled to be accomplished by compact end (year 5).

[b]This target ($28.8 million) was originally set for a similar indicator measuring the value of loans to program farmers, which was ultimately replaced by a number of indicators, including this indicator, and a lower target of $6 million.

[c]The value of this indicator ($10.7 million) includes the value of loans repaid and relent ($5.2 million) from the agricultural credit trust fund. This value ($10.7 million) does not include an additional $6.4 million in loans leveraged by financial institutions. According to MCC, adding the $6.4 million of funds leveraged by financial institutions to the $10.7 million of funds lent from the trust fund would result in double-counting of some funds. In addition, no target was established for the value of funds leveraged by financial institutions.

Honduras Transportation Project: MCC Upgraded Almost Half of Planned Highway Sections and All of Rescoped Secondary Roads

CA-5 highway. MCC disbursed approximately $90.3 million to reconstruct four sections of a major highway in Honduras. MCC completed two sections of highway, totaling about 50 kilometers, or 45 percent of the original compact target. The disbursement also partially funded the reconstruction of a third section, which MCA-Honduras did not complete by the end of the compact, and the relocation and design costs for reconstruction of a fourth section of the CA-5 highway activity.[25] MCA-Honduras established a management structure consistent with MCC's requirements to ensure work met quality standards and functioned as intended. MCA-Honduras officials identified three factors that affected their ability to achieve targets for this activity and resulted in a new estimated cost of $219 million for all four sections of highway:

- *Contract bid amounts.* Increases in project costs above initial estimates as a result of unit price increases for items such as asphalt, as well as additions to project scope and design, such as added travel lanes, were a principal cause of cost increases, according to MCC officials.
- *Land acquisition costs.* Due diligence studies conducted prior to construction did not include the cost of the full-market value of acquiring land and relocating households and businesses adjacent to roads. The original allocation increased from $3.1 million to about $20.2 million.
- *Contract modifications.* Contract modifications raised construction contract costs by about 6 percent primarily as a result of insufficient road designs that required work beyond that included in the contract plans.

Remaining work on a third and a fourth sections is being funded with a loan of about $130 million from the Central American Bank for Economic Integration (CABEI) and is expected to be completed by the middle of 2012.[26] Figure 5 shows the locations of the CA-5 highway activities.

Secondary roads. MCC disbursed $27.7 million to upgrade key secondary roads. MCC met its revised target for the construction of 65.5 kilometers of secondary roads, 72 percent of the original target of 91 kilometers. According to MCA-Honduras officials, the scope was reduced because updated estimated costs to upgrade the planned roads, after the first contract was bid, exceeded original estimates by 80 percent. MCA-Honduras established a management structure consistent with MCC's requirements to ensure work met quality standards and functioned as intended.

Weight control system. MCC disbursed almost $90,000 for a vehicle weight control activity but eliminated the activity when the Honduras compact was partially terminated due to Honduras' political situation.[27]

Honduras Rural Development Project: MCC Rescoped Some Project Activities, Meeting Certain Original Targets and All Key Final Targets

Farmer training and development. MCC disbursed approximately $26.6 million through the farmer training and development activity. MCC funded the training of 6,029 farmers to harvest high-value horticultural crops, meeting its final target of 6,000, or 82 percent of the original target of 7,340.[28] According to MCC, this target was reduced to provide additional technical assistance to those trained to increase the sustainability of the assistance provided. A number of farmers stated that, as a result of the training, they began growing different types of crops and using new techniques, which led to larger volumes and higher quality, and, thus, increased income.

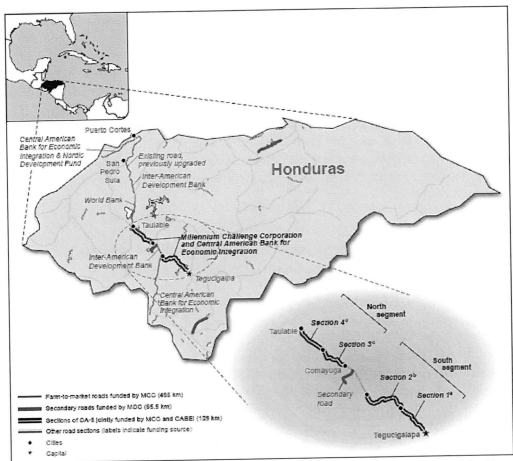

Sources: GAO synthesis of MCA furnished project maps; Map Resources (base map). Notes: Construction funding includes contract and construction supervision costs. aConstruction of section 1 is 100 percent funded by the Central American Bank for Economic Integration (CABEI).

Figure 5. CA-5, Secondary Road, and Farm-to-Market Road Locations, Honduras.

Farm-to-market roads. MCC disbursed approximately $20.1 million to upgrade farm-to-market roads. By the end of the Honduras compact, MCC had funded the reconstruction of 495 kilometers of farm-to-market roads—33 percent of the original target of about 1,500 kilometers and 99 percent of the final target of 499 kilometers. The farm-to-market roads activity was rescoped because the Honduran quality, environmental, and social standards on which the cost estimates were based did not meet compact requirements, which increased the cost from $14,300 to $42,000 per kilometer.[29] In addition, according to MCC officials, the change in target to reconstruct fewer kilometers was based on MCC's decision to improve the durability and life of the roads by adding drainage structures to reduce water damage, which increased the per-kilometer cost.

Farmer access to credit. MCC disbursed $12.8 million for the farmer access to credit activity. The activity consisted of three components designed to increase the supply of credit to rural borrowers—a $6 million agricultural credit trust fund designed to provide loans to financial institutions for rural lending, technical assistance to strengthen financial and nonfinancial institutions, as well as expansion of the national property registry.[30] Initial lack of interest in the trust fund among traditional banking institutions and a delay in demand for credit among farmers led MCA to refocus the activity on smaller sources of credit and to expand beneficiaries to nonprogram farmers, agribusinesses, and other producers and vendors in the horticultural industry.[31] By compact completion, the trust fund had disbursed $10.7 million in loans—37percent of the original target for the value of loans disbursed and 178 percent of the revised target.[32]

Agricultural public goods grant facility. MCC disbursed $8.8 million to fund 15 small competitive grants to enhance and accelerate the development of market-based commercial agriculture. MCC exceeded a key original and final target for this activity. Specifically, grants for irrigation projects connected 967 farmers to the community irrigation system—almost 250 percent of the target of 392 farmers.

MCC Took Steps to Enhance Project Sustainability, but Cape Verde and Honduras Face Long-Term Challenges in Maintaining Infrastructure Projects

MCC took steps to provide for the sustainability of compact projects, but certain activities in Cape Verde and Honduras face challenges to longterm sustainability. MCC's efforts included establishing specific conditions for compact funding disbursements. However, the governments of both Cape Verde and Honduras may have difficulty maintaining infrastructure projects in the long term due to the lack of funding, among other challenges. In addition, decisions to limit certain design features present challenges to maintaining rehabilitated roads. For noninfrastructure projects, steps taken by MCC enhanced the sustainability of some activities, but sustainability challenges remain for other activities.

Cape Verde

Infrastructure project. MCC took steps to enhance the sustainability of its infrastructure project investments by establishing specific conditions for compact funding disbursements. However, as can be seen in the following examples, in some cases the Cape Verde government has not been able to meet or has partially met these conditions, calling into question the long-term sustainability of the infrastructure project activities.

- MCC included privatization of port operations as a condition of the compact. The Cape Verde government agreed and developed a law enabling the port authority to enter into contracts with private operators. However, because the port is incomplete, the solicitation of such contracts has been delayed. The second phase of construction is expected to continue until March 2013. As a result, MCC no longer has leverage over the government to ensure this condition is met.
- MCC set a condition of the compact that the government of Cape Verde would establish and adequately fund a road maintenance account. In 2003, the government established a road institute that has since developed its capacity to raise revenue for maintenance work.33 However, government officials reported that the funds currently meet less than 50 percent of road maintenance requirements.

In the case of the MCC-funded roads and bridges activity, decisions made to control costs and limit the environmental impacts of construction—such as reducing the amount of earthwork to remove steep roadside slopes and installing or repairing fewer drainage structures— contributed to road maintenance requirements. The additional requirements may stress the Cape Verde government's ability to perform maintenance. Figure 6 depicts areas of erosion damage along one of the MCC-funded rehabilitated roads, and Cape Verde government-funded repairs, that we observed during our visit.

Source: GAO.

Figure 6. Damaged Areas and Government of Cape Verde-Funded Repair Activities along Road 2.

Watershed management and agricultural support project. MCC took steps to enhance the sustainability of activities completed under the watershed management and agricultural support project. Although these steps increased sustainability of certain activities, other activities face challenges.

- In January 2009, the government of Cape Verde established a water-fee structure for the three watersheds to fund infrastructure maintenance to meet an MCC condition for funding disbursements. MCA-Cape Verde also worked with community water management organizations, now responsible for maintenance, to develop water management plans. However, as of December 2010, water fees had not yet been collected in one of the three watersheds.
- The MCA-Cape Verde contractor took steps to promote the sustainability of the agribusiness development services activity, including helping to establish and train farmers associations and developing training materials for the Cape Verde agricultural ministry—which plans to continue training farmers. However, the contractor reported that ministry field staff do not have time to train farmers, given their workloads. According to the contractor, ministry staff have multiple responsibilities, including involvement in multiple donors' agriculture-related projects.
- MCA-Cape Verde determined that all MFIs performed well under the access to credit activity, and MCC converted the loans to grants at the end of the compact, which will sustain agricultural loan efforts for at least 2 years.[34]

Private sector development project. MCC required the Cape Verde Chambers of Commerce, the implementers of a new credit bureau, to secure a private sector partner and private sector investments to help support the bureau before MCC provided funding to the chambers.Private ownership may provide an incentive to enhance the sustainability of the credit bureau.

Honduras

Transportation project. To enhance the sustainability of its transportation project investments, MCC conditioned compact funding disbursements on the government meeting increased road maintenance funding levels and included a vehicle weight control activity in the project. However, the funding levels that the government achieved may not be sufficient to fund all road maintenance needs. In addition, the weight control activity was terminated. Both issues call into question the longterm sustainability of the infrastructure project activities.

- According to the compact, the key issue for sustainability of the transportation project is routine, periodic, and emergency road maintenance, such as sealing cracks, repainting the pavement markings, cleaning ditches and drainage structures, repairing potholes, resurfacing, and clearing landslides. As a condition of compact funding, MCC and the Honduran government agreed to increase funding levels for maintenance, which the government met, increasing funding from $37 million in 2005 to $64 million in 2010.[35] However, this funding is to maintain all Honduran roads, not specifically compact-funded roads and does not ensure road maintenance after 2010. According to MCC officials, they expect that the Honduran government will maintain the MCC-funded sections of CA-5 and some of the key secondary roads but are concerned that it may not be at the level required to maximize the roads' lifespan. Contractors and construction supervisors also expressed concerns that the roads will be adequately maintained. According to transportation ministry officials and documents, the government's maintenance allocation for 2010 represents less than half of the road maintenance allocation required by Honduran law and is about 30 percent of the amount officials estimate is needed to maintain the roads.
- The extent to which the Honduran government implements the vehicle weight control activity, which MCC eliminated in 2009 in response to the political situation, also affects sustainability.[36] According to government officials, a large number of truckers exceed legal weight limits.[37] Without enforcement of weight limits on the CA-5 and other MCC-funded roads, the roads will deteriorate faster and require additional maintenance.

In addition, decisions to limit certain design features may present challenges to maintaining the reconstructed roads. We observed quality deficiencies—erosion, roughness, and landslides—that will likely increase the amount and cost of maintenance needed over time (see fig. 7). Failure to perform needed maintenance will result in road deterioration decreasing the road-user cost benefits expected from the improved roads. Most of these deficiencies could have been mitigated during project design and construction. For example, the project designer could have included the International Roughness Index (IRI) measures in the contract documents as a performance specification, requiring the contractor to meet IRI targets set by MCC and MCA-Honduras—which would decrease long-term maintenance and road-user costs.[38]

Source: GAO.
Note: This landslide blocks the roadside drainage, resulting in long-term pavement damage, and needs to be removed as a part of road maintenance to eliminate a roadside safety hazard. MCC stated that existing natural conditions and extreme weather caused this slide.

Figure 7. Landslide on CA-5 Section 3 in Honduras.

Additionally, landslides and their associated maintenance costs could have been minimized if more detailed geotechnical analysis evaluating slope stability had been conducted during design. Such analysis would have enabled designers to include landslide stabilization and prevention measures in the construction plans. A more detailed geotechnical study regarding slope stability was completed for portions of CA-5 section 2 after a landslide occurred.

Rural development project. MCC took steps to increase the sustainability of activities under the rural development project. The sustainability of some activities was enhanced by these steps, but for other activities challenges remain.

- The contractor for the farmer training activity involved the private sector in program activities, including buyers, wholesalers, and input and equipment service providers to increase sustainability. The farmer training activity also helped farmers form associations to increase the sustainability of techniques and production practices. However, according to the contractor and Honduran farmers, some program farmers, who began receiving assistance late in the compact, are expected to face difficulty sustaining new techniques without the support of technicians.[39]

- In many cases, responsibility for maintenance of upgraded farm-to-market roads resides with the municipalities where the roads are located. However, according to MCA-Honduras officials, the municipalities lack equipment, expertise, and funding for road maintenance.
- MCA-Honduras took steps to increase the sustainability of the farmer access to credit activity in Honduras by enabling the agricultural credit fund to continue for 5 years beyond the end of the compact. In addition, according to the activity contractor, the financial products developed with the technical assistance are self-sustaining and self-financing.
- Local organizations supported the implementation of the agricultural public goods grants, which will help improve the activity's sustainability, according to MCA-Honduras officials. For example, local communities with new irrigation works were trained in the maintenance of such systems and put in place fee structures to fund maintenance costs.

IMPACT EVALUATIONS AND ERR ISSUES

Impact evaluations and ERR analyses assist MCC in estimating the impact of compact projects on long-term economic growth. MCC funds independent impact evaluations, which contribute to understanding whether an investment achieved its intended impact. According to MCC officials, these evaluations have been delayed because of delays in project implementation and a change in approach to the timing of the evaluations. MCC's ERR provides a means of estimating the proposed projects' impact on a country's economic growth relative to costs over a relatively long time period, typically 20 years. However, updated ERRs were not always well-documented or linked to revised targets. In addition, MCC has not issued guidance for re-estimating ERRs at compact completion or in subsequent years.

MCC Impact Evaluations Are Ongoing, and MCC Has Taken Steps to Revise Designs in Response to Implementation Challenges and Delays

Cape Verde. MCC plans to conduct impact evaluations, but project implementation delays have slowed progress.[40]

- *Port activity.* MCC has delayed contracting for an impact evaluator for the infrastructure project's port activity until the completion of phase 2 of port construction in 2013.[41] According to the 2010 Cape Verde monitoring and evaluation plan, it is unclear whether the originally planned impact evaluation is feasible, and MCC may revise the evaluation design if necessary.[42]
- *Roads and bridges activity.* MCC has not yet engaged an impact evaluator for the infrastructure project's roads and bridges activity. According to the 2010 Cape Verde monitoring and evaluation plan, if the collected baseline data do not support the planned evaluation design, MCC would accept a revised evaluation design.[43]

- *Watershed management and agricultural support project.* MCC engaged an impact evaluator in the last year of implementation of the watershed management and agricultural support project, and slower than expected project implementation has delayed final data collection for the impact evaluation.[44] According to the independent evaluator hired to assess the project, designing the evaluation after compact implementation may limit the quality of the results by, for instance, hindering the collection of quality baseline data. Baseline data were collected before project implementation, but the impact evaluator has cited concerns about the quality of this data. According to MCC officials, MCC plans to address these concerns about the quality of baseline data through additional data collection.

- *Private sector development project.* The private sector development project, which was significantly rescoped, will not be assessed using a quantitative evaluation since the technical assistance provided did not lend itself to a quantitative evaluation; however, a qualitative evaluation has been completed.[45]

- *Honduras.* Project delays and challenges in implementing originally planned impact evaluation designs have slowed progress of some impact evaluations. MCC initially anticipated completing impact evaluations for the Honduras compact projects by the end of the compact. However, according to MCC officials, MCC modified its approach to impact evaluations so that evaluations are completed after the end of the compact.[46]

- *Transportation project.* The impact evaluation for the transportation project began before project implementation, but delays in road construction led to delays in collecting necessary data and completing the evaluation. According to the impact evaluator, other than some delays in final data collection, the transportation impact evaluation was planned with a robust design and has been implemented as planned.

- *Farmer training and development activity.* Challenges encountered in implementing the original evaluation design led to potential limitations in the results. As a result, MCC added a supplemental design to enhance the methodology. Specifically, the impact evaluator had identified a certain group of farmers to participate in the program and serve as a sample for the evaluation. However, the activity contractor chose not to train a large portion of the selected group, reducing the sample size for the evaluation and potentially limiting the results. According to MCC, the challenge in implementing the original evaluation design arose because the contractor was focused on achieving targets set in the contract, instead of implementing the activity in parallel with the evaluation methodology, which was not outlined in the contract. MCC noted that this experience highlighted the importance of incorporating impact evaluation designs into implementation plans and contracts and the need to anticipate and manage potential tradeoffs.

- *Farmer access to credit activity.* According to the impact evaluator, the assessment of the farmer access to credit activity was complicated by changes that took place during implementation, such as the expansion of the activity beyond an exclusive focus on program farmers, as well as the delay in program implementation. By the time changes were made to the activity, no baseline data had been collected. Subsequently, MCA-Honduras hired a third-party contractor to collect qualitative data. However, when the impact evaluator's contract ended at the end of the compact, these data had not been analyzed and an evaluation report had not been completed as originally intended.

- *Agricultural public goods grants facility activity.* The impact evaluator conducted an economic rate of return calculation by comparing the costs and benefits that resulted from the agricultural public goods grants facility activity. For example, the report compared the expected costs and benefits as a result of certain grant activities with the estimated costs and benefits had the grant activity not been implemented. The evaluator produced a final report on the impact of a selection of the 15 public goods grants.[47]

ERR Analyses during Compact Implementation Were Not always Well-Documented or Linked to Key Revised Targets

MCC updated its ERR analyses for the Cape Verde and Honduras compacts when project activities changed significantly during implementation. However, the updated ERR analyses were not always well-documented or supported. In addition, the analyses were not consistently updated when projects or activities were rescoped or when key targets were revised, as stated in MCC guidance and policy documents.

Updated ERR Analyses Were Not Always Well-Documented or Supported

Updated ERR analyses were not well-documented or supported for projects constituting almost 50 percent of compact funds in Cape Verde and more than 65 percent of compact funds in Honduras.

- For Cape Verde, MCC increased its ERR for the port improvement activity from 23 percent to 29 percent as the investment cost tripled.[48] In re-estimating the ERR, MCC relied on a new model prepared by a French engineering consulting firm. The model incorporated efficiency gains leading to benefits to consumers and firms, such as reduced wait times and other cost savings.[49] The analysis assumes that these benefits also have an economywide effect. However, MCC does not have documentation for the modeling of the economywide effect. As a result, it is unclear how the analysis incorporates the project's effect on the overall economy. If the economywide effect is not taken into account, the activity ERR drops from 28.6 percent to 9.3 percent, which is below MCC's hurdle rate of 10 percent cited in the MCC Cape Verde restructuring memo. However, according to an MCC official, the prevailing hurdle rate was 4.8 percent, and thus the investment remained well above the minimum standard established for Cape Verde.[50] Furthermore, the extent to which consumers will benefit from the project is also not clear.
- For Honduras, the original economic analysis for the transportation project established an ERR of 24 percent. Updates of the monitoring and evaluation plan in 2008 and 2010 cite an ERR of 12 percent. However, documentation for the underlying quantitative analysis supporting the updated ERR is not available.

Updated ERR Analyses Were Not Always Linked to Key
Revised Targets

Updated ERR analyses do not always reflect changes in key targets revised after decisions about project rescoping have been made.

- For Cape Verde, when each of the three projects was rescoped, MCC updated all relevant ERR analysis.[51] However, the updated ERR analysis does not reflect the values or numerical ranges of key updated targets in the monitoring and evaluation plan. For example, the revised targets for the watershed management and agricultural support project include a revised volume of available water of 627,500 cubic meters, but in the updated ERR analysis, total water capacity is 17,000 cubic meters. In addition, the revised targets for the project include a farmer productivity target of 9.4 to 14.3 tons of crops per hectare, which overlaps only slightly with the range for farmer productivity of 13 to 20 tons of crops per hectare in the updated ERR analysis.

- For Honduras, where both compact projects were rescoped, MCC did not update the projected ERRs for the transportation and rural development projects to reflect all changes. For example, for the transportation project, MCC eliminated the weight control activity but did not update the project level ERR in the revised monitoring and evaluation plan to reflect this rescoping. In addition, the projected ERR for the farm-to-market roads activity was updated in the revised monitoring and evaluation plans, but this update was not incorporated in revising the rural development project level ERR. Moreover, MCC revised key targets, but the ERR analyses do not reflect those revisions. For example, the original ERR analysis for the farmer training and development activity of the rural development project is based on 14,400 hectares of high-value crops at the end of the compact.[52] The 2008 and 2010 monitoring and evaluation plans establish revised targets of 11,830 and 8,400 hectares, respectively, at compact completion but do not revise the ERR.[53]

MCC officials stated that when key indicators and targets were modified, MCC assessed the effects of these changes on ERRs using the existing models but did not formally document those assessments. MCC officials also attributed the lack of consistent linkage between ERR analyses and key revised targets to the fact that economist staffing shortages limited their ability to update the economic analysis every time key indicators and targets were modified.

MCC Has Not Issued Guidance for Re-estimating ERRs Following Compact Completion but, If Estimated, ERRs Are Likely to Be Lower than Predicted

MCC has not developed guidance for re-estimating project ERRs at compact completion or in subsequent years. Although MCC does not have guidance that requires re-estimation of ERRs, it plans to update ERRs for its investments in Cape Verde and Honduras. Since the initial ERR analysis is an estimate of the expected total increase in incomes over a typical 20-year period attributable to a proposed MCC-funded project relative to the total costs, ERR analysis at compact completion can provide updated estimates based on actual project costs. Further, for projects or activities that have been rescoped, revised estimates of benefits can be included in the ERR analysis. In addition, when data on actual benefits accrued to project beneficiaries are collected by impact evaluations, these data can also be used to re-estimate the ERRs. According to MCC officials, MCC requires independent evaluators to calculate ERRs at compact completion, but guidance is currently not available to guide this analysis. In the case of the sole Honduras ERR calculated at compact completion to date by an independent evaluator, in the absence of guidance, the evaluator prepared the ERR analysis in such a way that it cannot be compared to the initial ERR estimate.[54] Furthermore, even though the original ERRs are estimated over a 20-year period, according to MCC officials, MCC has not yet determined whether it will re-estimate the returns as additional benefit data from impact evaluations or other sources become available. Without an accurate estimate of the compacts' projected benefits, the extent to which the compacts further MCC's goal of poverty reduction, economic growth, and transformative development cannot be accurately evaluated.

Reductions in project scope and other factors are likely to reduce re-estimated ERRs. In one instance where MCC has revised the ERR at compact completion—the farmer training and development activity in Honduras—the revised ERR was lower than originally predicted, at 14.6 percent versus 21 percent. For any further re-estimates of Cape Verde and Honduras ERRs, several factors would likely contribute to lower estimates of returns on investments than originally predicted—as seen in the following examples.

Factors During Compact Implementation

- Reductions in projects' or activities' original scopes while MCC investments remained largely unchanged would lower expected benefits. For example, for the Honduras transportation project, MCC reduced the scope of the secondary roads construction activities to align actual costs with project allocations and terminated the weight control activity. Similarly, in Cape Verde, MCC funded about one-third of the port improvement activity.
- Measured results that lagged behind project or activity targets would lead to lower benefits than originally projected. For example, the original ERR analysis of the rural development project in Cape Verde assumed that the project would lead to 111 hectares under drip irrigation; however, by compact completion, about 13 hectares were under drip irrigation.

Factors Subsequent to Compact Completion

- Cost overruns for MCC-funded projects not finished by compact completion would lead to lower ERRs. Costs for the Cape Verde port improvement activity, which was not finished by compact completion, are currently estimated at about $148 million.[55] These costs exceed both the estimated investment costs of about $106 million for the activity in the updated ERR analysis and the cost contingency of 20 percent included in the updated analysis, totaling approximately $127 million.
- Factors affecting long-term sustainability, such as maintenance of the physical infrastructure and future training to prevent depreciation of acquired skills and human capital, can affect estimated benefits. For example, according to MCA-

Honduras officials, the sustainability of many of the farm-to-market roads constructed for the Honduras rural development project is in question because the municipal governments responsible for maintaining the roads lack equipment and expertise. If less than optimal maintenance is achieved, estimated benefits will be reduced, which would lead to lower ERRs.

CONCLUSIONS

MCC made significant investments in support of sustainable economic growth in Cape Verde and Honduras and will benefit from lessons learned during implementation of these compacts, which were among the first to enter into force. As we previously reported, insufficient planning, escalation of construction costs, and insufficient MCC review have led to project delays, scope reductions, and cost increases.[56] MCC directed the majority of funding in the Cape Verde and Honduras compacts to infrastructure projects, and for the economic benefits of these investments to be realized, the projects must be properly sustained over the planned 20-year benefit period. To promote sustainability, MCC took steps to require partner countries to plan to efficiently operate and maintain the infrastructure, including privatization of port operations in Cape Verde and the provision of road maintenance funding in Cape Verde and Honduras. The partner countries made progress meeting MCC's requirements in these areas, but they continue to face funding and other challenges that are key to sustainability. At the same time, MCC lost its ability to influence country decisions regarding sustainability once the compacts ended. In addition, MCC and MCA made design decisions that did not include measures to minimize landslides and erosion and did not include international roughness criteria among the contract specifications, which will result in higher long-term maintenance costs. In light of road maintenance funding deficits in both countries, these decisions put the sustainability of MCC-funded roads at risk.

MCC's ERR projections serve as the foundation and economic justification for MCC's investments. MCC guidance and policy statements indicate that key indicators and targets used for monitoring and MCC's ERR analyses should be directly linked. However, indicators and targets changed significantly over the 5-year implementation period, sufficient to alter the foundation of the initial ERR projection. In some instances, the lack of documentation on updated ERR analyses makes it difficult to know whether the revised ERR results are accurate and reliable. In other cases, MCC updated its ERRs during compact implementation, but the ERR analyses were not clearly linked to the revised targets in the monitoring and evaluation plans. Although MCC updated ERR projections in response to changes in implementation, it currently does not have guidance for re-estimating ERRs at compact completion or during the 20- year period when compact benefits are realized. Looking forward, if MCC plans to update ERRs at or following compact completion as a means of assessing project benefits relative to actual costs, it will be critical to use a consistent methodology that reflects final compact results and costs. Without an accurate representation of the compacts' projected benefits, MCC, Congress, and other key stakeholders and beneficiaries cannot accurately evaluate the extent to which the compacts further MCC's goals of poverty reduction and economic growth.

RECOMMENDATIONS FOR EXECUTIVE ACTION

We recommend the MCC Chief Executive Officer take the following three actions:

To maximize the sustainability of MCC-funded infrastructure projects and to reduce the amount of maintenance required after compact completion, work with partner countries to make project planning, design, and construction decisions that reduce long-term maintenance needs and costs.

To enhance the accuracy of MCC's ERR projections,

- ensure, during compact implementation, that updated ERR analyses are well-documented and supported and that key revised indicators and targets are reflected in updated ERR analyses; and
- develop guidance for re-estimating ERRs at compact completion and during the long-term period when compact benefits are realized to ensure that updated estimates reflect the most recent and reliable information available for MCC's compact investments and outcomes.

AGENCY COMMENTS AND OUR EVALUATION

In written comments on a draft of this report, MCC agreed with the intent of our recommendations and committed to developing specific actions to implement them. With respect to the first recommendation on the sustainability of MCC-funded infrastructure projects, MCC acknowledged the importance of maintenance and sustainability of its investments. MCC stated that, when designing projects, it works with partner countries to ensure that institutions and systems are in place to provide for the projects' long-term sustainability. In addition, MCC said that it looks to strike a proper balance between its initial capital investments and ongoing operations and maintenance costs. While MCC said that it pays considerable attention to minimizing operations and maintenance costs, MCC also stated that some maintenance-related measures raised in our report—such as slope protection along reconstructed roads—may not be justified in all cases. MCC further commented that financing maintenance is a challenge in both developed and developing countries. MCC agreed with both aspects of our second recommendation to enhance the accuracy of MCC's ERR projections. MCC agreed that, when project design and scope changes are proposed during compact implementation, updated ERR analyses should be adequately documented and the consistency between the updated ERR analyses and targets should be maintained. With respect to the third recommendation to develop guidance for reestimating ERRs following compact completion, MCC acknowledged the importance of measuring ERRs over the life of its projects and stated that it is committed to developing guidance to continue monitoring the results of compacts and measuring long-term impacts of MCC investments.

MCC also highlighted other positive contributions of the Cape Verde and Honduras compacts beyond the results achieved for key indicators and targets. Specifically, MCC stated that policy reforms in Cape Verde and new legislation in Honduras are expected to have positive lasting impacts in these countries. In addition, MCC noted that in response to implementation challenges, MCC was able to leverage its resources and obtain additional financing to support the completion of compact activities. Finally, MCC emphasized that country-led implementation of its compacts fosters good governance and effective administration of development assistance.

We have reprinted MCC's comments in appendix IV. We also incorporated technical comments from MCC in our report where appropriate.

We are sending copies of this report to the Millennium Challenge Corporation and interested Congressional Committees. In addition, the report will be available at no charge on the GAO Web site at http://www.gao.gov.

If you or your staffs have any questions about this report, please contact me at (202) 512-3149 or gootnickd@gao.gov. Contact points for our Offices of Congressional Relations and Public Affairs may be found on the last page of this report. GAO staff who made major contributions to this report are listed in appendix V.

David Gootnick
Director, International Affairs and Trade

APPENDIX I:
SCOPE AND METHODOLOGY

The fiscal year 2008 Consolidated Appropriations Act, Public Law 110- 161, mandated that GAO review the results of Millennium Challenge Corporation's (MCC) compacts. For the purpose of this engagement, we reviewed MCC compact results in Cape Verde and Honduras, the first compacts to complete the 5-year term at the initiation of our review. We examined the extent to which MCC (1) achieved performance targets and longer-term sustainability for projects in the Cape Verde and Honduras compacts and (2) assessed progress toward the compacts' goals of income growth and poverty reduction. We focused our review more heavily on infrastructure activities, which represented a higher portion of compact funds in both countries. We specifically focused on the port activity and roads and bridges activity in Cape Verde, and the CA-5 highway and secondary roads activities in Honduras.

To assess the extent to which MCC achieved expected performance targets and longer-term sustainability for compacts in Cape Verde and Honduras, we analyzed MCC documents, interviewed MCC officials and stakeholders, and observed project results in both countries. We reviewed the compact agreement for Cape Verde and Honduras, as well as MCC guidance on measuring and reporting compact results, including the agency's Framework for Results, Policy for Monitoring and Evaluation of Compact and Threshold Programs, Guidance on Quarterly MCA Disbursement Request and Reporting Package, Common Indicators Directive, and guidelines for monitoring and evaluation plans. We interviewed MCC officials in Washington, D.C., regarding their processes for overseeing compact activities. We traveled to Santiago and Santo Antão islands in Cape Verde in December 2010 and Tegucigalpa, Honduras, in November 2010. We interviewed MCC and Millennium Challenge Account (MCA) officials in both countries regarding the results of each compact activity, including the quality and sustainability of the projects. We visited infrastructure projects in both countries, including visits to the port and to roads and bridges in Cape Verde, and to the CA-5 highway, and secondary and farm-to-market roads in Honduras. We met with project construction contractors, independent construction supervisors, and MCA project management consultants. We interviewed contractors and grantees of noninfrastructure activities and held meetings with beneficiaries of certain projects. For Cape Verde, we interviewed the contractor and two grantees for the access to credit activity, the contractor for the credit bureau activity under the private sector development project, and the contractor and eight beneficiaries of the watershed management and agricultural support project, including the farmer training activity. For Honduras, we interviewed the contractor and more than 30 beneficiaries of the farmer training and development activity, contractors and several financial institutions participating in the farmer access to credit activity, and three grantees in the agricultural public goods grants activity. In addition, we interviewed officials from the governments of Cape Verde and Honduras about compact implementation, results, and sustainability, including Cape Verde's Ministry of Environment, Rural Development and Marine Resources, Port Authority, and Ministry of Infrastructure, Transport and Tele-communications, and Honduras' Ministry of Transportation, Ministry of the Presidency, Ministry of Agriculture, and Ministry of Finance. We also reviewed final reports submitted to MCA by contractors and grantees on compact activities.

We reviewed three versions of the monitoring and evaluation plans for each country to identify the performance indicators and associated targets to be achieved by compact end. MCC used these performance indicators and targets to track progress and assess results of compact activities; thus, we used these indicators and targets as criteria for assessing MCC results achieved. To track progress toward compact goals, MCA is required to compile and submit a performance indicator tracking table on a quarterly basis as part of its quarterly disbursement request package sent to MCC.[1] This tracking table displays performance targets and progress on all performance indicators included in a country's monitoring and evaluation plan. A complete indicator tracking table provides detailed information that shows cumulative past performance, recently completed performance, and the remaining annual targets for each performance indicator. We collected and analyzed all available indicator tracking tables for both countries to account for the actual results achieved against each performance target throughout the compact. We met with MCA staff in Cape Verde and Honduras about the steps they took to ensure that data used to track program results were valid, reliable, and timely, including conducting periodic data checks and hiring independent evaluators to review the reliability of data. We determined that these data were sufficiently reliable for the purposes of our review.

In assessing and reporting MCC's results, we compared actual results achieved at the end of the compact for each performance indicator to the original and, in some cases, the revised targets associated with each indicator. Given that there were three versions of the monitoring and evaluation plan for each country, we considered the original target to be the one listed the first time a performance indicator was introduced and the final target the one listed in the final 2010 monitoring and evaluation plan. In addition, in some cases, MCC revised the name or characterization of a performance indicator while the definition and type of measurement remained constant. In these cases, we chose to report the original target as that associated with the original or parent indicator, and the final target as that associated with the revised indicator. Given that MCC tracked several performance indicators for each compact project, we chose to report on a selection of key indicators that most closely represented the goal of each compact activity. For example, we reported the volume of available water for the water management and soil conservation activity in Cape Verde but did not report the value of irrigation construction contracts signed. In addition, we considered which performance indicators MCC selected to report on in its public communications about compact results. We did not report results for indicators that MCC eliminated and stopped tracking during the life of the compact, but we reported on such eliminated indicators in discussions of canceled or rescoped activities.

To examine the extent to which infrastructure projects met performance targets, met quality standards, and were sustainable, we interviewed MCA officials, project construction contractors, independent construction supervisors, project management consultants, the Cape Verde port design engineer, and officials with the Honduran ministries of transportation and finance. We also reviewed documents prepared by MCA officials, project construction contractors, independent construction supervisors, project management consultants, MCC independent engineers, and government officials, including monthly reports, special studies, testing reports, and daily inspections. Lastly, we conducted site inspections of projects that accounted for a majority of the MCC-provided infrastructure funding in Cape Verde and Honduras to verify the extent to which projects had been completed and to observe whether there were any visual deficiencies in construction. These interviews, document reviews, and site visits were used to determine if the MCAs had implemented MCC's quality assurance framework, if there was supporting documentation to verify that quality testing had been undertaken, if any quality deficiencies were encountered during construction, if any quality deficiencies remain, and whether the infrastructure projects would be sustainable. We were not able to view actual work in progress or visit testing facilities for most infrastructure contracts because the work had already been completed.

To examine the extent to which MCC assessed progress toward the compacts' goals of income growth and poverty reduction, we reviewed MCC's monitoring and evaluation guidance, Guidelines for Economic and Beneficiary Analysis, three versions of the monitoring and evaluation plans for each country, monitoring information MCC and MCA collected, data quality reviews, final reports prepared by contractors and grantees, documents related to impact evaluation contracts, impact evaluation design reports, final impact evaluations, and original and revised economic rate of return (ERR) analyses. We also interviewed MCC officials in Washington, D.C., regarding their processes for overseeing compact activities, developing monitoring plans, and carrying out assessments of progress toward the compacts' goals. During site visits, we interviewed MCC and MCA officials in Santiago and Santo Antão islands in Cape Verde and Tegucigalpa, Honduras, about monitoring procedures and data quality activities for compact projects. We also interviewed officials from the national statistical agencies in Cape Verde and Honduras, contractors, partner government agencies, and project contractors involved in data collection activities, as well as contractors implementing impact evaluations and other analysis.

To assess MCC's results framework, we analyzed the connection between the ERR estimates and related statements in the economic impact section of the monitoring and evaluation plans, the values of the variables that should translate into indicator targets in those plans, and the underlying economic analyses provided in support of the expected economic impact statements made in those plans. In addition, we studied the evaluation components of the plans and compared them with the evaluations' actual proposed designs and implementation to assess the extent to which the evaluations accurately reflected the designs envisioned in the plans, the likelihood that MCC would be able to gather reliable information on actual benefits attributable to the compact, and the ability of MCC to update the ERRs as that information becomes available. We reviewed MCC's evolving guidance for ERR and monitoring and evaluation analyses. We also examined spreadsheets MCC provided in support of their updated calculations. To further discuss MCC's approaches and to clarify aspects of the economic impact analysis, we interviewed MCC economists, impact evaluators, and other officials regarding MCC's monitoring and evaluation framework and estimated economic impact.

MCC enters into a legal relationship with partner country governments, which vest responsibility for day-to-day management of compact project implementation to the MCA, including monitoring and evaluation activities such as setting and revising targets, but such MCA actions require MCC's direct oversight and approval. Therefore, throughout this report, we attribute all decisions related to project rescoping and compact targets to MCC.

Finally, some of the reports and documents referenced above were written in Portuguese or Spanish. We translated these documents internally and created English summaries to enable our analysis.

We conducted this performance audit from September 2010 to July 2011 in accordance with generally accepted government auditing standards. Those standards require that we plan and perform the audit to obtain sufficient, appropriate evidence to provide a reasonable basis for our findings and conclusions based on our audit objectives. We believe the evidence obtained provides a reasonable basis for our findings and conclusions based on our audit objectives.

APPENDIX II:
CAPE VERDE COMPACT RESULTS

Cape Verde Compact Background

Located off the coast of West Africa, Cape Verde is a group of 10 islands, with a population of about 500,000. Cape Verde was classified as a lower-middle income country with a per capita income of $3,010 for fiscal year 2011.[1] U.S. development assistance accounts for about 9 percent of total assistance to Cape Verde over the last 10 years, making the United States its third-largest donor.

MCC and the government of Cape Verde signed a 5-year compact in July 2005, which entered into force in October 2005 and ended in October 2010. The compact, for which MCC provided $110.1 million in funding at compact signature, consisted of three projects.

- The *infrastructure project* was aimed at increasing integration of internal markets and reducing transportation costs. Activities include upgrading and expanding a major port and rehabilitating five roads and constructing four bridges. Expected beneficiaries of this project include consumers, importers and exporters, shippers, and residents.
- The *watershed management and agricultural support project* was aimed at increasing agricultural productivity in three targeted watershed areas on three islands. Activities include the development of water management infrastructure and activities

to increase the productive capacity of farmers. Expected beneficiaries of this project include individual farmers, farm households, and government and private sector participants.

- The *private sector development project* was aimed at spurring private sector development on all islands. Activities include investments in the private sector and technical assistance to microfinance institutions. Expected beneficiaries include individuals and companies, urban and rural poor, and existing microfinance institutions.

In addition, the compact included funding for program administration and monitoring and evaluation activities to support administration and implementation of the compact, program management, and reporting.[2]

Table 5 shows the Cape Verde projects' planned activities, objectives, and beneficiaries as of compact signature.

Table 5. Structure of Cape Verde Compact, at Signature

Project	Planned activities (funding allocation)	Objective	Expected beneficiaries
Infrastructure	• Port ($53.7 million): The upgrade and expansion of the Port of Praia • Roads and bridges ($25 million): The rehabilitation of 5 roads and construction of 4 bridges	Increase integration of internal markets and reduce transportation costs	1) Consumers, importers and exporters, shippers and residents of the island of Santiago, due to port efficiency gains and improved quality of transportation services 2) Rural and urban populations on two islands, due to road and bridge interventions
Watershed management and agricultural support	• Water management and soil conservation ($6.8 million): The development of water management infrastructure, including walls, terraces, dikes, and reservoirs • Agribusiness development services ($3.6 million): The promotion of drip irrigation technology and increased productive capacity and marketing of agricultural products among farmers and small agribusinesses • Access to credit ($0.5 million): The provision of access to credit for drip irrigation, working capital, and agribusiness investments	Increase agricultural productivity in three targeted watershed areas on three islands	1) Individual farmers and farm households in the three target watersheds and actors along the supply chain, due to increased access to water, training and extension opportunities, and the extension of credit 2) Government and private sector participants, due to capacity-building training and technical assistance

Table 5. (Continued)

Project	Planned activities (funding allocation)	Objective	Expected beneficiaries
Private sector development	• Partnership to mobilize investment ($5 million): collaboration with the government and World Bank to identify, prioritize, design, and implement interventions to increase investment in priority sectors of the economy • Financial sector reform ($2.2 million): The provision of technical assistance to support the development of microfinance institutions (MFI) and government efforts to expand access to the primary market for government securities	Spur private sector development on all islands	1) Individuals and companies, who will benefit from an improved investment climate, increased availability of jobs, and enhanced entrepreneurial opportunities 2) Urban and rural poor, who will gain access to a broader menu of financial services 3) Existing MFIs and nongovernmental organizations, due to technical assistance for institutional transformation 4) All investors and borrowers, including the government, due to a more open financial system and being better equipped to develop new financial products
Program administration and monitoring and evaluation	• Program administration ($8.4 million): Undertake institutional capacity-building • Program administration ($8.4 million): Undertake institutional capacity-building activities to upgrade the government of Cape Verde's electronic procurement and financial management systems • Monitoring and evaluation ($4.9 million): The measurement and evaluation of progress toward the achievement of the compact goal and objectives		

Source: GAO analysis of Millennium Challenge Corporation data.

CAPE VERDE
INFRASTRUCTURE PROJECT

Port Activity

Port: Objective

MCC allocated $53.7 million to fund infrastructure improvements at the Port of Praia—Cape Verde's largest port, accounting for approximately 50 percent of the total volume of port traffic—to support the country's goal of expanding the facility to promote continued economic development. The activity was planned to address constraints such as a lack of space for wharf-side cargo handling and lack of a breakwater to protect against waves that can impair stevedoring operations. The activity was planned with five components:

1) construction of a new cargo village—container storage yard—on a plateau above the wharves;
2) reconstruction of a wharf (wharf 2), including demolition of existing sheds and re-paving;
3) construction of a new access road to connect the wharves to the cargo village (lower access road) and public road system (upper access road);

4) expansion of a wharf (wharf 1) to extend its length and build a new storage yard on reclaimed land; and

5) construction of a new breakwater.

Port: Results

MCC disbursed $54.9 million for the port activity. MCC met a key final target and eliminated some indicators for this activity (see table 6 for key performance results for the port activity). After determining during the activity's planning and design that it would not be able to fund all planned port improvements, MCC and MCA-Cape Verde reduced the activity's scope by splitting it into two phases, with MCC funding the first phase (components 1, 2, and 3) and the Cape Verde government funding the second phase (components 4 and 5).

MCA-Cape Verde completed most of phase 1 in October 2010, and the Cape Verde government expects to complete phase 2 by March 2013.

Phase 1. MCA-Cape Verde funded phase 1 of the port activity at $45.3 million.[3] MCA-Cape Verde deleted the construction of some buildings from the contract scope to keep costs within funding limits, and the Cape Verde government subsequently funded construction of the buildings at approximately $16 million through a loan from a Portuguese bank.[4]

Phase 2. The Cape Verde government funded phase 2 of the activity (components 4 and 5) at approximately $87 million through a loan from the Portuguese government.[5] Work is to be completed over a 30- month period ending in March 2013 in accordance with the design initially funded by MCC.

Port: Challenges

Inaccurate early planning of the port activity led to cost increases and implementation delays.

- *Cost increases.* Costs increased as a result of inaccurate early planning assumptions concerning design details and construction materials. For example, the cargo village and access road were built in different locations than initially planned, and according to MCC, relocating these components resulted in significant cost increases. In addition, initial plans specified the use of a detached breakwater to protect the wharves, but subsequent analysis and model testing showed the need for an attached breakwater, which was more expensive to construct. Also, initial plans were based on an incorrect assumption that quarry materials would be available at minimal cost from government-owned quarries. However, by the time implementation began, the government no longer controlled the quarries, and materials had to be procured from private sources, increasing the activity's cost.[6]

- *Implementation delays.* Rescoping the port activity contributed to implementation delays that resulted in MCA-Cape Verde using more than half of the 5-year compact implementation period for planning, design, and contract procurement actions before awarding a construction contract.[7] As a result, implementation of the phase 1 components did not begin until year 3, when MCC had originally intended to have completed these components, and completion of phase 2 components is not expected until March 2013, approximately 29 months after compact end.[8]

Table 6. Key Performance Results for Port Activity, Cape Verde

Performance indicator	Original target (percentage)	Final target (percentage)	Final result (percentage)	Percentage of original target met	Percentage of final target met
Phase 1 Cargo village—percent complete	100 by year 3			Not determined[c]	100
Wharf 2 improvements—percent complete	100 by year 3	100 by year 5[a]	100 by year 5[b]		
Access road—percent complete	100 by year 3				
Phase 2 Breakwater—percent complete	100 by year 3	Activity eliminated[d]			
Wharf 1 extension and new container yard—percent complete	100 by year 5				

Source: GAO analysis of Millennium Challenge Corporation data.

Notes: We considered the original target to be that which was first documented for each performance indicator, in either the 2006, 2008, or 2010 monitoring and evaluation plan, and the final target to be that which was documented in the 2010 monitoring and evaluation plan. In addition, the final results in this table reflect the results achieved by compact completion, although some activities continue after the compact completion and continue to achieve results.

[a]MCC established a new indicator based on a combination of the original indicators for individual project components. The new indicator tracked the cumulative percentage of work complete as measured by disbursements. The change in target for this indicator was documented in the 2008 monitoring and evaluation plan.

[b]MCA-Cape Verde administered a $45.3 million construction contract for completion of port works (phase 1). Construction of buildings at the cargo village was removed from the scope of the contract at the time of award due to funding limitations. The Cape Verde government subsequently funded the construction of these buildings under a separate contract that MCC reported as costing approximately $16 million. At the end of the compact, approximately $530,000 of work related to the cargo village buildings that was part of MCA-Cape Verde's contract remained undone and will be performed upon completion of the buildings.

[c]Completion of all project components occurred after year 3 of the compact. We did not attempt to estimate the amount of work complete at the end of year 3.

[d]The Cape Verde government awarded a contract in September 2010 for completion of port activity elements (phase 2) that were removed from MCA-Cape Verde's scope of work due to funding limitations. MCC reported that the Cape Verde government awarded its contract in the amount of approximately $87 million. Contract completion is expected in March 2013.

Port: Quality

To provide management control and ensure quality for the port activity, MCA-Cape Verde established an organization consistent with MCC's management structure for infrastructure projects. The management organization for the Cape Verde port activity consisted of a project manager for MCA-Cape Verde; project managers for the activity's implementing entity, the Cape Verde transportation ministry;[9] an MCA-contracted independent construction supervisor; an MCA-contracted design engineer; and an MCC-contracted independent engineering consultant.

Work completed for the port activity was performed according to contractual requirements, generally met quality standards, and should enable the infrastructure to function for the duration of its design life,[10] according to the construction supervisor's progress reports and members of the management organization. However, a defect in construction of the shore protection structure built for the lower access road posed a threat to the road's stability, which MCC took steps to remedy. According to the design engineer, in May 2009 the construction contractor expressed concerns about building an underwater trench included in the design for the shore protection structure,[11] claiming that the seafloor was uneven and consisted of materials that were not shown on design documents. However, at the construction supervisor's direction, the contractor attempted to install the structure as specified in the design and completed work in July 2010. Subsequently, the design engineer determined that the underwater trench was not properly constructed and did not provide an adequate foundation for the shore protection structure.[12] To address this issue, MCC contracted the U.S. Army Corps of Engineers to inspect the as-built condition of the trench and develop alternatives for correcting the construction defects. In its initial assessment, the U.S. Army Corps of Engineers estimated that the cost of remedying the construction defects would range from approximately $1 million to $2.8 million.13 Costs for repairs to the underwater trench will be shared by the construction contractor and the Cape Verde government, according to an agreement between the two parties and MCA-Cape Verde in January 2011.[14]

Port: Sustainability

MCC determined that privatizing operations at the Port of Praia was critical to the sustainability of the port activity and included privatization of the port operations as a condition for disbursement of compact funding. MCC reasoned that privatization was needed to enable the port to handle current and projected traffic in a manner that would lead to improved financial performance. Although the government of Cape Verde agreed to this condition and developed a law to enable the port authority to enter into contracts with private operators, the port authority has been delayed in soliciting contracts for port operations services because construction of the port is incomplete, with phase 2 work expected to continue until March 2013. MCC reports that the port authority has taken initial steps in developing model contracts for port operations, but it no longer has leverage over the port authority to ensure that this condition is met.

Roads and Bridges Construction Activity

Roads and Bridges: Objective

MCC allocated $25 million to fund the rehabilitation of five roads on Santiago Island and construction of four bridges on Santo Antão Island. The activity was intended to support Cape Verde's goal of improving mobility on the two islands by closing road network gaps to ensure more reliable access both to intra-island markets and services and provide transportation linkages on the targeted islands.

Roads and Bridges: Results

MCC disbursed $27.7 million for the Cape Verde roads and bridges activity by compact completion. MCC met revised targets for the roads rehabilitation, after reducing the scope of the planned roads, and met its targets for the bridges construction (see table 7 for key performance results for the roads and bridges activity).

Table 7. Key Performance Results of Roads and Bridges Activity, Cape Verde

Performance indicator	Original target	Final target	Final result	Percentage of original target met	Percentage of final target met
Kilometers of road rehabilitated	63[a]	39.3[b]	40.6[c]	64	103
Percentage of roads and bridges work completed[d]	100 by year 3	100 by year 5[b]	100 by year 5	Not determined[e]	100

Source: GAO analysis of Millennium Challenge Corporation data.

Notes: We considered the original target to be that which was first documented for each performance indicator, in either the 2006, 2008, or 2010 monitoring and evaluation plan, and the final target to be that which was documented in the 2010 monitoring and evaluation plan.

[a]The scope of road rehabilitation initially identified in the construction contract was five roads totaling 62.2 kilometers. The 63 kilometers shown here is the value listed in the 2006 monitoring and evaluation plan.

bThe change in target for this indicator was documented in the 2008 monitoring and evaluation plan.

[c]Amount of rehabilitated roads consists of 39.6 kilometers along three road segments on Santiago Island and a 1 kilometer road associated with bridge construction on Santo Antão Island. Four bridges were constructed on Santo Antão Island as initially planned, although MCC did not have an associated indicator for tracking the number of bridges built.

[d]This indicator tracks completion as measured by cumulative progress payments to construction contractors divided by the total cost of the construction contracts.

[e]Completion of all roads and bridges occurred after the end of year 3 of the compact. We did not attempt to estimate the amount of work that was completed at the end of year 3.

MCC reduced the scope of road rehabilitations but maintained the scope of bridge construction work after redesigns of original plans led to increased costs.[15]

- *Roads.* MCA-Cape Verde awarded a $12.6 million contract to rehabilitate five roads, totaling 62.2 kilometers, in April 2006. Subsequent redesign of the road plans, to more accurately reflect the extent of work required,[16] increased the cost of the contract to $18.5 million and extended the contract completion date from 30 months to 44 months after the May 2006 work start date.[17] To keep the work within funding limits, MCC and MCA-Cape Verde reduced the scope of planned rehabilitation to three roads totaling 39.6 kilometers. Work was completed for the first road (Road 1) in June 2009; for the second (Road 4) in July 2009; and for the third (Road 2) in January 2010.[18]

- *Bridges.* MCA-Cape Verde awarded a $3.4 million contract in November 2006 to build the four bridges. Subsequent redesigns of the planned construction, intended to make the bridges more durable, increased the contract value to $5.8 million[19] and extended the completion date from 12 months to 34 months after the December 2006 work start date. Bridge work was completed in October 2009.

Figure 8 shows the locations of the planned roads, with photographs of the rehabilitated roads, on Santiago Island.

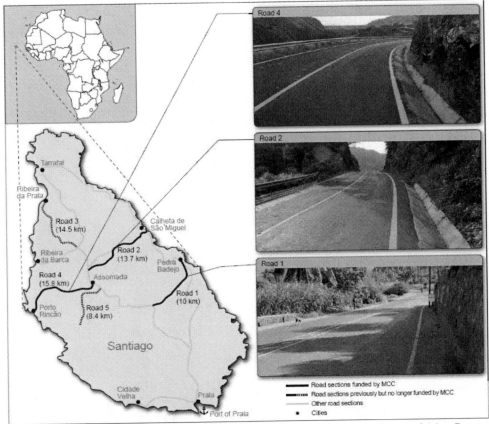

Sources: GAO synthesis of MCA furnished project maps; GAO (photographs); and Map Resources (base map)

Note: Roads 1, 4, and 2 were completed in June 2009, July 2009, and January 2010, respectively. Roads 3 and 5 were deleted from MCC's contract and are being constructed by the Cape Verde government with a loan from the government of Portugal.

Figure 8. Planned and Rehabilitated Roads on Santiago Island, Cape Verde Infrastructure Project.

Roads and Bridges: Challenges

On beginning work for the Cape Verde roads and bridges activity, MCA-Cape Verde found that the designs did not accurately represent the extent of work required. For example, inadequate topographic information in the road designs resulted in designs that did not accurately reflect the amount of earthwork involved in improving the roads. Revisions to the designs allowed for improvements to make the structures more durable: additional drainage culverts, concrete lining of ditches, rip-rap[20] placement to protect roads from erosion and landslides, and increased bridge heights to provide more clearance for water.

Roads and Bridges: Quality

To provide management control and ensure quality for the Cape Verde roads and bridges activity, MCA-Cape Verde established an organizational structure consistent with MCC's management structure for infrastructure projects. The management organization for the Cape Verde roads and bridges activity consisted of a project manager for MCA-Cape Verde; a project manager for the activity's implementing entity, the Cape Verde transportation ministry; two MCA-contracted independent construction supervisors, one for roads and one for bridges; and an MCC-contracted independent engineering consultant, who provided oversight on both the roads and bridges construction contracts.

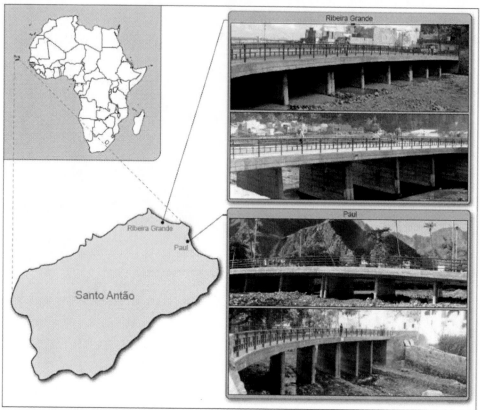

Sources: GAO synthesis of MCA furnished project maps; Map Resources (base map); and GAO (photographs).

Figure 9. Bridges Constructed on Santo Antão Island, Cape Verde Infrastructure Project.

In general, work on the roads and bridges activities met quality requirements. However, the new infrastructure is subject to damage from sometimes harsh environmental conditions, and the Cape Verde government faces challenges in funding needed maintenance and ensuring the infrastructure's sustainability.

Quality of roads. Work completed for the roads activity was performed according to contractual requirements, generally met quality standards, and should enable the infrastructure to function for the duration of its design life,[21] according to the construction supervisor's progress reports and members of the activity's management organization. However, the mountainous terrain through which the roads were built presents hazards such as landslides and erosion from storm water runoff. According to the construction supervisor, the low volume of traffic for which the roads were built influenced decisions to limit some design features, such as removing steep roadside slopes and installing or repairing drainage structures and retaining walls, to control costs. For example, in consideration of limiting costs and reducing environmental impacts, the construction supervisor authorized less earthwork than had been proposed by the construction contractor when the road activity was being redesigned. This resulted in the exposure of some road sections to potential damage from landslides and water runoff because they are adjacent to steep slopes.[22] We observed areas along Road 2, in particular, where the road structure had failed, apparently as the result of insufficient drainage or weakened retaining structures that were unable to withstand water flows during rain storms. We also observed repair efforts by the Cape Verde government's road maintenance contractor that illustrate how sustained attention to maintenance will be needed to keep the road network functional (see fig. 6 on page 27).

Quality of bridges. Work completed for the bridges activity was performed according to contractual requirements, met quality standards, and should enable the infrastructure to function for the duration of its 50- year design life, according to the construction supervisor's progress reports and the MCA-Cape Verde project manager. The construction supervisor's final report noted that the bridges may have been overdesigned, with more concrete and reinforcing steel than required for structural stability.[23] The report also indicated that the type of cement used in the concrete mix was different, and less resistive to corrosion, than the type originally specified. To protect the bridges from corrosion, due to their proximity to the ocean shore, the construction contractor applied a waterproofing treatment to the concrete that was used to construct the bridges. However, use of this waterproofing treatment creates a new maintenance requirement for the Cape Verde government to manage.

Roads and Bridges: Sustainability

MCC determined that stable maintenance financing was critical to sustaining its roads and bridges activity and established this as a condition for disbursement of compact funds. Over the course of the compact, the Cape Verde government's road institute developed its capacity for collecting user fees that it directed to funding maintenance for the national road network.[24] However, according to Cape Verde government officials, the agency lacks adequate funds for road maintenance. For example, road institute officials indicated that lack of funds for road maintenance is the greatest challenge facing the agency, and other Cape Verde government officials told us that current funding for road maintenance would meet less than half of requirements.

CAPE VERDE WATERSHED MANAGEMENT AND AGRICULTURAL SUPPORT PROJECT

Water Management and Soil Conservation Activity

MCC disbursed approximately $6 million for the water management and soil conservation activity, which was designed to improve natural resource management and increase agricultural productivity in three watersheds—Faja (São Nicolau Island), Mosteiros (Fogo Island), and Paul (Santo Antão Island)—through the construction of water management and distribution infrastructure.

Water Management and Soil Conservation: Results

MCC met some key original and final targets for the water management and soil conservation activity (see table 8 for key performance results for the water management and soil conservation activity). Because the activity was rescoped and construction delayed, the agency expects that agricultural productivity will be delayed. For example, MCC did not meet its original or final target for the volume of water available in the three watersheds at compact end. MCC achieved approximately 353,000 cubic meters for the volume of available water in the three watersheds at compact end, which was about 40 percent of the original target of approximately 875,000 cubic meters and about 76 percent of the final target of approximately 466,000 cubic meters. According to MCC, since the water was delayed, the agency does not expect immediate changes in agricultural productivity.

**Table 8. Key Performance Results for Water Management
and Soil Conservation Activity, Cape Verde**

Indicator	Original target	Final target	Final result	Percentage of original target met	Percentage of final target met
Reservoirs constructed	28	28	28	100	100
Volume of available water (m3)	875,355	465,800[a]	352,978	40	76
Tons of solid material retained through dikes[b]	25,552	25,552	46,763	183	183

Source: GAO analysis of Millennium Challenge Corporation data.

Notes: We considered the original target to be that which was first documented for each performance indicator, in either the 2006, 2008, or 2010 monitoring and evaluation plan, and the final target to be that which was documented in the 2010 monitoring and evaluation plan. In addition, the final results in this table reflect the results achieved by compact completion, although some activities continue after the compact completion and continue to achieve results.

[a]The target for this indicator was changed to 627,500 cubic meters in the 2008 monitoring and evaluation plan and further changed to 465,800 in the 2010 monitoring and evaluation plan.

[b]MCC established this indicator to measure the amount of arable land conserved through the use of rural soil conservation and water catchment infrastructure.

Responding to environmental concerns identified during implementation, MCC rescoped the activity from a combination of wells and reservoirs to only reservoirs, which delayed completion and operation of water management infrastructure as well as the adoption of drip irrigation. Following a 2-year delay in constructing water management infrastructure, not all reservoirs were operational at compact end.[25] As of January 2011, MCC reported all 28 reservoirs constructed were operational. MCC officials, the contractor, and some farmers we met with in Cape Verde said that farmers were slow to adopt drip irrigation because of the delay in the construction of infrastructure and the low water availability. MCC also reported that, for fully functional water systems, adoption of drip irrigation was slow, partially due to the completion of works coinciding with the rainy season. For example, during our visit to one reservoir in the Paul watershed in December 2010, we found that five of the seven available drip irrigation connections were hooked up to farm plots. Figure 10 shows a connected farm plot.

Source: GAO.

Figure 10. Irrigated Participant Farm, Cape Verde Watershed Management and Agricultural Support Project.

Water Management and Soil Conservation: Sustainability

MCC and the government of Cape Verde took some initial steps to enhance the sustainability of completed water management infrastructure. For instance, in January 2009, the government of Cape Verde's National Water Council established a water-fee structure for the three watersheds. MCC reported that it was actively engaged with the government to develop the water-fee policy, which was a condition required for MCC disbursements. In addition, communities and water users are responsible for maintenance of the water management infrastructure. The Cape Verde agricultural ministry and an MCA-Cape Verde contractor also worked with local community water associations, composed of farmers and other water users, to develop water management plans for each watershed. However, during our visit to Cape Verde, we found that the National Water Council had not begun collecting water fees in one of the three watersheds.

Table 9. Key Performance Results for Agribusiness Development Services Activity, Cape Verde

Indicator	Original target	Final target	Final result	Percentage of original target met	Percentage of final target met
Number of farmers trained[a]	800	800	553	69	69
Number of farmers adopting drip irrigation	337	337	106	32	32
Hectares under improved or new irrigation[b]	121	111	13.4	11	12
Construct and equip postharvest centers[d]	3	1[e]	1[f]	33	100

Source: GAO analysis of Millennium Challenge Corporation data.

Notes: We considered the original target to be that which was first documented for each performance indicator, in either the 2006, 2008, or 2010 monitoring and evaluation plan, and the final target to be that which was documented in the 2010 monitoring and evaluation plan. In addition, the final results in this table reflect the results achieved by compact completion, although some activities continue after the compact completion and continue to achieve results.

[a]The "number of farmers trained" indicator is the number of farmers trained in at least three of five training areas.

[b]MCC renamed the original indicator "Area irrigated with drip irrigation" to reflect a modified definition in its 2010 monitoring and evaluation plan.

[c]The change in target for this indicator was documented in the 2008 monitoring and evaluation plan.

[d]MCC revised this process milestone indicator to "construct and equip postharvest center in Santo Antão island," one of the three watersheds, in its 2010 monitoring and evaluation plan.

[e]The change in target for this indicator was documented in the 2010 monitoring and evaluation plan.

[f]The Cape Verde agricultural ministry indicated that it plans to pursue construction of the two postharvest centers designed under the MCC project on the islands of São Nicolau and Fogo. The Ministry reported that it has committed to fund the construction of the two postharvest centers in its 2011 budget.

Agribusiness Development Services Activity

MCC disbursed approximately $5 million for the agribusiness development services activity, which consisted at compact signature of several activities to increase the productivity and marketing of agricultural products by farmers and agribusinesses, including training of farmers,[26] technical assistance in postharvest agricultural techniques, and construction of postharvest packing and quality control centers.

Agribusiness Development Services: Results

MCC did not meet key original targets and most final targets for the agribusiness development services activity (see table 9 for key performance results for the agribusiness development services activity). For example, MCC reported that 553 farmers were trained in at least three out of five subject areas by compact end, achieving 69 percent of the target of 800 trained farmers.

MCC rescoped the agribusiness development services activity following implementation challenges, and the contractor reported challenges in implementing the activity and achieving targets.

- *Small agribusiness sector.* MCC reported that it eliminated the activity's focus on the agribusiness sector after finding that sector in Cape Verde to be small, but continued to work with the broader agricultural sector.
- *Limited training capacity of Cape Verde agricultural ministry staff.* MCA-Cape Verde reported that it had originally planned for the Cape Verde agricultural ministry to implement the farmer training activity; however, when it found that the ministry did not have the capacity to train farmers, it hired a contractor to assist in implementation of the farmer training activity and other aspects of the agribusiness development services activity.
- *Limited authority of contractor over Cape Verde agricultural ministry staff.* The contractor reported that its inability to directly train farmers and lack of authority over ministry field staff trainers made it difficult to meet the training targets.[27]
- *Limited targeting of farmer trainings.* The contractor reported that using the Cape Verde agricultural ministry's farmer training list, which was not targeted, resulted in a significant portion of time and resources spent on beneficiaries that had little interest in the training and saw little value in attending training sessions.[28] We spoke with several farmers in one watershed in Cape Verde who said the training had been helpful, but most were unable to specify which training they had taken, new information they had learned, or new techniques they had applied on their farms.

Agribusiness Development Services: Sustainability

The MCA-Cape Verde contractor took steps to promote sustainability of agribusiness development activities, and the Cape Verde agricultural ministry has expressed interest in continuing certain activities beyond the end of the compact, but MCC and the contractor have expressed concern about the sustainability of some activities. For example, the contractor took steps to promote the sustainability of the agribusiness development services activity after compact completion, including developing training materials for the Cape Verde agricultural ministry, helping establish and train farmers associations, and implementing a farm-to-market pilot project for testing postharvest practices along the produce value chain. The Cape Verde agricultural ministry reported that it will continue training farmers through its extension centers using training materials developed under the compact activity. However, the contractor reported that even after receiving training under the compact, all ministry field staff did not have the capacity to train farmers, given their work loads. For example, the contractor stated that ministry field staff had multiple responsibilities, including involvement in multiple donors' agriculture-related programs.

The Cape Verde agricultural ministry has also taken steps to privatize management of the postharvest center, including a commitment in February 2010 to finance the costs of operating the postharvest center and advertisement in June 2010 for a private management team. However, the postharvest center was not in operation as of December 2010 and had not yet been privatized.[29] According to MCC officials, the ministry did not contract with a private management team and has established a government management team to manage operations for the next 2 years. MCC reported that it has flagged privatization of the postharvest center as an issue critical to the sustainability of the project. MCC stated that it has received assurances from the ministry that it intends to privatize operations, but MCC is unclear about the timeline.

Access to Credit Activity

MCC disbursed $600,000 for the access to credit activity, which was designed to meet demands in the three watersheds for financing drip irrigation, working capital, and agribusiness development.

Access to Credit: Results

MCC exceeded key original and final targets for the access to credit activity (see table 10 for key performance results for the access to credit activity). For example, four eligible microfinance institutions (MFI) accessed the $600,000 MCC credit line to provide $617,000 agricultural loans. MCC and the contractor stated that they were optimistic about continued demand for drip irrigation credit once water management infrastructure was fully operational and the rainy season ended.

Table 10. Key Performance Results for Access to Credit Activity, Cape Verde

Indicator	Original target	Final target	Final result	Percentage of original target met	Percentage of final target met
Value of agricultural and rural loans	$600,000	$600,000	$617,000	103	103
Percentage of MFI loan portfolio past due more than 90 days[a]	5	5	4	Exceeds target[b]	Exceeds target[b]

Source: GAO analysis of Millennium Challenge Corporation data.

Notes: We considered the original target to be that which was first documented for each performance indicator, in either the 2006, 2008, or 2010 monitoring and evaluation plan, and the final target to be that which was documented in the 2010 monitoring and evaluation plan. In addition, the final results in this table reflect the results achieved by compact completion, although some activities continue after the compact completion and continue to achieve results.

[a]The "Portfolio Risk above 90 Days" indicator is the value of all MFI loans with one or more installment of principal past due more than 90 days as a percentage of the gross loan portfolio.

[b]According to MCC, repayment rates were very high for the project, exceeding the target, due to strong portfolio management.

Access to Credit: Sustainability

According to MCC, as a result of the strong performance of the four MFI loan portfolios, MCC converted its loans to each MFI into grants at the end of the compact, enhancing the sustainability of agricultural credit efforts. Following an evaluation of the MFIs' operational and financial performance, MCA-Cape Verde determined that all four MFIs were eligible for conversion of MCC loans under the credit line to grants. MCC converted its loans into grants by the end of 2010. Two MFIs reported that they had not previously provided loans in the agricultural sector in certain locations, but following a positive experience with the MCC credit line, they anticipate continued growth of these loan portfolios.

MCC did not require that an oversight entity monitor the MFIs' use of grant funds for agricultural purposes beyond the end of the compact, but the agency included limited oversight terms in the grant conversion that may promote sustainability. The agency specified in its grant terms that funds are to be used solely for agribusiness and drip irrigation credit and are subject to MCC audit for the first 2 years.

CAPE VERDE PRIVATE SECTOR DEVELOPMENT PROJECT

Partnership to Mobilize Investment Activity

MCC disbursed about $400,000 for the partnership to mobilize investment activity, which was intended to help the Cape Verde government identify, prioritize, design, and implement interventions to increase investment in priority sectors.

Table 11. Key Performance Results for Partnership to Mobilize Investment Activity, Cape Verde

Indicator	Original target	Final target	Final result	Percentage of original target met	Percentage of final target met
Value added in priority sectors above current trends	none set			Activity eliminated[a]	
Volume of private investment in priority sectors above current trends	none set			Activity eliminated[a]	
Volume of public investment in priority sectors above current trends	none set			Activity eliminated[a]	

Source: GAO analysis of Millennium Challenge Corporation data.

Notes: We considered the original target to be that which was first documented for each performance indicator, in either the 2006, 2008, or 2010 monitoring and evaluation plan, and the final target to be that which was documented in the 2010 monitoring and evaluation plan.

[a] All components of this activity were eliminated except the establishment of a private credit bureau, which did not have an associated indicator.

Partnership to Mobilize Investment: Results

MCC had not funded private sector investments in priority sectors for the partnership to mobilize investment activity by the end of the compact, but had funded the creation of a private credit bureau during the administrative closeout period (see table 11 for key performance results for the partnership to mobilize investment activity). MCC had initially allocated $5 million for this activity, but MCC, the World Bank, and the government of Cape Verde were unable to agree on which priority sectors should receive investment support. Therefore, MCC reallocated funds from this activity to the compact's infrastructure project. However, MCC funded technical assistance to support the creation of a private credit bureau. In January 2011, after the end of the compact and during the administrative closeout period, the Chambers of Commerce signed a contract with an investment partner to create a private credit bureau. Upon signature of this contract, MCA-Cape Verde provided $250,000 to the Chambers of Commerce to invest in the credit bureau.[30]

Partnership to Mobilize Investment: Sustainability

MCC took steps to support the new credit bureau's operational and financial sustainability by requiring a private sector partnership and private sector investments to be in place before MCC provided support for the activity. Private ownership may provide an incentive to enhance the sustainability of the credit bureau.

Financial Sector Reform Activity

MCC disbursed $1.4 million for the financial sector reform activity, which consisted of technical assistance to support the development of microfinance institutions and government efforts to expand access to the primary market for government securities.

Table 12. Key Performance Results for Financial Sector Reform Activity, Cape Verde

Indicator	Original target	Final target	Final result	Percentage of original target met	Percentage of final target met
Microfinance institutions operationally self-sufficient	4 of 8	4 of 5[a]	5 of 5	125	125
Microfinance institutions financially self-sufficient	3 of 8	3 of 5[a]	3 of 5	100	100
Percentage of MFI loan portfolio past due more than 30 days[b]	14%	14%	10%	139	139
Percentage of government securities held outside of financial institutions and government agencies	8%		Activity component eliminated		

Notes: We considered the original target to be that which was first documented for each performance indicator, in either the 2006, 2008, or 2010 monitoring and evaluation plan, and the final target to be that which was documented in the 2010 monitoring and evaluation plan.

[a]The change in target for this indicator was documented in the 2010 monitoring and evaluation plan.

[b]This indicator measures the value of all MFI loans that have at least one installment of principal past due for more than 30 days as a percentage of the gross loan portfolio.

Financial Sector Reform: Results

MCC met or exceeded its original and final targets, but eliminated a key target for the financial sector reform activity (see table 12 for key performance results for the financial sector reform activity). For example, MCC met or exceeded its targets for MFI operational and financial self-sufficiency. According to MCC officials, technical assistance to the government of Cape Verde under the compact also helped produce financial sector reforms, but MCC eliminated funding for financial software to implement reforms following procurement delays.[31]

Under this activity, MCC funded technical assistance to eight MFIs in several areas, including accountability and internal controls, lending methodologies, and client services, to support their operational efficiency and financial sustainability. According to two MFI representatives we spoke with during our visit to Cape Verde, the assistance they received helped professionalize MFI credit agents and provided them with technical competence to develop and market loan products for the agricultural sector.

Financial Sector Reform: Sustainability

The MFIs that received technical assistance achieved operational and financial self-sufficiency, which will enable them to continue their agricultural loan operations. In addition, according to MCC, the Cape Verde government agreed to fund the software with country funds and completed the financial sector reforms, showing strong country ownership and commitment to compact goals.

APPENDIX III:
HONDURAS COMPACT RESULTS

Honduras Compact Background

Honduras, with a population of about 7.2 million, was classified as a low-income country with a per capita income of $1,820 for fiscal year 2011.[1] U.S. development assistance accounts for about 13 percent of total assistance to Honduras over the last 10 years, making the United States its fourth-largest donor.

Table 13. Structure of Honduras Compact, at Signature

Project	Planned Activities (funding allocation)	Objective	Expected Beneficiaries
Transportation	• Highway CA-5 ($96.4 million): The improvement of two segments of Highway CA-5 totaling 109 kilometers, including 50 kilometers between Taulabe and Comayagua (the "North Segment") and 59 kilometers between Vila de San Antonio and Tegucigalpa (the "South Segment") • Secondary road ($21.3 million): The upgrade of key secondary routes to improve the access of rural communities to markets, totaling an upgrade of 91 kilometers of secondary roads • Weight control system ($4.7 million): The construction of an effective vehicle weight control system and the issuance of contracts to operate it effectively • Transportation project manager ($3.3 million)	Reduce transportation costs between targeted production centers and national, regional, and global markets	1) Users of improved roads that result in lower transportation costs to markets and social service delivery points (e.g., hospitals, schools) 2) Employees and owners of urban and rural businesses that rely on the Honduran road network The Transportation Project was also expected to have a significant economic impact in the greater Central American region since it constitutes a key component of the Atlantic Corridor

Table 13. (Continued)

Project	Planned Activities (funding allocation)	Objective	Expected Beneficiaries
Rural development	• Farmer training and development ($27.4 million): The provision of technical assistance in the production and marketing of high-value horticulture crops • Farm-to-market roads ($21.5 million): The construction and improvement of feeder roads to connect farms to markets, totaling approximately 1,500 kilometers of rural roads • Farmer access to credit ($13.8 million): The provision of technical assistance to institutions, loans to such institutions, and support in expanding the national lien registry system • Agricultural Public Goods Grant Facility ($8 million): The provision of grants to fund agricultural "public goods" projects that the private sector cannot provide on its own • Rural development project manager ($1.5 million	Increase the productivity and business skills of farmers who operate small and medium-size farms and their employees	1) Program farmers whose productivity and business skills are improved 2) The communities of the program farmers who experience increased employment and reduced transportation costs to markets and social service delivery points (e.g., hospitals, schools) 3) The agricultural sectors, due to public goods and quasi-public goods funded by the Agricultural Public Goods Grants Facility
Program administration and monitoring and evaluation	• Program administration ($12.1 million): Support administration and implementation of the compact, including program management, oversight, and audit • Monitoring and evaluation ($5 million): The measurement and evaluation of progress toward the achievement of the compact goal and objectives.		

Source: GAO analysis of Millennium Challenge Corporation data.

MCC and the government of Honduras signed a 5-year compact in June 2005, which entered into force in September 2005 and ended in September 2010. The compact, for which MCC provided $215 million in funding at compact signature, consisted of two projects.

- The *transportation project* was aimed at reducing transportation costs between targeted production centers and national, regional, and global markets. Activities include reconstructing portions of highways and secondary roads. Expected beneficiaries include road users and urban and rural businesses.
- The *rural development project* was aimed at increasing the productivity and business skills of farmers who operate small and medium-size farms and their employees. Activities include providing technical assistance to farmers in the production of high-

value crops and constructing and improving selected farm-to-market roads. Expected beneficiaries include trained farmers, their communities, and the agricultural sector.

HONDURAS TRANSPORTATION PROJECT

CA-5 Highway Reconstruction Activity

CA-5 Highway: Objective

MCC allocated $96.4 million to reconstruct 109 kilometers of the CA-5 highway.[2] The northern portion of the CA-5 highway connects Tegucigalpa—the capital of Honduras—to Puerto Cortes on the north coast, providing the primary route for import and export traffic between Puerto Cortes and the major production and consumption centers in and around San Pedro Sula, Comayagua, and Tegucigalpa. Figure 5 shows the locations of the CA-5 highway activities.

CA-5 Highway: Results

MCC disbursed $90.3 million for the CA-5 highway reconstruction activity by contract completion. MCC did not meet its target for kilometers of highway upgraded, completing 49.5 kilometers, or 45 percent of the target (see table 14 for key performance results for the CA-5 highway activity).[3]

Table 14. Key Performance Results for CA-5 Highway Reconstruction Activity, Honduras

Indicator	Original target	Final target	Final result	Percentage of original target met	Percentage of final target met
Kilometers of highway upgraded (km)	109	109	49.5	45	45

Source: GAO analysis of Millennium Challenge Corporation data.

Note: We considered the original target to be that which was first documented for each performance indicator, in either the 2006, 2008, or 2010 monitoring and evaluation plan, and the final target to be that which was documented in the 2010 monitoring and evaluation plan. In addition, the final results in this table reflect the results achieved by compact completion, although some activities continue after the compact completion and continue to achieve results.

MCC originally planned to fund all reconstruction included in four contracts for the four sections of the CA-5 highway. However, while completing final design, acquiring right-of-way, and beginning to award contracts, MCC determined that, because estimated costs had increased, it would be unable to complete the 109 kilometers within the 5-year compact timeframe and within the funding allocation of $96.4 million. Consequently, the Honduras government, working with MCC, arranged for a loan from the Central American Bank for Economic Integration (CABEI) to fund up to $130 million of the CA-5 reconstruction, and MCC reduced its allocation to $89.3 million. This brought total funding for the CA-5 reconstruction to $219 million, more than double the original estimate.[4] The $219 million MCC and CABEI allocated for the CA-5 reconstruction included $20.2 million—$19 million from MCC and $1.2 million from CABEI—for land acquisition and relocation costs; $195 million—$70.3 million from MCC and $124.8 million from CABEI—for construction supervision and construction contract costs; and $3.4 million from CABEI for other consulting and administrative costs.

Varying amounts of the $195 million in construction supervision and construction contract work were completed in each section of the highway by the end of the compact.[5]

- *Section 1.* After completing the design for section 1 of the CA-5 highway, MCC lacked sufficient funding to construct the 24.3-kilometer section. Construction began in June 2010 with about $75 million in CABEI funds and was about 5 percent complete when the compact ended. MCC expects section 1 to be completed by June 2012.

However, in March 2011, MCC officials stated that additional work added to the contract may require MCA-Honduras to extend that date.[6]

- *Section 2.* Construction began in February 2009 on the $68 million, 33.3-kilometer section 2 of the CA-5 highway and was about half completed when the compact ended. MCC allocated about $21 million (31 percent) and CABEI allocated about $47 million (69 percent) for section 2, with MCC's allocation covering the cost of about 10 kilometers of constructed road. Construction was scheduled to be completed by March 2011, but MCA-Honduras is considering extending the completion date to September 2011 because of additional construction work, rain, and other delays.
- *Sections 3 and 4.* Reconstruction is 100 percent complete for 49.5 kilometers of the highway's two northernmost sections—sections 3 and 4—with about $52 million allocated to the activities. This amount included MCC funding of about $49 million (94 percent) and CABEI funding of about $3 million (6 percent). See figure 11 for before and after pictures of section 4.

Source: MCA-Honduras.

Note: After reconstruction, pavement includes four through lanes, added turn lanes, and improved pavement surface.

Figure 11. CA-5 Section 4 before and after Reconstruction, Honduras Transportation Project.

CA-5 Highway: Challenges

Contract bid amounts, land acquisition costs, and contract modification costs exceeded MCC's estimates, causing overall costs for reconstructing the CA-5 highway to exceed allocations for the activity and preventing MCC from achieving its original target, according to MCA-Honduras officials.

- *Construction contract bid amounts.* Construction contract bid amounts for reconstructing each section of the CA-5 highway were significantly higher than MCC's initial estimates, owing in part to requests from the Honduras government for changes in scope and changes in design, according to MCA-Honduras officials.
  Section 1. The construction contract bid for section 1 exceeded estimated costs by 15 percent.
  Section 2. The construction contract bid for section 2 exceeded estimated costs by 112 percent. The original design was to increase the road from two to three lanes in some areas. However, the Honduras government requested that the entire section have four lanes, increasing the travel lane pavement area by 43 percent.
  Section 3. The construction contract bid for section 3 exceeded estimated costs by 11 percent, after the Honduras government requested a third lane for passing to improve traffic flow in a few areas with steep inclines.
  Section 4. The construction contract bid for section 4 exceeded estimated costs by about 75 percent. The Honduras government requested that four lanes be installed in some portions of the section and that concrete, rather than asphalt, be used for the pavement. In addition, according to MCA-Honduras officials, 12 kilometers of a special base treatment were added to support the concrete pavement.[7]
- Land acquisition costs. The additional costs of acquiring right-of-way for the additional lanes and relocating adjacent housing and businesses exceeded initial estimates by almost 600 percent. According to MCA-Honduras officials, the original estimate for land acquisition and relocation was $3.1 million, but the final budgeted cost was about $20.2 million. Officials said that due-diligence studies conducted before the design phase had not included the costs of resettling residents and business owners from acquired land. In addition, the original land acquisition costs were estimated based on the land's official value for tax purposes rather than on its market value (which is typically higher), in accordance with normal practice in Honduras, and did not include relocation costs. MCA-Honduras officials said that, to accelerate the acquisition of land for the CA-5, they worked with the Honduras government to pass legislation that allows citizens to be reimbursed for market value land costs and relocation costs. According to MCC officials, relocation of the businesses provided economic benefits by allowing the business owners to retain their livelihood. In addition, businesses were grouped together to reduce traffic congestion related to cars stopping along the road and small chambers of commerce were developed to promote the businesses (see fig. 12).
- *Contract modifications.* Modifications of contracts during construction for sections 2, 3, and 4 raised CA-5 costs by about 6 percent, according to our review of construction supervision reports. A construction supervision official for section 2 stated that some of these increases were the result of road design plans with

insufficient detail, which required the construction of additional retaining walls, earthwork, and drainage pipes beyond those included in the contract plans. The construction supervision official for section 4 stated that the increases were due to the addition of drainage pipes and other items.

Source: MCA-Honduras.

Figure 12. Relocated Businesses (in front) and Homes (in rear), Honduras Transportation Project.

Secondary Roads Reconstruction Activity

Secondary Roads: Objective
MCC planned to reconstruct 91 kilometers of secondary roads, which connect rural roads to primary roads such as the CA-5 highway.[8]

Secondary Roads: Results
MCC disbursed $27.7 million to reconstruct 65.5 kilometers of secondary roads by compact completion. MCC met the final target of 65.5 kilometers of secondary road reconstructed after a reduction in the original target from 91 kilometers (see table 15 for key performance results for the secondary roads activity).

After accepting bids for the first secondary road construction contract, MCC agreed to a reduction in the target for reconstructing secondary roads because the cost of the reconstruction work greatly exceeded original estimates, according to MCA-Honduras officials. The officials also stated that the amount of planned MCC funding increased after the first contract was let because the bid amounts were more than estimated. According to the officials, the original estimated reconstruction cost was about $235,000 per kilometer, but the actual cost was about $422,000 per kilometer—an 80 percent increase.

Table 15. Key Performance Results for Secondary Roads Activity, Honduras

Indicator	Original target	Final target	Final result	Percentage of original target met	Percentage of final target met
Kilometers of secondary road upgraded (km)	91	65.5[a]	65.5	72	100

Source: GAO analysis of Millennium Challenge Corporation data.

Notes: We considered the original target to be that which was first documented for each performance indicator, in either the 2006, 2008, or 2010 monitoring and evaluation plan, and the final target to be that which was documented in the 2010 monitoring and evaluation plan.

[a]The target for this indicator was changed to 62 kilometers in the 2008 monitoring and evaluation plan and further changed to 65.5 kilometers in the 2010 monitoring and evaluation plan.

For the reduced target, MCA- Honduras selected 65.5 kilometers of secondary roads from among a group of roads expected to provide the highest rate of economic return by increasing vehicle speeds and reducing vehicle maintenance costs. The selected roads, located in three different parts of the country, were constructed through three separate contracts and were completed by the end of the compact. According to MCA-Honduras officials, the reconstructed roads have brought benefits such as improving the health of residents near the road by reducing airborne dust, improving access to land near the roads, attracting new farmers and laborers, and improving access to health clinics. Figure 13 shows the secondary roads before and after the reconstruction was completed.

Weight Control System Activity

Weight Control: Objective

MCC allocated $4.7 million to facilitate the implementation of a weight control system, including activities such as constructing eight truck weigh stations and the purchase of ancillary equipment along the CA-5, to help limit damage to the roads from overweight vehicles.[9]

Weight Control: Results

MCC disbursed about $90,000 for the weight control system activity. MCC terminated funding for this activity in 2009 in response to the country's political situation (see table 16 for key performance results for the weight control activity).

MCC officials stated that prior to the decision to eliminate the activity, they worked with the Honduran government to enact legislation allowing Fondo Vial—the Honduran road maintenance agency[10]—to regulate and enforce weight limits on Honduran roads. According to the Honduran government and MCA-Honduras officials, the government is trying to develop a smaller weight control activity, with one permanent weigh station and two portable stations, to start enforcing weight limits on the CA-5. However, at the time of our visit in November 2010, the government had not established a definite plan or obtained funding for the activity, and MCC is no longer monitoring the activity to provide us with an update.

Comayagua-Ajuterique-La Paz

Sonaguera-KM-35 (El Coco)

Source: MCA-Honduras.

Note: The top two pictures show that the road was widened (requiring the reconstruction of a building), the road surface was paved, and sidewalks were added. The bottom two pictures show that the road was widened with shoulders, the road surface was paved, the culvert under the road was repaired and widened, and pavement markings were added.

Figure 13. Secondary Roads before and after Reconstruction, Honduras Transportation Project.

Table 16. Key Performance Results for Weight Control Activity, Honduras

Indicator	Original target	Final target	Final result	Percentage of original target met	Percentage of final target met
Number of weight stations built	8[a]	Activity eliminated			

Source: GAO analysis of Millennium Challenge Corporation data.

Notes: We considered the original target to be that which was first documented for each performance indicator, in either the 2006, 2008, or 2010 monitoring and evaluation plan, and the final target to be that which was documented in the 2010 monitoring and evaluation plan.

[a]The target for this indicator was changed to 3 in the 2008 monitoring and evaluation plan, and the indicator was removed in the 2010 monitoring and evaluation plan.

MCC officials stated that prior to the decision to eliminate the activity, they worked with the Honduran government to enact legislation allowing Fondo Vial—the Honduran road maintenance agency[10]—to regulate and enforce weight limits on Honduran roads. According to the Honduran government and MCA-Honduras officials, the government is trying to develop a smaller weight control activity, with one permanent weigh station and two portable stations, to start enforcing weight limits on the CA-5. However, at the time of our visit in

November 2010, the government had not established a definite plan or obtained funding for the activity, and MCC is no longer monitoring the activity to provide us with an update.

Transportation Project: Quality

To provide management control and ensure quality for the Honduras transportation project, MCA-Honduras established an organization consistent with MCC's management structure for infrastructure projects.

The management organization for infrastructure projects included a MCA-Honduras transportation director and staff; contracted project management consultant who also performed design engineer services; and contracted independent construction supervisors, who reviewed the work of the project construction contractors for the CA-5 highway and secondary roads.[11] MCC hired an independent engineering consultant to provide them with independent reviews and recommendations of MCA-Honduras' design and construction activities.

In addition, MCA-Honduras implemented a quality control process, with independent construction supervisors and contractors ensuring that construction of the CA-5 highway and secondary roads followed designs.[12] The contractors were responsible for the primary testing, or quality control, and independent construction supervisors were responsible for a smaller amount of testing to confirm that the contractor's tests were accurate. In our review of contracts, we found that to implement the quality control plan, the independent construction supervisors and contractors conducted testing on certified testing equipment and kept records of daily activities and test results (see fig. 14).[13]

Concrete strength testing equipment   Soil strength testing equipment

Source: GAO.

Figure 14. Testing Equipment in Contractor's Laboratory for CA-5 Section 2, Honduras Transportation Project.

While the work on the CA-5 highway sections and secondary roads was conducted with a quality control process in place, we observed instances of roadside erosion, pavement roughness, surface slickness, landslides, steep slopes, and limited use of roadside safety measures that raised concerns about the quality of the completed works.

- *Roadside erosion.* We found problems with erosion in some areas that had not been adequately revegetated, resulting in drop-offs at the edge of pavement, undermining of sidewalks, and filling of drainage areas (see fig. 15). At one site, construction supervision officials stated that revegetation was included in the contract to control erosion, but they decided not to have the contractor install it because it was dry season and the revegetation would not survive. At another location, there was no erosion control included in the design of a drainage way, resulting in erosion from rains. If these erosion problems are not resolved during construction, they will present maintenance challenges that will require additional funding.

Proper revegetation of fill slopes along CA-5

CA-5 Section 4: Lack of revegetation along edge of drainage ditch resulting in erosion

Secondary road: Lack of revegetation of fill slope resulting in erosion of fill behind and under sidewalk

Source: GAO.

Figure 15. Revegetation along Reconstructed CA-5 Highway and Secondary Road, Honduras Transportation Project.

- *Pavement roughness.* Pavements on the CA-5 section 3, the CA-5 section 4,[14] and secondary roads met contractual requirements for pavement smoothness; however, these CA-5 sections and secondary roads did not meet the International Roughness Index (IRI) targets that MCC and MCA-Honduras had set (see table 17).[15] The project designer had not included the IRI measures in the contract documents as a performance specification; thus, the contractor was not required to meet IRI targets, which resulted in increased long-term maintenance and user costs.

Table 17. Targeted and Achieved International Roughness Index (IRI) for CA-5 and Secondary Roads, Honduras

Road	Target IRI (meters/kilometer)	Achieved IRI (meters/kilometer)
CA-5 Section 1	1.9	Not completed
CA-5 Section 2	1.9	Not completed
CA-5 Section 3	1.9	2.2
CA-5 Section 4	1.9	3.2
Secondary roads	2.5	3.2

Source: GAO analysis of Millennium Challenge Corporation data.

Note: A lower IRI indicates greater smoothness, with 0 meters per kilometer indicating a perfectly smooth surface.

- *Surface slickness.* On two of the completed secondary roads, we observed some areas of asphalt seepage to the road surface—a condition known as asphalt flushing, which can affect road safety by reducing skid resistance, making the surface slick, or obscuring pavement markings (see fig. 16). According to MCA-Honduras officials, the contractor previously had taken action to mitigate the deficiency on the road with the worst flushing and felt it was satisfactorily repaired; however, it still existed at the time of our visit in November 2010.

Source: GAO.

Figure 16. Flushed Asphalt on Secondary Roads, Honduras Transportation Project.

- *Landslides.* Landslides were found along CA-5 in sections 2, 3, and 4. For example, in the unfinished section 2 of the CA-5, a large landslide made the uncompleted road almost impassable and caused delays in construction of section 2 (see fig. 17).[16] The geotechnical analysis identified by MCC as being those used to assess the risks of landslides in the original CA-5 highway designs did not include detailed analysis identifying how specific slopes would be stabilized, prevention measures that could be included in the construction plans, or an analysis of sections 3 and 4 of the CA-5. If such detailed analysis had been conducted during the design of the highway, the construction plans could have included such measures, thus reducing landslides and maintenance costs.

- *Steep slopes.* In several locations along one secondary road, we observed that the contractor had excavated soil to construct the road and left steeps slopes that were almost vertical, with soil eroding along the face of the excavation and filling drainage areas (see fig. 18). Construction supervisor officials said that this type of design and construction was typical in Honduras because there was limited right- of-way available to construct gentler slopes that were less subject to erosion. However, we observed some locations where there appeared to be sufficient right-of-way and the slope was still vertical. For example, on one contract where right-of-way was available, the construction supervision officials stated that the work was constructed with a steep slope to save the cost of the excavation. Although the decision to limit right-of-way acquisitions and reduce the amount of excavation reduces costs and reconstruction time, it increases the cost of long-term maintenance to ensure the pavement does not deteriorate due to inadequate drainage.

Source: GAO.

Note: The landslide occurred in an area of a new road construction. The rock and soil collapsed and almost covered the entire roadway, delaying construction until a new construction plan was designed.

Figure 17. Landslide in CA-5 Section 2, Honduras Transportation Project.

Erosion of cut area into drainage due to slope of cut and lack of revegetation.

Source: GAO.
Note: In part due to the steep slope, the excavated area is eroding and blocking the roadside drainage.

Figure 18. Erosion of Steep Slope along Secondary Road, Honduras Transportation Project.

Inadequate or inconsistent traffic safety measures. We found inadequate or inconsistent use of traffic safety measures on the completed CA-5 sections and secondary roads:[17]

- Concrete barrier wall was installed along retaining walls with drop-offs, but guardrail was not generally installed along steep embankments and drop-offs (see fig. 19).
- Guardrail with safety end treatments or crash cushions to protect motorists was not installed at the ends of most concrete barrier walls and concrete bridges (see fig. 19).
- Guardrail was installed to protect vehicles from concrete bridge railing ends on one secondary road but not on another, in part due to limited funding for the second road, according to MCC officials.
- Solid pavement centerlines were installed in a different manner on one secondary road than on the other two roads, with the one road not following design standards that MCC officials said they generally used for the activity. MCC officials attributed the lack of uniform centerlines to one road contract having less detailed specifications than the other two road contracts, resulting in the contractor using a different standard supplied by the Honduran transportation ministry. MCC asserted that motorist safety was not affected; however, this approach differs from the traffic controls used in the United States, where uniformity of traffic control devices, such as pavement markings, is considered vital to their effectiveness, promoting highway safety and efficiency and minimizing the occurrence of crashes.[18]

MCC officials expressed confidence in the safety of the completed CA-5 sections and secondary roads, stating that the design of the road reconstruction had met Central American standards; that the Honduras transportation ministry had accepted and approved the proposed designs; and that the traffic safety devices included in the reconstruction exceeded those traditionally used on Honduran roads. However, MCC officials acknowledged that they did not perform a cost-benefit analysis of additional traffic control and traffic safety devices during the design of the contracts and that funding limitations had affected the extent to which safety improvements were included in the construction contracts. According to MCC, additional safety improvements were installed when funding was available.[19]

No guardrail protecting vehicles from dropping into the drain or hitting the retaining wall at the outlet of the culvert

Source: GAO.

No safety end treatment (crash cushion or guardrail) to protect motorists from colliding with the end of the concrete bridge rail (see circled area).

Source: MCA-Honduras.

Figure 19. Locations on Completed CA-5 without Traffic Safety Devices, Honduras Transportation Project.

Transportation Project: Sustainability

Uncertainty over Honduras government funding for road maintenance calls into question the likely sustainability of the MCC-funded roads. According to the compact, the key issue for sustainability of the transportation project is routine, periodic, and emergency road maintenance, such as sealing cracks, repainting the pavement markings, cleaning ditches and drainage structures, repairing potholes, resurfacing, and clearing landslides. Several of the quality deficiencies we observed— erosion, roughness, slickness, and landslides—will increase the amount and cost of maintenance needed over time, and failure to perform the planned maintenance may result in escalating maintenance needs. For example, without required maintenance,

- erosion may block drainage, causing road deterioration and undermining the sidewalks, pavements, or drainage structures, causing them to fail;
- increasingly rough pavement, as measured by the IRI, will likely require the road to be resurfaced sooner than planned and raise road user costs; and
- landslides may close roads, produce unexpected safety hazards, or block drainage, causing road deterioration.

However, several circumstances call into question the Honduran government's ability to provide the required maintenance over the 20-year period specified in the compact. MCC expressed concerns about whether the reconstructed roads would be maintained so as to sustain reductions in road users' travel costs. Contractors and construction supervisor officials also expressed a concern that, unless the Honduras government improved its level of road maintenance, the reconstructed roads would likely not be maintained.

Although MCC officials worked with the Honduras government to increase its funding of road maintenance from a precompact amount of $37 million in 2005 to $64 million in 2010, this funding is for maintenance of all roads on the official Honduran road network and not specifically for compact-funded roads.[20] In addition, the commitment did not specifically address road maintenance after 2010. With the increased funding, MCC officials stated that they expect that the Honduran government will maintain the MCC-funded sections of CA-5 and some of the key secondary roads, but are concerned that it may not be at the level required to maximize the road's life span.

The amount that the Honduran government has committed for road maintenance is less than required by law and needed for the roads. According to officials from the Honduras transportation ministry and documents prepared by Fondo Vial, the government's allocation for 2010 represents less than half of the road maintenance allocation required by Honduras law. These documents show that Honduras law requires the government to allocate 40 percent of a fuel tax for road maintenance.[21] However, according to our analysis of Fondo Vial documents, the percentage of fuel tax allocated for road maintenance has varied, from 27 percent in 2000 to 14 percent in 2006 to 19 percent in 2010, even though Fondo Vial's road maintenance plan recommends road maintenance be funded at $210 million annually—or about 60 percent of the fuel tax.

MCC's elimination of the vehicle weight control activity from the Transportation Project and the extent to which the Honduran government completes the activity in the future will affect the sustainability of the CA-5 road reconstruction. According to one Honduras government official, there is currently no control of overweight trucks shipping goods, and a large number of truckers exceed legal weight limits.[22] Without enforcement of weight limits on the CA-5 and other MCC-funded roads, the roads will deteriorate faster, reducing transportation cost savings and increasing road maintenance costs.

HONDURAS RURAL DEVELOPMENT PROJECT

Farmer Training and Development Activity

MCC disbursed $26.6 million for the farmer training and development activity, which was designed to improve the techniques and business skills of farmers, assist farmers in improving agricultural productivity, and achieve higher incomes from the production of high-value horticulture crops.[23]

Table 18. Key Performance Results for Farmer Training and Development Activity, Honduras

Indicator	Original target	Final target	Final result	Percentage of original target met	Percentage of final target met
Total recruited farmers receiving assistance	8,255	8,255	7,265	88	88
Program farmers harvesting high-value horticulture cropsa	7,340[b]	6000[c]	6029	82	100
Hectares harvesting high-value horticulture crops[a]	11,830[b]	8,400[c]	9,287	79	111
Business plans prepared by program farmers with technical assistance	6,480	6,960[d]	16,119	249	232

Source: GAO analysis of Millennium Challenge Corporation data.

Notes: We considered the original target to be that which was first documented for each performance indicator, in either the 2006, 2008, or 2010 monitoring and evaluation plan, and the final target to be that which was documented in the 2010 monitoring and evaluation plan. In addition, the final results in this table reflect the results achieved by compact completion, although some activities continue after the compact completion and continue to achieve results.

[a]To be counted for this indicator, the program farmer must (1) in the first year of participation, have a crop mix demonstrated to have an expected annual net income of at least $2000 per hectare; and (2) in the second year of participation, have earned a net income of at least $2000.

[b]This indicator was originally set with a higher target that was meant to be achieved after compact completion. As a result, this target represents the target that was originally scheduled to be accomplished by compact end.

[c]The change in target for this indicator was documented in the 2010 monitoring and evaluation plan.

[d]The target for this indicator was changed to 5,520 in the 2008 monitoring and evaluation plan and further changed to 6,960 in the 2010 monitoring and evaluation plan.

Farmer Training and Development: Results

MCC did not meet some of its original key targets, but it met or exceeded three of its four final targets for the farmer training and development activity (see table 18 for key performance results for the farmer training and development activity). For example, 6,029 farmers harvested high-value horticulture crops, which is 82 percent of the original target of

7,340 and which exceeds the final target of 6,000.[24] According to MCC, this target was reduced to provide additional technical assistance to those trained, to increase the sustainability of the assistance provided.

The farmer training activity provided a number of benefits for participating farmers. The program provided farmers with improved skills in crop choice and site selection, land preparation, soil and water management, and crop protection. A number of farmers in Honduras stated that, as a result of the training, they began growing different types of crops—for instance, switching from corn and beans to new higher-profit crops such as plantains, peppers, and onions—and using new agricultural techniques. Several farmers said they increased crop volumes, quality, and income. Figure 20 shows irrigation on a training participant farm.

Source: GAO.

Figure 20. Irrigation on Farmer Training and Development Activity Participant Farm, Honduras Rural Development Project.

Farmer Training and Development: Sustainability

According to the compact, the farmer training activity is to be sustained by program farmers who are able to maintain their new level of productivity and expand their business. In addition to providing technical assistance directly to farmers, the farmer training and development activity involved working with entities along the farm production value chain to enhance the sustainability of the activity after compact completion. For instance, the contractor emphasized involving the private sector in program activities, including buyers, wholesalers, processors, and input and equipment service providers. In addition, the farmer training activity also helped farmers form associations for growing and selling their products to increase the sustainability of techniques and production practices. According to farmers we spoke with, forming associations helped them sell to larger producers and encouraged certain producers to purchase goods directly from these farms, which had not happened previously.

However, according to the contractor and farmers we spoke with in Honduras, sustainability remains a concern for more than half of farmers receiving assistance. In its final report submitted to MCA, the contractor estimated that it takes approximately four to six production cycles for the new skills farmers obtain to become sustainable. According to the report, 90 percent to 95 percent of program farmers who began receiving assistance in the first 2 years of the program will continue using the new technologies. However, of the farmers who were recruited late—more than 50 percent of the total number of program farmers—half are expected to reach sustainability. Farmers in Honduras stated that, although they intended to continue using the new techniques, they were concerned about the ability of some farmers to sustain their new skills and overcome future challenges after the program ended. According to MCC officials, both the contractor and the farmers have an incentive for overstating potential sustainability challenges, as the contractor is interested in receiving additional funding and the farmers are seeking additional services.

Farm-to-Market Roads Activity

MCC disbursed $20.1 million for the farm-to-market roads activity, which was designed to improve rural roads that directly serve farms, providing durable, all-weather access to secondary and primary roads and ultimately improving access to markets and to social services.[25]

Farm-to-Market Roads: Results

MCC did not meet its original target but nearly achieved the revised target for the farm-to-market roads activity (see table 19 for key performance results for the farm-to-market roads activity). MCC funded the reconstruction of 495 kilometers of farm-to-market roads, or 33 percent of the original target of about 1,500. The target was reduced to 692 kilometers in the 2008 monitoring and evaluation plan and further reduced to 499 in the 2010 plan. Ultimately, MCC achieved 99 percent of the final revised target.

MCA-Honduras and MCC officials cited cost increases and compact changes as the primary reasons for the reduction in kilometers of farm-tomarket roads reconstructed. The partial termination of the Honduras compact in 2009, in response to the country's political situation, included termination of the uncommitted portion of the farm-to-market roads activity, representing approximately 93 kilometers of farm-to-market roads.

Table 19. Key Performance Results for Farm-to-Market Roads Activity, Honduras

Indicator	Original target	Final target	Final result	Percentage of original target met	Percentage of final target met
Kilometers of farm-to-market road upgraded	1,500	499[a]	495	33	99

Source: GAO analysis of Millennium Challenge Corporation data.

Notes: We considered the original target to be that which was first documented for each performance indicator, in either the 2006, 2008, or 2010 monitoring and evaluation plan, and the final target to be that which was documented in the 2010 monitoring and evaluation plan.

[a]The target for this indicator was changed to 692 kilometers in the 2008 monitoring and evaluation plan and further changed to 499 in the 2010 monitoring and evaluation plan.

In addition, in generating the original target, MCC used a per-kilometer cost estimate of $14,300, based on Fondo Vial quality, environmental, and social standards, but revised the estimate to $42,000 per kilometer because the Fondo Vial standards did not meet compact requirements. Furthermore, according to MCC officials, MCC chose to improve the durability of the roads built to increase the life of the roads by, for instance, adding drainage structures that reduce water damage. As a result, MCC funded fewer total kilometers of road.

The farm-to-market roads reconstructed were selected based on a list of proposed roads with an estimated economic rate of return of at least 12 percent. The reconstructed roads included 38 stretches of roads in 29 different municipalities and 10 departments throughout Honduras. With the completion of the roads, MCA-Honduras officials said that rural residents' travel times to more urbanized areas for access to markets and health centers had been reduced from 6 hours to 1 hour in some cases (see fig. 21).

Source: MCA-Honduras.

Figure 21. Farm-to-Market Roads before and after Reconstruction, Honduras Rural Development Project.

Farm-to-Market Roads: Sustainability

Lack of equipment, expertise, and funding for road maintenance by the municipalities where many reconstructed roads are located may affect the sustainability of the roads. Although Fondo Vial is responsible for maintaining some farm-to-market roads in Honduras, in many cases the roads are maintained by municipalities. According to MCA-Honduras officials, MCA-Honduras required municipalities to agree to co-finance a percentage of the road reconstruction activities, based on the poverty level of the community, as a condition for receiving funding. This co-financing could be made up of cash and in-kind contributions, such as materials. In addition, the municipality had to agree to permanently maintain the roadway.

However, the maintenance of the road and its associated benefits is a concern. MCA-Honduras officials stated that, although some municipalities may be acquiring additional equipment, the municipalities generally lack the equipment and expertise to maintain the roads. We found an example of this in one section of farm-to-market road where the road had washed out in a low area and maintenance was being performed by hand with little progress. MCA-Honduras had intended to help improve the municipalities' expertise in proper road maintenance procedures through training. However, no funds were available for the training after MCC funding was partially terminated partially as a result of the country's political situation.

Farmer Access to Credit Activity

MCC disbursed $12.8 million for the farmer access to credit activity, which consisted of three components—an agricultural credit trust fund, technical assistance for financial institutions, and a national property registry activity. This activity was designed to increase the supply of credit to rural borrowers, including program farmers and other agribusiness borrowers. The agricultural credit trust was a $6 million fund that was designed to provide loans to financial institutions to improve the availability of credit for rural lending. The technical assistance program provided assistance to financial and nonfinancial institutions to strengthen the institutions and assist them in developing products to more effectively serve the horticulture industry. The expansion of the national property registry activity was designed to create a new registry of movable property and facilitate implementation of legislation required to institute such a new system.[26]

Farmer Access to Credit: Results

According to MCA-Honduras officials, implementation challenges led to scope modifications and delays in the farmer access to credit activity. An initial lack of interest in accessing the agricultural credit fund among traditional banking institutions led MCA-Honduras and the contractors to refocus these activities on smaller sources of credit, such as financial intermediaries and input suppliers. These early challenges and resulting modifications meant that the agricultural credit fund was not effectively operating until late in the compact.

In addition, the agricultural credit fund, which was initially intended to target program farmers, was modified to include horticulture producers and businesses. According to MCC, small farmers making the transition to high-value horticulture used existing resources and savings and did not require access to credit until market opportunities expanded. Due to this delay in demand for credit and an interest in enhancing the sustainability of the lending activity, MCC and MCA-Honduras decided to expand the scope to include nonprogram farmers. Additionally, according to MCA-Honduras and MCC officials, some initial opposition to reforming collateral laws and a political transition in Honduras significantly increased the time it took to enact the new law.

MCC met most key original and all final targets for the farmer access to credit activity, following modifications and delays in implementation (see table 20 for key performance results for the farmer access to credit activity). For example, the total value of loans disbursed to farmers, agribusinesses, and other producers in the horticulture industry was $10.7 million—more than 170 percent of the revised target of $6 million and 37 percent of the original target of $28.8 million.[27] MCC noted that the updated indicator reflected changes in the operational guidelines for the use of loan fund resources that allowed nonprogram farmers, agribusinesses, and vendors in the horticulture industry to access credit. An MCC official noted that, as a result of rescoping the activity, MCA-Honduras was better able to reach beneficiary populations that likely would not have been served under the original design.

Table 20. Key Performance Results for Farmer Access to Credit Activity, Honduras

Indicator	Original target	Final target	Final result	Percentage of original target met	Percentage of final target met
Funds lent to financial intermediaries (millions of U.S. dollars)	6	6	7.2	120	120
Value of loans disbursed to the horticulture industry (millions of U.S. dollars)	28.8[a]	6[b]	10.7[c]	37	178
Lien registry equipment installed (percentage)	100 in year 3	100 in year 4b	100 in year 5	100 in year 5	100 in year 5

Source: GAO analysis of Millennium Challenge Corporation data.

Notes: We considered the original target to be that which was first documented for each performance indicator, in either the 2006, 2008, or 2010 monitoring and evaluation plan, and the final target to be that which was documented in the 2010 monitoring and evaluation plan. In addition, the final results in this table reflect the results achieved by compact completion, although some activities continue after the compact completion and continue to achieve results.

[a]This target ($28.8 million) was originally set for a similar indicator measuring the value of loans to program farmers, which was ultimately replaced by a number of indicators, including this indicator, and a lower target of $6 million.

[b]The change in target for this indicator was documented in the 2008 monitoring and evaluation plan.

[c]The value of this indicator ($10.7 million) includes the value of loans repaid and relent ($5.2 million) from the agricultural credit trust fund. This value ($10.7 million) does not include an additional $6.4 million in loans leveraged by financial institutions. According to MCC, adding the $6.4 million of funds leveraged by financial institutions to the $10.7 million of funds lent from the trust fund would result in double-counting of some funds. In addition, no target was established for the value of funds leveraged by financial institutions.

Financial institutions participating in both the agricultural credit fund and technical assistance activity also said that these activities helped them increase the credit they provide to the agricultural sector in Honduras. Representatives of one financial institution in particular said that the training helped them develop special products, which they were previously unfamiliar with, to provide credit to the agricultural sector.

Farmer Access to Credit: Sustainability

MCC took steps to increase the sustainability of the farmer access to credit activity through continuation of certain activities beyond the end of the compact. According to MCA-Honduras officials, since the agricultural credit fund activity started late, MCC arranged for the activity to continue after the end of the compact to achieve the intended effects. The agricultural credit fund will continue operating for 5 additional years after the compact is complete, which will enhance the sustainability of these loans to the horticultural industry.

Since MCA-Honduras and MCC will no longer oversee the agricultural credit fund after compact end, a committee chaired by Honduras's Ministry of Finance was set up to oversee the administration of the agricultural credit fund. According to the contractor of the technical assistance activity, many of the new financial tools adopted by financial institutions as a result of the technical assistance are self-sustaining, as they do not require external updates and are self-financing. In addition, we spoke with representatives of several financial institutions in Honduras who stated their intentions to continue lending to the agricultural sector and taking out loans with the agricultural credit fund after compact completion.

Agricultural Public Goods Grants Facility Activity

MCC disbursed $8.8 million for the agricultural public goods grants facility activity,[28] which funded 15 small competitive grants designed to support activities that enhance and accelerate the development of market-based commercial agriculture, particularly the horticultural sector.[29]

Agricultural Public Goods Grants Facility: Results

MCC met or exceeded some original and most final targets for the agricultural public goods grants facility activity (see table 21 for key performance results for the agricultural public goods grants facility activity). For example, irrigation systems reached more than 950 farmers, or almost 250 percent of the target for the number of farmers connected to the community irrigation system.

**Table 21. Key Performance Results for Agricultural Public
Goods Grants Facility Activity, Honduras**

Indicator	Original target	Final target	Final result	Percentage of original target met	Percentage of final target met
Number of hectares under irrigation	203	203	400	197	197
Number of farmers connected to the irrigation system	392	392	967	247	247
Number of farmers testing biological control agents	100	100	80	80	80
Number of coffee plants cloned	375	250[a]	259	69	104

Source: GAO analysis of Millennium Challenge Corporation data.
Notes: We considered the original target to be that which was first documented for each performance indicator, in either the 2006, 2008, or 2010 monitoring and evaluation plan, and the final target to be that which was documented in the 2010 monitoring and evaluation plan. In addition, the final results in this table reflect the results achieved by compact completion, although some activities continue after the compact completion and continue to achieve results.
[a]The change in target for this indicator was documented in the 2010 monitoring and evaluation plan.

Agricultural Public Goods Grants Facility: Sustainability

Agricultural public goods grants facility took longer than expected to implement, but MCA-Honduras officials were positive about sustainability. Public goods grants were planned for 18 months, but almost every activity had to be extended beyond the end of the originally planned completion date. Public goods grants were implemented by local organizations with the support of the local community to improve sustainability. According to some public goods grantees, local communities with irrigation systems received training in the maintenance of such systems and help establishing a user-fee structure that would fund maintenance costs. According to those grantees and MCA-Honduras officials, such arrangements will bolster the sustainability of the irrigation systems.

APPENDIX IV: COMMENTS FROM THE MILLENNIUM CHALLENGE CORPORATION

MILLENNIUM
CHALLENGE CORPORATION
UNITED STATES OF AMERICA

June 23, 2010

Mr. David Gootnick
Director, International Affairs and Trade
U.S. Government Accountability Office
441 G Street, NW
Washington, DC 20548

Re: MCC Comments to Draft Report GAO-11-728

Dear Mr. Gootnick:

Thank you for the opportunity to review and comment on the U.S. Government Accountability Office's draft report "Compacts in Cape Verde and Honduras Achieved Reduced Targets" (GAO-11-728). We at MCC are appreciative that your report has highlighted many of the impressive results achieved by the first two compacts to fully complete. The report further reflects MCC's deep commitment to results and transparency, and will serve as an important learning tool for management as we continually seek to improve the investment of taxpayer dollars.

In Cape Verde, MCC assistance resulted in the completion of the first phase of a major port modernization project, the improvement of roads and construction of new bridges, as well as training for farmers. In Honduras, MCC supported the rehabilitation of several key roads, including a critical stretch of the Central American Highway, and training in improved farming techniques for over 7,000 farmers.

These results were achieved under challenging circumstances, requiring MCC and its partners to make significant changes to projects and reduce some initial targets. The report demonstrates, however, that in making changes to projects, MCC remained focused on results, meeting the majority of the revised targets and making substantial progress toward achieving the shared development objectives of the United States and MCC's partner countries. Moreover, the report highlights that independent evaluations are already in process that will assess the cost-effectiveness of these interventions, a further reflection of both the rigor of MCC's evidence-based approach to investment and our commitment to learn from our experiences

As set forth in more detail in the attached comments, MCC agrees with the intent of GAO's recommendations. The long-term sustainability and monitoring of MCC's investments are central to our mission, and MCC commits to work with GAO to develop specific actions to implement the recommendations. MCC has applied many of the lessons learned from its early compacts and prior GAO reports. As a result, we are already implementing aspects of GAO's current recommendations and expect that future compacts will benefit as we incorporate these lessons into our programs.

Finally, we wish to thank you and the GAO staff for the professional manner in which the audit was conducted and the opportunities given to MCC to provide additional information and feedback.

Sincerely,

Patrick C. Fine
Vice President
Department of Compact Operations

MCC Comments to the Draft GAO Report (GAO-11-728):
Compacts in Cape Verde and Honduras Achieved Reduced Targets

GAO Recommendation: To maximize the sustainability of MCC-funded infrastructure projects and to reduce the amount of maintenance required after compact completion, work with partner countries to make project, planning design, and construction decisions that reduce long term maintenance costs.

MCC Comments: MCC takes seriously the maintenance and sustainability of its investments. Prior to signing a compact, MCC systematically assesses sustainability and formulates meaningful and pragmatic actions that our partner countries must take during implementation of the compact to move towards self-sufficiency. MCC monitors progress on those actions, and takes action during implementation to correct non-compliance.

The rehabilitation of infrastructure improves the condition of assets such that the need for maintenance is reduced, for at least a period of time. Of course this is not sufficient, and in designing projects, MCC seeks to strike a proper balance between front end capital investment costs and ongoing operations and maintenance costs. Thus, among the steps that MCC has taken, in its pre-construction activities, is systematic analysis – such as value engineering and life cycle cost analysis – to consider the effects of durability and maintenance costs and to reflect these in the final designs. For example, MCC could invest more in slope protection and some of the measures GAO has cited in its draft report, but such measures may not be justified in all cases, particularly in a developing country context.

During the design phase, considerable attention is paid by MCC to minimization of operations and maintenance costs. In many instances, MCC has insisted on upgraded drainage standards on road projects over the objections of country counterparts who may prefer to rehabilitate more kilometers. The same applies to MCC's insistence on installation of the appropriate pumps and other equipment on water treatment and irrigation projects in a way that is both cost effective and maintainable in the local setting.

The concern with maintenance carries over to the attention MCC pays to long term operations of facilities. As part of the design of implementation arrangements, MCC works to ensure that institutions and systems are put into place to provide for the sustainability of projects over the long term. Examples include the establishment of and provision for capacity building of water users associations for irrigation projects, capacity building of maintenance organizations in the road sector, and the purchase of maintenance equipment for government agencies that will be entrusted with the care of MCC funded projects when completed.

In order to cover the inevitable maintenance costs, many of MCC's compacts require governments to set aside funding for maintenance from the general treasury or to set up maintenance funds with dedicated sources of funding (e.g., fuel levies, other targeted user fees, or taxes) as a condition to disbursements of the grant. MCC has also supported the formation of agencies to manage maintenance planning, funding and contracting in some cases. More recently, we have allocated funding toward periodic (as opposed to routine) maintenance costs of roads in a country. MCC's policy engagement to increase country capacity to undertake needed maintenance for all sector assets, not just MCC-funded assets helps countries to adopt plans to move towards full-funding, resulting in a lasting benefit for the sector.

In the draft report, GAO concludes that "MCC took steps to require partner countries to plan to effectively operate and maintain the infrastructure, including privatization of port operations in Cape Verde and the provision of road maintenance funding in Cape Verde and Honduras. The partner countries made progress meeting MCC's requirements in these areas, but they continue to face funding and other challenges that are key to sustainability." MCC agrees that the Cape Verde and Honduras compacts are examples of both the positive effects that the MCC compacts achieved toward sustainability and the challenges that remain. All infrastructure projects around the globe face challenges to long term sustainability, and financing maintenance is a challenge in both developed and developing countries.

In Cape Verde, MCC took significant measures to improve road maintenance systems, and the GAO witnessed the maintenance program working. MCC incentivized the establishment of the road maintenance fund, which is functioning, and all MCC-funded roads and bridges are being maintained. For instance, the GAO report shows a photograph of a Government of Cape Verde-funded contractor making needed repairs to a road, financed by the road levy that was instituted to meet the conditions in the compact.

Similarly, in Honduras, as a result of conditions that MCC placed on disbursements of funding, GAO notes that the government increased its road funding from $37 million in 2005 to $64 million in 2010 (a 73% increase. While this amount remains short of what would be required to cover the entire network, the willingness to make this increase has helped change the priority and direction of road maintenance funding in the country. There can be no guarantee that partner countries will continue to make these investments now that the MCC compact is over. MCC believes, however, that this is ultimately the responsibility of the country and is one of the reasons why MCC selects countries based on good governance criteria and fosters country ownership so that countries will meet this responsibility going forward.

GAO Recommendation: To enhance the accuracy of MCC's ERR projections, ensure, during compact implementation, that updated ERR analyses are well documented and supported and that key revised indicators and targets are reflected in updated ERR analyses.

MCC Comments: This recommendation has two components, the first related to our economic work and the second related to the monitoring and evaluation (M&E) targets. MCC agrees with both aspects of this recommendation.

With respect to the economic analysis during implementation, MCC's pre-investment economic rates of return (ERRs) represent our best assessment of the future returns of a project as designed at that time. When the anticipated scope of the project changes, however, it is MCC's policy that ERRs should be updated (resources permitting, with exceptions documented and explained). When ERRs are updated, MCC agrees that these changes should be adequately documented, so that informed stakeholders can follow the logic and the sources of the data of the project as conceptualized at that time.

4

With respect to the consistency between ERR models and M&E targets, MCC's current M&E policy requires that these be linked to the extent possible. When changes to the project design or scope are proposed, MCC agrees that the economic implications of these changes should be assessed and documented, and that the consistency between M&E targets and the current ERR model should be maintained.

In Honduras and Cape Verde, the GAO found that in some instances the lack of documentation on updated ERR analyses made it difficult to know whether the revised ERR results are accurate and reliable, and that the ERR analyses were not clearly linked to the revised targets in the M&E plans. MCC has taken significant steps to correct this issue. As GAO notes, MCC adopted a new policy on the approval of modifications to compact programs in 2010. Among other measures which improve the process for analyzing the impact of program modifications on ERRs and beneficiaries, the policy requires that significant changes be documented prior to approval and that changes to M&E indicators and targets must be verified by the appropriate staff.

GAO Recommendation: To enhance the accuracy of MCC's ERR projections, develop guidance for re-estimating ERRs at compact completion and during the long-term period when compact benefits are realized to ensure that updated estimates reflect the most recent and reliable information available for MCC's compact investments and outcomes.

MCC Comments: Again, this recommendation encompasses two distinct ideas, the re-estimation of ERRs at compact completion and the re-estimation of ERRs at some future point(s) well after completion, consistent with the long-term returns of our infrastructure and other investments. MCC acknowledges the importance of measuring ERRs over the life of its projects, and will develop guidance that takes the following considerations into account:

In some cases, the calculation of ERRs at the time of compact completion could provide useful information, if MCC has preliminary evidence regarding observed program impact. But in many cases, MCC may not have much more than input and output data at compact completion, and re-estimation of the ERR at that time may produce little or no new information over an existing model. Alternatively, MCC has committed resources for independent evaluators to undertake estimations of ERRs based on impact evaluation data. These ERRs, which will be produced one-two years after completion, will provide more useful information.

A more significant issue is the re-estimation of ERRs beyond the current evaluation plan. MCC recognizes that the persistence of benefits over time is an important issue for compact evaluation, but notes that our assistance to partner countries is restricted by statute to five years. This limits the terms and types of commitments MCC could make with partner countries to sustain an effective monitoring program over the lifespan of a project.

MCC is committed to working with GAO to agree on guidance to achieve the shared objective of the recommendation, which is to continue to transparently monitor the results of the compacts, so that the long-term impacts of MCC investments are known and the lessons learned are incorporated into future programs. Any such guidance will need to take into consideration, however, the limitations on MCC's assistance to a country in the long term and the administrative and funding constraints of committing to actions up to 20 years in the future.

Additional MCC Comments to GAO Findings:

Given that the GAO report focuses on indicators and targets, MCC would like to highlight a couple of other important results of the compacts in Cape Verde and Honduras that are not fully reflected in the report.

In Cape Verde, the compact contributed to significant policy reforms that will have long-term impacts on their respective sectors. For example, the government issued a national decree lifting a 20-year embargo on agricultural exports from the island of Santo Antão, and a new microfinance law was passed to authorize collection of savings by microfinance institutions.

In the case of Honduras, the compact led to the passage and implementation of legislation to permit secured transactions of equipment, movable and other personal property, the introduction of a new and higher standard for resettlement, and the near doubling of road maintenance funding. These are key policy changes which are expected to make lasting contributions to Honduran economic development. The secured transaction legislation and security interest registry has been instrumental in improving the credit opportunities for small and medium-sized enterprises. The resettlement legislation developed and enacted during the compact enabled the resettlement of affected parties in accordance with a higher standard for social safeguards, coordination and efficiency.

Financing and implementation challenges meant that not all of the sections of the CA-5 Highway in Honduras that were initially projected could be completed during the compact. With the support of MCC's compact, however, the Government of Honduras was able to obtain concessional financing from the Central American Bank for Economic Integration (CABEI) to complete all of the sections, currently scheduled for 2012. This is a clear example of the ability of MCC to leverage its resources and partner with other donors. The fact that the CABEI-financed sections of the project will continue to be implemented by MCA-Honduras is also a testament to the good governance and effective administration of development assistance that MCC is fostering in its partner countries.

APPENDIX V: ACKNOWLEDGMENTS

Emil Friberg Jr. (Assistant Director), Michael Armes, Diana Blumenfeld, Lynn Cothern, Gergana Danailova-Trainor, Miriam Carroll Fenton, Ernie Jackson, Leslie Locke, Reid Lowe, Amanda Miller, and Suneeti Shah Vakharia made key contributions to this report. Additional technical assistance was provided by Lucas Alvarez, Juan Avila, Chloe Brown, Thomas Costa, Martin DeAlteriis, Michael Derr, Kevin Egan, Vanessa Estevez, Etana Finkler, Rachel Girshick, Kieran McCarthy, Lauren Membreno, Werner Miranda-Hernandez, Mark

Needham, Nelson Olhero, Joshua Ormond, Marisela Perez, Kyerion Printup, Cristina Ruggiero, Carla Rojas, Jena Sinkfield, and Omar Torres.

End Notes

[1] 22 U.S.C. § 7708(j).

[2] MCC commits funding when a compact is signed and obligates funds after the compact enters into force. As of June 2011, MCC had signed compacts with, in order of signature, Madagascar, Honduras, Cape Verde, Nicaragua, Georgia, Benin, Vanuatu, Armenia, Ghana, Mali, El Salvador, Mozambique, Lesotho, Morocco, Mongolia, Tanzania, Burkina Faso, Namibia, Senegal, Moldova, the Philippines, Jordan, and Malawi.

[3] Consolidated Appropriations Act, 2008, Pub. L. No. 110-161, § 668(d)(1)(A). The act also required us to examine the financial control and procurement practices of MCC and its accountable entities. We responded to this requirement separately in GAO, Millennium Challenge Corporation: MCC Has Addressed a Number of Implementation Challenges, but Needs to Improve Financial Controls and Infrastructure Planning, GAO-10-52 (Washington, D.C.: Nov. 6, 2009).

[4] We did not include the Madagascar compact in this review because, as the result of a pattern of actions inconsistent with MCC policy, MCC formally terminated the compact effective August 31, 2009. Protests and instability in Madagascar in January 2009 ultimately led to the forced resignation of the country's elected president.

[5] Other board members are the U.S. Trade Representative, the Administrator of the U.S. Agency for International Development, the CEO of MCC, and up to four Senate-confirmed nongovernmental members who are appointed by the President from lists of individuals submitted by congressional leadership.

[6] Candidate countries must not be statutorily barred from receiving U.S. assistance.

[7] To be eligible for MCA assistance, a country must pass the indicator for control of corruption and at least one-half of the indicators in each of the following three categories: ruling justly, investing in people, and encouraging economic freedom. To pass an indicator test, a country must score better than at least one-half of the other candidates (above the median) in its income group.

[8] In our November 2009 report on MCC's compact development and implementation processes for infrastructure projects, we recommended that MCC (1) improve fiscal accountability plans and ensure comprehensive policies for all MCA expenses, (2) reinforce MCC's price reasonableness analysis guidance, and (3) improve project design reviews and cost estimates prior to issuing contract solicitations. MCC has implemented the second of these recommendations and has indicated that it has taken steps to implement the remaining recommendations where applicable. See GAO-10-52.

[9] There are four types of indicators, including (1) goal indicators, which measure the economic growth and poverty reduction changes that occur during or after compact implementation; (2) objective indicators, which measure the intermediate and long-term effects of an activity or set of activities and are related to output indicators; (3) output indicators, which measure, describe, and quantify the goods and services produced by the activity; and (4) process milestone indicators, which measure progress toward the completion of project activities.

[10] MCC and MCAs monitor the progress of compact activities using an indicator tracking table, which is a reporting tool that displays targets and tracks progress against them. The tracking table is designed to help MCC and MCAs track interim progress toward compact goals. MCA staff in Cape Verde and Honduras conducted periodic checks to ensure that data used to track compact results were valid, reliable, and timely. In addition, MCC also hired independent evaluators to review the reliability of data collected by contractors in both countries.

[11] According to MCC's 2009 annual report, MCC is conducting impact evaluations for every MCC compact. Specifically, approximately 50 percent of all MCC compact activities representing almost 60 percent of all MCC compact funds are assessed using independent impact evaluations.

[12] In our July 2006 report on the status of MCC's compact implementation, we recommended that MCC (1) ensure that economic analyses of compact proposals better reflect country conditions and involve country participation and (2) improve monitoring and evaluation by obtaining more reliable baseline data, ensuring a clear linkage to economic analyses, developing criteria for establishing and adjusting targets, and ensuring timely development of evaluation designs. MCC has implemented these recommendations. See GAO, Millennium Challenge Corporation: Compact Implementation Structures Are Being Established; Framework for Measuring Results Needs Improvement, GAO-06-805 (Washington, D.C.: July 28, 2006).

[13] During MCC's due diligence review, MCC determines whether the proposal that an eligible country has submitted meets MCC criteria to ensure that proposed programs will be effective and funds well-used.

[14] The results of the due diligence assessment are reported in an investment memo—an internal document that analyzes the compact—submitted to MCC's investment management committee. The investment management committee consists of MCC's vice presidents and other senior officials and reports to the Chief Executive Officer. The committee reviews the memo and decides whether to recommend proceeding to compact negotiations. This ERR information is also found in MCC documents such as compacts, compact summaries, annual reports, and congressional notifications and budget justifications.

[15] According to MCC's 2006 guidelines for monitoring and evaluation plans, the economic analysis determines the main variables that drive program results, which can become indicators, and values of these variables can become targets. As a result, targets are usually directly linked to and derived from the economic analysis. In addition, according to earlier MCC guidelines for monitoring and evaluation plans issued in January 2006, indicators proposed should be linked as much as possible to the economic assessment justifying the program.

[16] In our June 2008 report on MCC's projections for ERRs and compact impact on income and poverty, we recommended that MCC (1) adopt and implement written procedures for a secondary independent review of its economic analyses and (2) improve MCC's guidelines by identifying a consistent approach with preferred methods for projecting compacts' impact on income and poverty. MCC has implemented these recommendations. See GAO, Millennium Challenge Corporation: Independent Reviews and Consistent Approaches Will Strengthen Projections of Program Impact, GAO-08-730 (Washington, D.C.: June 17, 2008).

[17] The organization of the management structure may vary across compacts and projects.

[18] In some cases, project designs already exist and MCAs do not engage a design engineer in implementing the project.

[19] Construction quality management is a joint responsibility of the contractor and construction supervisor. The construction contractor is responsible for quality control, which involves, among other tasks, material and construction testing. The construction supervisor provides quality assurance through its oversight activities, which may include, for example, independent material and construction testing.

[20] Testing is typically completed to ensure construction materials meet performance characteristics. For example, compaction tests are done to ensure underlying soils are able to support pavement structures. In addition, completed work is tested to ensure it was installed properly and performs as intended. For example, smoothness tests can be performed on newly placed pavements.

[21] We previously reported on the effect of insufficient planning on Cape Verde's infrastructure project and steps that MCC has taken to improve planning for future compacts. See GAO-10-52.

[22] A small amount of phase 1 work remained undone at the end of the compact because its completion is contingent upon the completion of other work that was not funded by MCC. In addition, MCC is currently providing technical support to resolve one issue of defective construction related to the new access road.

[23] Phase 2 work is being performed based on the MCC-funded design for the port improvement activity.

[24] The reservoirs funded by MCC are water storage tanks ranging in size from 200 cubic meters to 1,000 cubic meters; the reservoirs are fed by springs, wells, or rain.

[25] The targets do not reflect the extent to which the scope of the CA-5 was expanded to improve traffic flow. Targets are based on centerline kilometers (one kilometer of road length measured along its center), which do not identify the number of traffic lanes reconstructed. If the targets had been based on lane kilometers (one kilometer per lane in length), additional traffic lane lengths completed would have been reflected as progress toward the target.

[26] MCC funded the preparation of the final design documents, the environmental impact assessment, and the development and implementation of resettlement action plans for the entire highway project.

[27] In June 2009, Honduran President Zelaya was removed from office after attempting to change the constitution to allow for his re-election, which the Honduran congress and judiciary opposed. In response to the Honduran president's removal and the failure to reestablish democratic order, which demonstrated a pattern of actions inconsistent with MCC's eligibility criteria, MCC's Board of Directors terminated $10 million of MCC assistance, reducing the compact total to $205 million. The partial termination of the compact eliminated funding for the weight control activity and the uncommitted portion of the farm to market roads activity, corresponding to the cancellation of approximately 93 kilometers of farm-to-market roads. MCC also placed a hold on funding for a section of the CA-5 highway activity, under the transportation project; the hold on funding was lifted in early 2010.

[28] To be "a Program Farmer harvesting high-value agricultural products," the Program Farmer must (1) in the first year of participation, have a crop mix demonstrated to have an expected annual net income of at least $2000 per hectare; and (2) in the second year of participation, have earned a net income of at least $2000.

[29] The partial termination of the Honduras compact in 2009, in response to the political situation, included termination of the uncommitted portion of the farm-to-market roads activity corresponding to the cancellation of approximately 93 kilometers of farm-to-market roads.

[30] The movable property registry activity also involved the facilitation of a new law that allowed credit seekers to use a new type of property—such as equipment, shop inventory, future crops, tractors, supply contracts, sewing machines, and more—as collateral, and also established a registry system to monitor the property.

[31] According to MCC, small-program farmers moving into high-value horticulture used existing resources and savings and did not require access to credit until market opportunities expanded. As a result of the delayed demand for credit, MCC and MCA decided to expand the scope to include nonprogram farmers.

[32] The value of this indicator ($10.7 million) includes the value of loans repaid and relent ($5.2 million) from the agricultural credit trust fund. This value ($10.7 million) does not include an additional $6.4 million in loans leveraged by financial institutions. According to MCC, adding the $6.4 million of funds leveraged by financial institutions to the $10.7 million of funds lent from the trust fund would result in double-counting of some funds. In addition, no target was established for the value of funds leveraged by financial institutions.

[33] The road institute was created in June 2003 as the Cape Verde government's authority for operating the national road network. The institute collects user fees that are allocated to a maintenance fund (85 percent), local municipalities (10 percent), and operating expenses (5 percent). Maintenance funds are used to service approximately 425 kilometers of roads—including the MCC-funded roads, which are part of the national road network of approximately 1,500 kilometers.

[34] MCC did not plan for an oversight entity to oversee use of the grant funds, but MCC's grant agreements provide the agency with audit authority over the grant finds for the 2 years following the compact.

[35] The Honduran government agreed to the increase in its funding in 2007.

[36] Roads are designed to carry estimated numbers of vehicles with specific weight loads. When the numbers and weights of vehicles are higher than those planned for in the design, roads deteriorate more quickly.

[37] Targets set for this activity indicated that the percentage of overweight vehicles using the CA-5 would be reduced from 23 percent to 7 percent. The due diligence report stated that the current levels of overweight vehicles are expected to reduce the 15-year life of the road by 2 years and further reduce the life of bridges.

[38] IRI is a measure of roughness of the road pavement in terms of meters per kilometer. The IRI affects vehicle operating costs, ride quality, and road damage. For example, according to an MCC analysis used to determine the benefits of the new pavement, the IRI for CA-5 section 4 pavement, which was planned to be 1.9 upon completion of construction, was not expected to degrade to an IRI of 3.2—the IRI for the newly completed section of pavement—until almost 14 years after the project was complete.

[39] According to MCC officials, both the contractor and the farmers have an incentive for overstating potential sustainability challenges. The contractor is interested in receiving additional funding and the farmers are seeking additional services.

[40] Due to MCC restrictions, MCA cannot incur new commitments or make expenditures with MCC funding after the compact end date. Therefore, due to project implementation delays in Cape Verde, the evaluations of the port, roads and bridges, and agricultural activities will be funded with MCC due diligence funds instead of compact funds. Due diligence funds are used by MCC to cover costs associated with assessing compact proposals and providing compact implementation oversight.

[41] MCA-Cape Verde hired the impact evaluation consultant to develop an impact evaluation design from September 2009 to August 2010. However, MCC reported the contract was terminated because the suggested design did not reflect the approach proposed by the government of Cape Verde.

[42] According to MCC, baseline data were collected before implementation of the port activity as part of normal operations by the port authority. In addition, five baseline surveys were conducted before compact closeout.

[43] According to MCC, baseline data were collected through a World Bank socioeconomic study and traffic surveys in 2004 and 2005.

[44] According to MCC, MCA-Cape Verde contracted an impact evaluation consultant in November 2006 to develop an impact evaluation design. However, MCC reported that, due to rescoping of the project, MCA-Cape Verde did not accept the impact evaluation design recommendations. This contractor was subsequently rehired to conduct the impact evaluation for this project.

[45] The qualitative evaluation of five local MFIs found that all reported growth in their loan portfolios and improvements in their operational and financial sustainability, some of which the institutions attributed to the

MCC compact. The MFIs reported that growth was due to several factors, including access to funds under MCC's access to credit activity and other programs such as Cape Verde's National Program for the Fight Against Poverty and the U.S. African Development Foundation.

[46] MCC determined during implementation of the first several compacts that, in most cases, it is not advisable to assess the impact of activities before they have been completed and have demonstrated tangible, measurable results. Accordingly, MCC has modified its evaluation strategy to collect final data after the investments have been completed, in some cases as much as 12 to 24 months after compact closeout. Therefore, MCC issued a new contract totaling $1.06 million for the continuation and completion of the Honduras transportation and farmer training and development impact evaluations, which were initially to be completed under an MCA contract by the compact's end. This contract does not include the outstanding access to credit activity impact evaluation for which MCC plans to issue an additional contract.

[47] The evaluator estimated the ERR for 8 of the 15 grants, with a weighted average, to be 38 percent.

[48] The updated port ERR is based on the completion of both Phases I and II and includes a 20 percent cost increase contingency.

[49] For the port improvement activity's original ERR estimate of 23 percent, MCC assumed that improvements to the Port of Praia would prevent a slowdown in growth in the tourism sector that would have resulted from congestion and higher transportation costs at the port. However, the model for the original ERR estimate rejects the notion that efficiency gains would be passed on to consumers, owing to the monopoly position of shippers and shipping lines. From the updated analysis, MCC reported a return of 29 percent. MCC's updated analysis was based on studies undertaken by a French engineering consulting firm, which modeled the results of MCC investments in operational detail. In particular, the model captures explicitly the contribution of MCC investments to relieving constraints on handling capacity, productivity, and, ultimately, port traffic.

[50] MCC stated that the 10.1 percent cited in the Cape Verde restructuring memo was referenced in error.

[51] The Partnership to Mobilize Investment, an activity of the private sector development project, was mostly eliminated, but as that project activity was not included in the original ERR analysis, there was no reason to adjust the ERR. In addition, the two social roads of the roads and bridges activity of the infrastructure project were also eliminated, but because those roads were not included in the original ERR analysis either, there was no need for an adjustment.

[52] According to the Honduras compact, the target of 14,400 hectares was to be achieved by the end of year 5 of the compact and was fully consistent with the modeling of the benefit stream in the original ERR model. The compact was to remain in force for 5 years from the entry into force, dated September 29, 2005.

[53] MCC officials stated that they checked whether these target changes shifted the ERR beyond the hurdle rate.

[54] The independent impact evaluator for this activity has estimated the ERRs for 8 of the 15 agricultural public goods grants in Honduras. The selected 8 projects were chosen because they have completed their financing and infrastructure construction phase with support from MCA-Honduras. While the estimated ERR for these projects shows a high economic rate of return of 38 percent, the rate cannot be compared to the original ERR since it does not include all 15 grants and the original ERR is based on the expected rate of return for the activity as a whole.

[55] The cost estimate for the port improvement activity includes both phase 1, which was finished in October 2010, and phase 2, which was not finished by compact completion.

[56] See GAO-10-52.

End Note for Appendix I

[1] The granting of a disbursement request is contingent on MCC finding the quarterly package satisfactory in form and substance.

End Notes for Appendix II

[1] For fiscal year 2011, MCC's cutoff for lower-middle-income candidates was a per capita income of $3,945.

[2] Using program administration and monitoring and evaluation funds, MCC funded capacity-building activities, including strengthening e-government systems. According to MCC, these activities contributed to building the capacity of the Cape Verde government.

[3] MCC awarded in July 2008 a fixed unit price contract to a Portuguese construction consortium in the amount of $42.3 million. Contract modifications increased the contract value to $45.3 million by the time work was completed in October 2010. The $3 million (7 percent) increase resulted from changes such as realigning the access road and providing additional shore protection.

[4] Buildings eliminated from the scope of the phase 1 contract were in the proximity of the cargo village and included offices for customs and port operations staff, warehouses, entrance gates, and a workshop. These buildings were subsequently constructed by the same contractor that built the phase 1 works under a separate contract with the Cape Verde government.

[5] According to MCC, in September 2010, the Cape Verde government awarded a contract for phase 2 works to the same contractor that constructed phase 1 of the port improvement activity.

[6] According to MCC, the cost of quarry materials amounted to about 5 percent of the total construction cost.

[7] Planning, design, and contract procurement actions continued over a 33-month period from the compact's entry into force in October 2005 through award of a construction contract in July 2008.

[8] Implementation delays contributed to cost increases as a result of construction prices rising approximately 30 percent, according to MCC, from the beginning of the compact to the time the phase 1 construction contract was awarded in July 2008.

[9] The proper title of this government agency is the Ministry of Infrastructure, Transport, and Telecommunications.

[10] Design life is the minimal time that constructed infrastructure is expected to provide reliable performance without major investments to keep it safe and efficient. According to the design engineer for the port improvement work, the design life of components varies. For example, the design life of the rehabilitated wharf (wharf 2) is 50 years and the design life of the cargo village container lot and access roads is 20 years.

[11] The lower access road is positioned along the coast and is protected by a structural system designed to mitigate the effects of hydraulic forces created by waves and currents. The design of the shore protection structure specifies that the base of its outer layer is to be set in a trench along the seafloor. The structure's outer layer consists of specially shaped interconnected CORE LOC™ concrete units—the units measure approximately 4 cubic meters and weigh about 10 tons—that provide for structural stability.

[12] As part of the quality assurance process, the design engineer conducted site visits on five separate occasions while the shore protection structure was being built, diving to inspect the underwater work. These dives, as well as a sixth dive in October 2010, found, among other things, that the trench was not built in some areas, so that the base of the shore protection structure rested on the seafloor; in other areas, the trench was built to the wrong dimensions, so that the trench was wider than the base of the shore protection structure and the resulting fit was loose.

[13] In October 2010, U.S. Army Corps of Engineers submitted a report on the basis of its initial assessment that identified repair alternatives. Following the initial report, an underwater survey was conducted to obtain greater detail of seafloor conditions. Data obtained from the survey is being used to develop physical model tests of the alternative solutions. MCC expects that results of the model tests will be available in August 2011. These results will then be used to determine which repair alternative will be implemented.

[14] Under the agreement, the parties committed to activating a Dispute Adjudication Board with binding authority to resolve outstanding issues, such as determining the split of costs for repairs to the underwater trench and the outcome of the construction contractor's $4.3 million claim for increased costs associated with its initial construction of the trench. The three-member board is to be composed of a member nominated by the Ministry of Transportation, a member nominated by the construction contractor, and a president chosen by agreement between the two members. As of the beginning of May 2011, the board was still being constituted and its deliberations had not yet begun.

[15] The initial designs of both the roads and bridges construction activities were funded by the World Bank and completed prior to the compact. After it had awarded construction contracts for the roads and bridges, MCA-Cape Verde found that the designs were of poor quality and inadequate as a basis for construction. MCA-Cape Verde subsequently took steps to redesign the roads and bridges activities, which led to implementation delays and increased costs as the new designs were generally to a higher standard than the original designs.

[16] The construction contractor initially completed work to redesign the road rehabilitations and incorporate enhanced features such as the addition of drainage culverts. MCA's construction supervisor reviewed the contractor's design and made modifications based on technical and cost considerations. Construction was completed on the basis of the construction supervisor's modified design.

---

[17] According to MCC, construction costs rose during the time the activity was being redesigned, and a price escalation allowance in the construction contract contributed to a cost increase of approximately $1.8 million.

[18] Construction of the two roads deleted from MCA-Cape Verde's contract was completed under a separate contract administered by the Cape Verde transportation ministry and funded through a loan from the government of Portugal; MCC reported that the cost of the contract to build the deleted roads was approximately $9.8 million.

[19] The $2.4 million increase in the total value of the bridges construction contract included approximately $1.1 million to compensate the contractor for delays and for escalation of prices.

[20] Rip-rap consists of rocks, rubble, or preformed concrete shapes that are put in place to prevent erosion to an embankment or structure.

[21] The duration of the roads' design life varies by component. For example, the pavement has a design life of 15 years, while culverts and retention structures have design lives that range from 20 to 50 years.

[22] Other methods, such as installation of walls at the base of slopes to prevent soils from falling onto the road, were implemented in an effort to mitigate damage from potential landslides. [23]According to the supervisory engineer, the overdesigned elements account for approximately 8 percent of the total construction cost.

[24] The institute collects user fees that are allocated to a maintenance service fund (85 percent), local municipalities (10 percent), and operating expenses (5 percent). Maintenance funds are used to service approximately 425 kilometers of roads—including the MCC-funded roads, which are part of the national road network of approximately 1,500 kilometers.

[25] According to an October 2010 report by an independent engineer, the water management infrastructure constructed with MCC funds was not complete or operational on all islands. For example, some reservoirs were not yet filled with water, some water distribution systems were incomplete, and some water meters were nonfunctioning.

[26] The contractor developed the farmer training curriculum in five subjects—agronomy, drip irrigation, marketing, pest management, and postharvest techniques—as well as training materials on these topics for the Cape Verde agricultural ministry, among other activities.

[27] The contractor reported that it was not able to train farmers directly under this activity and, instead, implemented a training of trainers program for the Cape Verde agricultural ministry's field extension workers, or field staff.

[28] The contractor reported that it provided technical assistance to several farmers who expressed interest in learning new agricultural techniques and additional assistance. According to the contractor, these farmers were more likely to encourage others to apply such techniques.

[29] In September 2010, the government of Cape Verde lifted a long-standing embargo on agricultural imports from the island of Santo Antão, contingent on the operation of a postharvest quality control and inspection center that would mitigate the effects of a millipede pest prevalent in agriculture on the island.

[30] MCC disbursed funds to MCA-Cape Verde for the creation of the credit bureau, allowing MCA-Cape Verde to sign a grant with the Chambers of Commerce. The grant agreement specified that receipt of funds by the Chambers of Commerce was contingent on the contract signed between the Chambers of Commerce and its investment partner.

[31] MCC reported that the government of Cape Verde passed legislation that brought MFIs into the formal, regulated financial sector. In addition, MCC reported that the government of Cape Verde modified legislation permitting the sale of government securities to individuals, and the Ministry of Finance approved a new auction process for government securities. MCC required these financial sector legislative reforms for disbursements.

End Notes for Appendix III

[1] For fiscal year 2011, MCC's cutoff for low-income candidates was a per capita income of $1,905.

[2] Reconstruction of the roads is generally on existing roadway routes. MCC funded CA-5 reconstruction included widening and resurfacing the road in some sections and replacing the existing pavement in one section with new concrete pavement.

[3] MCA-Honduras awarded four fixed unit price contracts to reconstruct the four sections of the CA-5 highway. A contract for Section 1 was awarded to a Honduran construction firm in February of 2009 in the amount of $39.7 million. A contract for Section 2 was awarded to a Costa Rican construction consortium in September of 2008 in the amount of $48.4 million. Contracts for Section 3 and Section 4 were both awarded to an Italian construction firm in May of 2008 in the amounts of $16.2 million and $23.2 million, respectively.

[4] According to MCC officials, because CABEI's loan to the Honduras government provided sufficient funding for CA-5 reconstruction, MCA-Honduras reallocated, with MCC approval, about $7 million of the $96.4 million previously allocated for the activity to the secondary roads activity, bringing the allocation to $89.3 million. The $90.3 million that MCC had disbursed for CA-5 reconstruction as of March 31, 2011, represented about 41 percent of total reconstruction costs. 5According to MCC officials, the length of the CA-5 Highway reconstructed and still under construction totaled 107 kilometers, compared with MCC's final target of 109 kilometers.

[6] MCA-Honduras officials stated that they plan to continue operating under the MCA- Honduras name for about 2 years, until the construction of CA-5 sections 1 and 2 are completed. MCC officials said they agree to the continued use of the name until the projects are completed, provided MCA-Honduras does not take any actions that would risk MCC's reputation.

[7] Because the concrete pavement is expected to reduce long-term maintenance costs, according to an analysis by the design engineer, MCA-Honduras allowed an adjustment of $2.3 million when evaluating bids for construction with concrete pavement.

[8] Secondary road reconstruction generally included widening the existing unpaved roads, improving drainage, adding additional base material to the road, and applying an asphalt chip and seal pavement surface. In some areas, sidewalks were included and pavers were used for the road pavement.

[9] Administration of the weight control stations was to be the Honduran government's responsibility.

[10] Fondo Vial is the Honduran agency responsible for maintaining all primary roads (such as the CA-5), secondary roads, and some rural roads. Some rural roads are the responsibility of Honduran municipalities.

[11] The project management consultant, who was responsible for the final design of the CA- 5 activities and management of all transportation project activities and the farm-to-market road activities, was terminated after 3.5 years. As a result, the MCA-Honduras staff worked directly with the construction supervisors they had hired to oversee each contractor. According to MCC officials, to hire a replacement consultant would have taken time, delayed the activities past the end of the compact, and would not have guaranteed improved performance. MCA-Honduras staff also coordinated project designs and changes with the Honduras transportation ministry, but the ministry did not take an active role in the direct supervision of work.

[12] We visited the construction sites and interviewed independent construction supervisors and contractors for three of the four CA-5 contracts (sections 2, 3, and 4 contracts); and two of the three secondary road contracts (the Comayagua–Ajuterique-La Paz contract and the Choluteca–Orocuina contract).

[13] According to a construction supervision official, Honduras has no certification processes to ensure the qualifications of those responsible for quality control, however construction supervisors and contractors generally used a combination of on-the-job training, inspectors with many years of training, and oversight by a professional engineer to ensure that the tests were conducted properly. In addition, all of the construction supervisors and contractor officials we interviewed were certified as having a quality management system that met the requirements of the International Organization for Standardization (ISO), although this certification was not required in their contracts with MCA-Honduras. The ISO 9001 specifies the requirements for a quality management system to consistently provide a product that meets customer requirements and all statutory and regulatory requirements.

[14] After the MCA-Honduras quality control process identified unacceptable concrete pavement roughness on section 4 of the CA-5, the construction supervisor required the contractor to mill the new concrete pavement until it met contract requirements.

[15] New pavement IRI ratings generally range from 1.5 to 3.5; the higher the IRI, the rougher the pavement, with an IRI of 0 being perfectly smooth. IRI is used in determining the reduction in road-user costs and is an indicator of when additional resurfacing work is needed. As IRI increases, traffic speed can be reduced, suspension damage increases, and fuel, oil, and tire consumption is increased. In an MCC analysis used to determine the benefits of the new pavement, the IRI for CA-5 section 4 pavement was not expected to degrade to an IRI of 3.2—the IRI for the newly completed section of pavement—until almost 14 years after the project was complete.

[16] After the landslide, MCA-Honduras commissioned a geotechnical study to develop solutions to modify the reconstruction of several landslide areas. For this location, the study suggested cutting the slope back at a less steep incline, installing monitoring equipment to notify officials if it starts to slide again, and stabilizing other slide locations. When we visited the site in November 2010, MCA-Honduras had not yet determined a final course of action or estimated the cost of the remediation work; however, construction supervision officials estimated that it could cost around $1.1 million. In April 2011, MCC officials were not able to provide updated

information on the status or cost of the remediation effort for the section 2 landslide because it is now the Honduran government's responsibility.

[17] As a part of evaluating compact proposals, MCC uses a due diligence review process to determine whether the proposal meets MCC criteria, to ensure that proposed programs will be effective and that funds will be well-used. The due diligence outline for the Honduras proposal stated that increased vehicle speed and risk of accidents would be negative consequences of the improvements and that road safety had been adequately factored into the design. The proposed use of safety measures was more closely in keeping with those used on U.S. highways than those previously used in Honduras, including signage to keep drivers informed about the road ahead and steel guardrails on dangerous curves and other locations.

[18] U.S. Department of Transportation, *Federal Highway Administration, Manual on Uniform Traffic Control Devices for Streets and Highways*, 2009 Edition (Washington, D.C.: December 2009).

[19] MCA officials also stated that, although crash statistics are not available in most countries to identify the economic benefits of installing improved traffic safety measures, the cost of addressing key safety issues should be included in project cost assessments prior to compact implementation.

[20] The Honduran government agreed to increase its funding in 2007.

[21] Fondo Vial documents show that the percentage of the fuel tax required by law to be allocated to road maintenance was 35 percent in 2000, 38 percent in 2001, and 40 percent from 2002 through 2010.

[22] The objective for this activity was to reduce the percentage of overweight vehicles using the CA-5 from 23 percent to 7 percent. The due diligence report stated that the current levels of overweight traffic are expected to reduce the 15-year life of the road by 2 years and further reduce the life of bridges.

[23] The farmer training and development activity, which began in September 2006, provided technical assistance and training to farmers in crop management, business skills, marketing, and postharvest handling.

[24] An original target of 8,255 was planned to be achieved after the end of the compact in September 2010. In the second monitoring and evaluation plan, MCC noted that since it is unclear that program funds and monitoring and evaluation resources will be available after the compact ends, the compact target of 7,340 will be used, which was scheduled to be completed by May 2010, before the compact ends.

[25] Reconstruction of the roads was generally on the existing routes. The farm-to-market road reconstruction included widening the road, improving drainage, and building an aggregate road in place of a dirt road.

[26] According to MCC, the new law allowed credit seekers to use an entirely new set of property—such as equipment, shop inventory, future crops, tractors, supply contracts, and sewing machines and more—as collateral and also established a registry system to monitor the property.

[27] The original target ($28.8 million) was set for a similar indicator measuring the value of loans to program farmers, which was ultimately replaced by a number of indicators, including this indicator, and a lower target of $6 million. The final result ($10.7 million) does not include an additional $6.4 million in loans leveraged by financial institutions. According to MCC, adding the $6.4 million of funds leveraged by financial institutions to the $10.7 million of funds lent from the trust fund would result in double-counting of some funds. In addition, no target was established for the value of funds leveraged by financial institutions.

[28] According to the public goods grants manual, a public good is both nonexcludable and nonrival and, as a result, cannot be profitably provided by the private sector. Nonexcludable means that it is not feasible to exclude use and, as a result, everyone may use the good or service; therefore, the private sector cannot recover investment costs. Nonrival means that one person's use does not preclude or diminish another person's use, and multiple users may enjoy the benefits. To qualify as a public good for the purposes of this activity, the good does not need to be completely nonexcludable, but excludability must be cost-prohibitive such that the private sector is unlikely to provide the good.

[29] Ten of the selected grants were for irrigation works designed to increase hectares under irrigation and the number of farmers with access to irrigation water. Three grants were for research projects focused on different topics related to agricultural productivity, including potato seed production, reproduction of coffee hybrids, and biological pest control. One grant was for an activity focused on fruit pest eradication in a particular region of Honduras with an agricultural competitive advantage. One grant was for a technology transfer activity focused on increasing productivity and income of micro, small, and medium-scale processing agribusiness in Honduras.

INDEX

T

U